# PEONIES

*Paeonia, Paeonies, Paeony*

## Claire Austin

Published in 2021 by White Hopton Publications, Sarn, Newtown, Powys SY16 4EN.

Design, text, photography copyright © Claire Austin 2021.

Claire Austin has asserted her right to be identified as author of this work in accordance with the Copyright, Designs and Patents Act, 1988.

All rights reserved. No part of this publication may be reproduced, stored in a retrieval system, or transmitted, in any form or by any means, electronic or mechanical, by photocopying, recording or otherwise, without prior permission in writing from the publisher.

A CIP catalogue record for this book is available from the British Library.

ISBN 978-0-9931647-3-6

**Editor** Anna Kruger
**Proofreader** Jo Weeks
**Indexer** Marie Lorimer

Printed and bound in Great Britain using materials
accredited by the Forest Stewardship Council by
Pureprint Group
Uckfield, East Sussex TN22 1PL
www.pureprint.com

Claire Austin Hardy Plants,
White Hopton Farm,
Wern Lane, Sarn,
Newtown,
SY16 4EN
www.claireaustin-hardyplants.co.uk

**Front cover**
Paeonia 'June Rose'
with common red soldier beetle

**This page top to bottom**
Paeonia officinalis subsp. 'Anemoniflora Rosea'

Paeonia 'Shirley Temple'

Paeonia 'Marchioness'

**Next page top and middle**
Paeonia 'Unique'

Paeonia 'Moonrise'

**Next page left to right**
Paeonia 'Paula Fay'

Paeonia 'Angel Cheeks'

Paeonia 'Kansas'

**Back Cover**
Paeonia 'Mrs. Franklin D. Roosevelt'

# CONTENTS

INTRODUCTION 5

A ROUGH GUIDE TO PEONIES 6

GROWING PEONIES 12

PEONIES IN THE GARDEN 16

PEONIES IN HISTORY 30

MY PEONIES 36

LACTIFLORA PEONIES 44

GARDEN-WORTHY SPECIES PEONIES 104

HYBRID PEONIES 112

INTERSECTIONAL PEONIES 142

TREE PEONIES 154

THANKS & BIBLIOGRAPHY 171

INDEX 172

# INTRODUCTION

There are three types of garden writers. Botanists, who produce studious works on the what, where and why of plants are the first type. Creative writers who aim to help gardeners make the space outside look even more lovely are the second type and lastly, there are those who speak through experience on a subject they know and love. I hope I fit into the last category because I am neither a botanist nor a garden designer, but a nurserywoman who just happens to love taking photographs and writing about the plants I grow.

With nearly 40 years experience of growing perennials, peonies have become a permanent feature in my horticultural life. I must admit that, when asked what is my favourite perennial, peonies have not always been the first choice. But, over the years my respect for these beautiful, love-lived plants has increased markedly. Despite a relatively short flowering season, the peony's enduring ability to bloom whatever the season, and thrive in a situation that can be far from ideal, makes it the perfect garden plant.

Over the decades I have grown hundreds of different peony varieties, which is why I decided to write this book. Not all have travelled with me as I moved from one nursery to another, but most are included in this book and available from a nursery somewhere in the world. It has taken 30 years to gather the information. Each peony has been closely observed, details noted and photographs taken - perhaps in more detail than a gardener might need - but for those who want to identify a plant it is these little details that make the difference.

**WHY PEONIES?**

Long-lived and hardy, peonies have been admired and grown by gardeners for many centuries. They thrive almost anywhere in parts of the world where the temperature drops below freezing in winter and they need almost no attention once established. The flowers are so breathtakingly beautiful you simply want to rub your nose in the large, soft-petalled, often fragrant blooms. The whole plant is handsome from the minute the thick red shoots emerge in early spring until the leaves start to die back as the summer evenings get shorter.

**Top right:** *Paeonia* 'Nosegay'
**Above:** *Paeonia* 'Claire de Lune'
**Left:** *Paeonia* 'Madame Calot' (front) with *Paeonia* 'Barbara' (behind) growing in our field at White Hopton Farm

# A ROUGH GUIDE TO PEONIES

There is nothing quite like the opulent, multi-petalled blooms of a classic peony. Some compare them to roses, but peonies easily surpass roses in size and sheer numbers of petals. Of course, not all peonies are over the top; some species produce small, delicate flowers. But when you add scent, handsome foliage and ease of maintenance to the mix, you have a perfect plant – one that gardeners have been growing for centuries.

## THE GENUS *PAEONIA*

Peonies grow wild only in the northern hemisphere. They have been found in areas ranging from western and central Europe, the Middle East, Russia, China, northern India and Pakistan as well as in one region in far northwest United States. All plants are classified into groups and with peonies this process began in the early 19th century. As more species were discovered, however, the names became confused. Quite often, plant hunters on expeditions found specimens that they subsequently took to their chosen expert, who then allocated a name. By the end of the 19th century, the same peony might have had up to 10 different names and it became obvious these needed sorting out.

### Clarifying Botanical Confusion

Several botanists from Britain and America started classifying peonies, but it was F. C. Stern who produced the most important work of the 20th century. Having grown peonies for years in his garden at Highdown, West Sussex, in 1946 he published his findings in a very beautiful book: *A Study Of The Genus Paeonia*. In it, Stern divided peonies into the three sections outlined opposite. In recent years, however, botanist have again muddied the waters and there is currently no consensus. Some experts attribute 28 species to the genus while others, such as the American Peony Society, list 33. Some organise the genus according to roots, others by flowers, some refer to the dried and pressed leaf specimens in the herbariums of botanical gardens. In 1995 an American, Tao Sang, published a study of the genes of peonies and concluded that many were the result of natural hybridisation – a conclusion I applaud.

*Paeonia humilis* var. *villosa* is now listed under *P. officinalis*

*Paeonia steveniana,* a rare plant from the Caucasus region of Georgia

*Paeonia mlokosewitschii* likes a very well-drained soil

An outline of the *Paeonia* family is given below. I make no apologies for ignoring most of the subspecies, mainly because they are almost impossible for gardeners to acquire. Those marked with an * are included in this book.

### Onaepia

(Herbaceous peonies) An anagram of *Paeonia*, this group includes just two plants, both grow in northwestern states of the USA. I have grown neither.
P. brownii
P. californica

### Moutan

(Tree or woody peonies) Divided into two groups, these plants are all found growing in Asia, particularly in China. I have not included all the current subspecies.

#### Subsection *Delavayanae*
P. delavayi *
P. ludlowii *

#### Subsection *Vaginatae*

| | |
|---|---|
| P. cathayana | P. qiui |
| P. decomposita | P. rockii * |
| P. jishanensis | P. rotundiloba |
| P. ostii * | |

### Paeon

(Herbaceous peonies) This group includes the peonies we mostly grow in gardens. Some species are divided into subspecies, but most are stand-alone. As no two botanists or lists agree on the subspecies, I am including only the few that are in general use.

| | |
|---|---|
| P. algeriensis | ssp. *velebitensis* |
| P. anomala | ssp. *wittmanniana* * |
| P. arietina | P. emodi * |
| P. broteri | P. intermedia |
| P. californica | P. kesrouanensis |
| P. cambessedesii | P. lactiflora * |
| P. clusii | P. mairei |
| ssp. *clusii* | P. mascula |
| ssp. *rhodia* | P. obovata * |
| P. coriacea | ssp. *willmottiae* |
| P. corsica | P. officinalis |
| P. daurica | P. parnassica |
| ssp. *coriifolia* | P. peregrina * |
| ssp. *daurica* | P. steveniana |
| ssp. *macrophylla* | P. tenuifolia * |
| ssp. *mlokosewitschii** | P. veitchii * |
| ssp. *tomentosa* | |

## TYPES OF GARDEN PEONY

There are three basic types we grow in our gardens. Each has its own charm and use in the border. All are deciduous, losing their leaves in autumn.

**Herbaceous peonies** die right back from late summer onwards with nothing showing above ground in winter. They are divided into two distinct groups. Peonies in the largest group, lactiflora, have large, opulent flowers that bloom from early to late June in colours ranging from white to cerise-pink, dark crimson and, in more recent years, yellow. There are no true 'fire-engine' reds.

Hybrid peonies are the other type of herbaceous peony and are the result of crossing species peonies. Unlike lactiflora peonies, which all have similar mid-green leaves, the foliage of hybrid peonies varies from shiny to dull green, and the leaf shape from round-ended to deeply divided. Their flower colour is also different and can range from white and pale- to very bright pink, shades of apricot or true red. Many also bloom earlier than lactiflora types, from late April onwards.

**Intersectional peonies**, a relatively new group, are created by hybridising herbaceous with tree (woody) peonies. The leafy stems emerge each spring from the base of the plant and by autumn some have turned woody, while some die back just like herbaceous peonies. The flowers are very large, usually single or semi-double and range from white, apricot and lilac-pink to true red and yellow. In addition, the petals of some start out one colour then gradually change in tone as the bloom matures. Intersectional peonies are grown in the same way as herbaceous peonies and bloom at similar times to lactiflora and hybrid peonies.

**Tree peonies** should be more accurately called 'woody' peonies because their form is not a tree but a shrub, with woody stems that remain over winter. The flowers and leaves are usually much bigger than herbaceous peonies, although they bloom at the same time. The hybrids are organised into four groups: Japanese, Chinese, plus lutea and rockii hybrids, each creating a different shrubby shape. Throughout this book I have chosen to refer to these as tree peonies, the term that is most familiar to gardeners.

*Paeonia lactiflora* 'Adolphe Rousseau' with semi-double, reddish-pink flowers

Hybrid peony *Paeonia* 'Eliza Lundy' with double, bright-red flowers

*Paeonia* 'Hillary' is typical of an intersectional peony with big flowers that are evenly spaced and open just above the mound of deeply divided leaves

Lutea hybrid *Paeonia* 'Hesperus' with sideways-facing flowers

Japanese tree peony *Paeonia* 'Shimane Chojuraku' with upward-facing flowers

## PARTS OF THE FLOWER

To choose the right type of peony for your garden, it's very helpful to know about the different flower parts and shapes, and this also assists in identification. Below is a list of the terms used to describe peony flowers within this book.

**Carpels** are the female reproductive part of the flower. With peonies, each carpel contains ovules where seeds develop when pollinated. At the top is a stigma, often a different colour to the carpel. It is also called a pistil.

**Guard petals** are the outer petals that, at first, cover the bud. As the bud opens these petals get bigger and sit around the base of the inner petals. They can be very large or the same size as the other petals.

**Petaloids** are found in the middle of the flower and look like slender petals. Originally stamens, these have evolved over time to become wider and are sometimes forked or ragged at the tops. Unlike stamens, petaloids are sterile.

**Side buds** are carried on shorter stems below the flower, which blooms at the top. Largely characteristic of lactiflora peonies, they allow the plant to bloom for longer. Removing them enables the main flower to increase in size.

**Stamens** form a ring around the carpels and consist of male, pollen-bearing anthers on very fine, long filaments that can be a different colour.

**Staminodes** are modified stamens with anthers that no longer produce pollen. Instead, they have become flattened, are usually ridged along the edges and often yellow, although the colour may change. They are usually a feature of Japanese peonies. *Paeonia* 'Bowl of Beauty' (below) has both petaloids and staminodes.

Close-up of pollen and carpels of *Paeonia* 'Flame'

*Paeonia* 'Inspecteur Lavergne' has large outer guard petals

*Paeonia* 'Cora Stubbs' with a mound of almost white petaloids

Buds and side buds clearly visible on *Paeonia* 'Lemon Chiffon'

*The* yellow staminodes of *Paeonia* 'Moon of Nippon'

**Eyes** is a term used to describe the dormant leaf buds on herbaceous and intersectional peonies that sprout from the peony root. The new leaves and flowers are within the eyes. The outside of the eye is covered by a sheath that turns red as the bud starts to grow, eventually pushing the sheath apart. On intersectional peonies, eyes are produced on any woody stem that is beneath the soil. When herbaceous and intersectional peonies are sold bare-rooted, they are often priced according to the number of eyes on the plant.

*Paeonia* 'Bowl of Beauty' with petaloids and staminodes

Eyes on an intersectional peony

Eyes on a herbaceous peony

## FLOWER SHAPES

The eye-catching blooms of peonies are not only large, they can also change in shape with age. In some varieties the inner petals get larger, while those of others may become shorter towards the centre and form a dip. Petals can also change in tone and colour, giving the flower a different appearance at each stage. When describing peony flowers, different terms are used based on the number of petals. In this book I have used the following four terms for the flower shapes:

**Single** flowers have between 5 and 10 petals, although some experts include plants with 13 petals. They are arranged around a centre of carpels and pollen-bearing stamens. In the first few days of flowering, single peonies close up at night to protect the pollen, thereby prolonging the life of the flower.

**Semi-double** flowers display simple rings of petals or a fluffy mix of many petals. In both cases, the stamens are always visible and can be seen either between the petals or in the centre of the flower. Sometimes they produce a further crop of inner petals and when these grow as the bloom ages, it can be mistaken for a double flower.

**Japanese** flowers have an outer ring of large guard petals and an inner mound of staminodes that may change colour as the flower evolves. Sometimes Japanese peonies are referred to as 'imperial' peonies, while others are more correctly categorised as 'anemone-flowered'. The latter form describes flowers with inner petals made up of petaloids rather than staminodes. Personally, I prefer not to use the term anemone-flowered because this shape can often resemble a double peony and easily lead to confusion.

**Double** flowers are those that produce lots of petals. To be botanically accurate, all the petals of double forms, including the guard petals, should be evenly sized. Also, technically speaking, the inner petals of doubles are really petaloids but are not always described as such unless they are of a different colour. Double flowers can be further divided by shape. Some open into a dome, which can also be called a crown. Others form a bomb, making the flowers look like a scoop or ball of ice-cream, with layers of interwoven petals sitting on large guard petals. This inner ball can consist of more than one colour.

The single flowers of *Paeonia* 'Picotee'

Semi-double flowered *Paeonia* 'Buckeye Belle'

Japanese type *Paeonia* 'Tom Eckhardt'

Bomb-shaped double *Paeonia* 'Bridal Icing'

## FLOWER STEMS

**Lactiflora** peonies have strong stems but these vary in thickness. Those with thin, wiry stems and big, double flowers can topple over, especially in wet and windy weather. The fewer petals a flower has the more self-supporting it is.

**Hybrid** peonies, by and large, have thick stems but those with big flowers and long stems, don't always stay upright. Some, like the blooms of *Paeonia* 'Red Charm' (below) stand up because the stems are short as well as strong.

**Intersectional** peonies produce stems that are similar to those of herbaceous peonies, in spring. As summer trundles towards autumn, these turn woody.

**Tree peonies** have distinctive woody stems that are long, thick and branched – like any other shrub. The 'bark' is ridged.

## PEONIES THAT NEED NO SUPPORT

Single, semi-double and Japanese peonies don't need support to stay upright, nor do intersectional and tree peonies. Here is a short list of double peonies I have found to be reliably self-supporting:

'Adolphe Rousseau'
'Alexander Fleming'
'Barbara'
'Bouquet Perfect'
'Bunker Hill'
'Eliza Lundy'
'Emma Klehm'
'Inspecteur Lavergne'
'Joker'
'Karl Rosenfield'
'Madame Calot'
'Marie Lemoine'
'Myrtle Gentry'
'Nancy Nora'
'Red Charm'
'The Fawn'

*Paeonia* 'Red Charm' has strong, short flower stems

The leaves protect the flower buds

Yellow leaves of Paeonia 'Golden Frolic'

Intersectional peony leaves and pods

Paeonia 'Catharina Fontijn' leaves during October

## FLOWER BUDS

Peonies emerge in spring as the soil warms up. Lactiflora peonies produce young leaves the colour of rhubarb that tightly encase the flower buds. If you gently prise the leaves apart you should see the tiny buds. Hybrid flower buds are often bigger and the young stems are naked of leaves. Tree peonies and some intersectional peonies have big, pointed buds that are extremely beautiful. As the petals inside the buds form they gradually increase in size. It can take three months for a double-flowered peony to fully open.

## STEMS & LEAVES

Peony leaves are borne in pairs up the leaf stem and may consist of three to five leaflets or segments. These can be pointed, as on lactiflora types, or rounded as with many hybrid and species peonies. The leaves of tree peonies are much larger and, although not unlike those of herbaceous peonies, the leaf buds grow directly from the woody stem.

As the flower buds develop and the leaves unfurl in spring, the dark-red colour of the young stems diminishes. Although the stems often retain some red tints, the leaves change from red to bronze and eventually turn green. Leaf tones range from grass-green to dark green, or in the case of Paeonia 'Golden Frolic' (left), to yellow-green. The leaf edges can also vary. Some are smooth while others can be distinctly wavy or rippled.

## AUTUMN LEAVES

Peony leaves begin to decline at different rates and times. Those of herbaceous peonies are the first to die back, quickly turning from green to dull brown as early as late August. When foliage does produce autumn tints, the amount of colour seems to vary according to season and location, not peony variety. In some years our peony field is displaying autumn colours in October; in others it's just a sea of brown. By early autumn herbaceous peonies have gone dormant.

Owing to the thickness of their leaves, intersectional peonies and some tree peonies can look particularly impressive in autumn. Foliage can often maintain tones of yellow and red for some time. By late autumn, however, the leaves have simply, and neatly, dropped off and the plant persists as a clump of bare sticks.

## CLUMP SHAPE

Most herbaceous peonies carry the leaves low on the flower stem. As a result, on taller plants the flowers sit proud of the lush mound of foliage. If the flower stems are very long they can create a leggy clump and the stems may topple over. Intersectional peonies are different. The leaves are densely packed in a neat ground-hugging dome that can be short, round or more upright. Like tree peonies, they need no support and both types remain upright all year, adding structure over winter.

Jewel-like seeds of Paeonia 'Picotee'

## SEEDS & PODS

Once the flower has finished blooming the carpels in the centre get to work and fill the pod, either with or without seeds. Eventually they look rather like a jester's hat. As the pod ages it starts to dry and crack down the central groove, opening to reveal the seeds. Both seeds and seed pods of peonies are unique. Large and structurally attractive, they add autumn interest to what might otherwise be a dull end to a plant.

Each type of peony produces a different style of pod. Lactifloras have the least interesting pods, but those of intersectional and tree peonies can look and feel furry to the touch. Peony seeds also differ according to type. Tree peony seeds can be as big as a pea, those of herbaceous peonies are smaller. All turn black as the outer coat hardens. Often, seeds that are red in colour are revealed when the pod opens. These are unfertilised seeds and although not viable they look most attractive. Intersectional peonies almost never produce seeds.

## SCENT

Fragrance and the ability to smell it differs from person to person. Not all peonies are scented and with some the fragrance is hard to detect. For each herbaceous peony in this book, its scent has been assigned to one of four categories: none (does not exist), light (may be elusive), medium (obvious scent) and heavy (powerful scent). Pinpointing a scent is also difficult. Some heavily scented flowers are reminiscent of roses; others are what I can only describe as pollen-scented and not dissimilar to the perfume of lilies. Some peonies are said to smell of honey, but I've never detected that fragrance. The scent of others can be quite unpleasant. Make the most of any attractively scented peonies by placing your vase of cut stems in a warm room. As the fragrance warms, the more obvious it is. Below is a list of some of the most fragrant peonies:

**Lactiflora peonies**
  'Alexander Fleming'
  'Amalia Olsen'
  'Ann Cousins'
  'Best Man'
  'Bouquet Perfect'
  'Bridal Icing'
  'Edulis Superba'
  'Florence Nicholls'
  'Germaine Bigot'
  'Gilbert Barthelot'
  'Glory Hallelujah'
  'Golden Frolic'
  'Krinkled White'
  'Marie Lemoine'
  'Marietta Sisson'
  'Monsieur Jules Elie'
  'Myrtle Gentry'
  'Nancy Nora'
  'Nice Gal'
  'Nick Shaylor'
  'Pink Parfait'
  'President Wilson'
  'Surugu'
  'Vivid Rose'
  'Vogue'

**Hybrid peonies**
  'Claire de Lune'

**Intersectional peonies**
  'Bartzella'
  'Hillary'
  'Garden Treasure'

## FOR CUTTING

Peonies as cut flowers have become much more popular in recent years, especially in wedding bouquets. The soft colours and folds of the petals perfectly complement floaty wedding gowns. The increased availability of peonies as cut flowers has also been a factor. Most supplies are grown in the Netherlands; the roots are then sold for planting in the garden.

As a cut flower, peonies can last for up to 10 days in a vase, although this does depend on the variety. Cerise-red peonies tend to have a short vase life, whereas white and pink ones, especially those with thick petals, last particularly well.

Always cut the flowers before the weather gets too warm and preferably when in bud rather than in full bloom. Gently squeeze the bud between your fingers: if it's soft and squashy then it's ready to cut. Try to leave a few sets of leaves on the stem or you will deplete the plant's energy reserves.

Peonies picked as the blooms are just opening

Those who are serious about growing peonies for cutting and arranging might want to remove the side buds, as this will encourage bigger flowers. Cutting the flower stems under water may also prolong their life, as will adding flower food to the vase water. I've found the flowers last well simply by cutting them early in the day and putting them straight into water. Here is a list of peonies I find last well:

**Lactiflora peonies**
  'Alexander Fleming'
  'Alice Harding'
  'Amalia Olson'
  'Barbara'
  'Bouquet Perfect'
  'Bowl of Cream'
  'Bridal Icing'
  'Dinner Plate'
  'Duchesse de Nemours'
  'Edulis Superba'
  'Festiva Maxima'
  'Gay Paree'
  'Lady Alexandra Duff'
  'Monsieur Jules Elie'
  'Myrtle Gentry'
  'Nancy Nora'
  'Pillow Talk'
  'Sarah Bernhardt'
  'Shirley Temple'
  'Solange'
  'Vogue'

**Hybrid peonies**
  'Coral Charm'
  'Coral Sunset'
  'Cytherea'
  'Red Charm'
  'Scarlet O'Hara'

*Paeonia* 'Bouquet Perfect', one of the most scented peonies

A vase of peonies and roses in late June

Wedding bouquet of May-blooming peonies, roses and a dahlia

# GROWING PEONIES

### HARDINESS, SUN & SOIL

Peonies are extremely hardy plants. They cope with winters that drop to -30° C and summer heat up to 40° C. What's more, once established they will live for many years with very little attention.

#### Soil

Peonies prefer a deep, rich loam that has plenty of nutrients, although they will happily grow in other soils. A clay soil is perfect, provided it is well-drained. The one thing peonies do not like is soil that remains waterlogged for any length of time, especially through winter. This can cause the roots to rot. At the other extreme, peonies won't flourish if they are very dry at the roots, particularly in spring when the flower buds are swelling. Sandy, stony or chalky soils can be dry for much of the year, but as long as there is sufficient moisture in spring and autumn you can grow peonies, although they may take longer to establish than in richer soils.

#### Sun & Shade

To be absolutely sure that peonies will flower well, plant them in a sunny place. They will, however, grow in spot that is shaded for some of the day. *Paeonia wittmanniana* subsp. 'Rosea' is happy with more shade than most as it grows naturally along the outskirts of lightly wooded areas. In my garden lactiflora *Paeonia* 'Shirley Temple' also does well. Planted about 15 years ago on the north side of the house, this gets around half a day of sun in summer, but none in winter.

### BUYING PEONIES

There are two ways of buying peonies: as bare-rooted plants or in containers. From experience, I'd recommend buying bare-rooted plants that have been lifted from the ground when the peony is dormant in autumn. These are available from late October until just before the leaves emerge in early spring, usually around mid-February. Do bear in mind that planting before the days get longer and lighter is preferable as peony growth is triggered by light.

Potted plants are fine, but peonies don't grow well if confined in a pot for more than a year. Peony roots are very large and a pot will simply restrict their growth.

Container-grown plants are available, but bare-rooted peonies make better plants

### HOW TO PLANT BARE-ROOT PEONIES

Dig a hole wide enough and deep enough to accommodate the roots. Place the plant in the hole following the planting rules below, and cover with soil. Unless a period of dry weather is forecast, they don't need watering. Label your peony immediately – unless it's a tree peony, you won't remember where you have put it. I have always understood that it is best not to plant peonies where they have been grown before. The reason? I'm not sure.

**Herbaceous peonies** need to be planted with the eyes (see p.8) no more than 5cm below the soil surface. If they are planted too deeply the plant may struggle to produce flowers.

**Intersectional peonies** are planted in a similar way to herbaceous peonies. Ignore the level of the woody stems and, using the red eyes on the wide crown as your guide to depth, plant these around 5cm below the soil.

**Tree peonies** are planted in a totally different way to herbaceous peonies, especially if the plant has been grafted. On a grafted plant (see below), the lower section of root will be thicker than the upper, which is the graft. The point where the two sections meet should be at least 8cm below the soil surface, which might mean that very little of the 'stick' is visible. Don't worry, in spring new shoots will emerge from beneath the soil. Seed-raised peonies, such as *Paeonia delavayi*, are quite happy planted as deep as you wish.

Lifted in December, this bare-rooted herbaceous peony has new fine roots

A bare-rooted intersectional peony with some woody stems left on

Grafted tree peony showing the thick rootstock at the base

## TIDYING UP

**Herbaceous peonies** can suffer from fungal diseases, and spores persist in the soil over winter. Once the plant is looking tatty, the leaves and the old flower stems should be cut down and removed. I generally do this in spring when the new shoots start to show. Here in mid-Wales, that can be as early as late February.

**Intersectional peonies** are generally disease free, but to keep a plant looking tidy you can always remove leaves when they drop in autumn. I also prune the woody stems before the leaves start to emerge in spring so the clump looks neat and domed, rather than an unbalanced mix of a few tall and many shorter stems.

**Tree peonies** will provide winter shelter for birds and small creatures when the leaves are left on the plant. If you wish to tidy up the plant in autumn, this can be done by simply snapping the leaves off the plant. However, the old foliage is much easier to pull off in spring when the new leaf shoots start to grow. Spring is also the time to tame a plant that has lost its shape or grown too big. Use clean secateurs to prune the woody stem just above a red leaf bud. Take out the amount of stem you need to create a neat shrub, but not so much that the pruned stem is left with no leaf buds. Removing one or two stems entirely won't harm the plant.

## FERTILISING

Fertilising peonies can help them flourish, although poor growth can be due to lack of water or sun (see Troubleshooting p.15). I rarely fertilise my peonies but if you do, never use fresh farmyard manure. If this sits too near to the peony stems it will cause them to rot. Make sure you use very well-rotted manure and apply in a ring at least 15cm from the plant before the new shoots appear. Alternatively, apply a general-purpose granular fertiliser according to the instructions.

## SUPPORT

Some peonies need support to keep the flower stems from tumbling over. The sturdiest and most elegant are made of metal, but a ring of thick stakes can look attractive when secured at the top with a circle of intertwined willow stems. Supports should be put in place before the flower stems become too tall.

The leaves of herbaceous peonies start to die off in late August

Tree peony shoots after pruning in early spring

The tall flower stems of *Paeonia* 'Coral Charm' need supporting

## MOVING A PEONY

Although peonies can thrive in the same spot for decades there may come a time when they need to be relocated, perhaps because you are moving house or the plant has outgrown its space. There is a long-held but totally unfounded gardening belief that peonies cannot be moved. On the nursery we have lifted and divided many peonies. And what's more, they have often flowered in their first year. Success in replanting depends on the size of the peony in question, the number of eyes on the plant and the amount of root.

Peonies should be moved when they are dormant. With lactiflora peonies the leaves start to die back at the end of August. Tree peonies and intersectionals go dormant in early autumn. I have found that leaving a plant a little longer in the soil before lifting allows the eyes to fatten. This also makes it easier to see where to divide it.

## LIFTING

First, dig the plant out of the ground using a fork or a spade. Old plants will be very large and we often use a mini-digger! It is likely that you won't be able get the whole peony out and some thick roots may snap. This won't harm the plant, but try to lift as much of it out of the ground as you can. You will find that peonies with bulbous roots, such as *Paeonia officinalis* types, will sprout again if roots are left in the soil.

## MAKING DIVISIONS

Having lifted the peony out of the ground, blast it with water from a hose pipe to clear away the soil. This will also help you to find the eyes. First, cut the thick roots back, but to no less than 15cm in length. At the top of the roots, the eyes – next year's leaf shoots – should now be clearly visible. For the plant to have a chance of flowering the next year, each division should have 3 eyes, although 5 to 8 eyes is even better. Take a good look at the plant and, starting from the eyes, seek out those attached to the biggest root. It is very easy to slice away and end up with eyes but no roots. Using a large, sturdy knife or pair of sharp secateurs, insert the tip of the blade around the top of the plant and carefully slice downwards. With luck and a bit of practice you will be able to divide the plant into some nice, healthy pieces ready for planting out (see p.12).

## GROWING FROM SEED

Growing peonies from seed requires patience. Not all peonies set seeds, and even when they do, the seed may not turn out like the parent, even if they are from a species peony. To check for seeds, gently squeeze the pod and if it feels hard it may well have seeds. Single-flowered peonies form seeds more readily than other types.

### Collecting

Seeds are ready to gather when the pod begins to split down the central groove. This can happen at any time from late August onwards. If the pod has not opened fully, prise it gently open and take out the seeds, which may be sticky to the touch. Seeds with a soft or sticky coating will germinate more readily than those where the outer coat has hardened.

### Sowing

Sow the fresh seeds into deep plastic pots (these won't dry out quickly) that you have filled with multi-purpose, peat-free compost and cover them with twice their own depth of sieved compost. Alternatively, seeds can go straight into the soil, but they might get eaten by mice.

Put the pot outside where it will remain cold or even freeze over winter. A cold spell will aid germination. Now comes the part that requires patience: the seeds need to be ignored for at least two years. Once germination has taken place, only the roots are produced in the first year. Leaves don't appear until the second year.

Another word of warning: although seeds can produce a flowering plant within four years, this may take up to seven years.

The dried outer coat of this single seed means it could take longer to germinate

Rootstock (left) with V-shaped incision and the scion (right) with wedge-shaped end

Seedlings of *Paeonia delavayi*

The new growth on a grafted tree peony after a year

## GRAFTING TREE PEONIES

There are no short cuts when propagating tree peonies by grafting. It is one of the most difficult ways to increase your stock and requires skill. Having made a few attempts, I have so far had little success. But don't be put off. If you are a keen gardener, enjoy tasks that require precision, and have access to a mature tree peony, it could be very rewarding.

### Equipment

You will need two sharp blades, such as a scalpel or box cutter, and grafting tape (thin strips of cling film also work). Make sure everything is very clean.

1. Grafting should be done in August and September, before the stems that were produced in spring become woody. First select your stock plant: you will be using its root (the rootstock) to take grafts. Some choose a vigorous hybrid peony such as *Paeonia* 'Scarlet O'Hara'. Lift this plant and cut some thick pieces of disease-free root that are about 2cm in diameter and 15–20cm long. Wash off any soil.

2. Select a stem (called the scion) from your dormant tree peony. This should have 2 or 3 eyes, and be at least 15cm long. I have found that removing the top bud from the stem gives a better chance of success.

3. Cut a V-shaped incision into the top of the root. This will accommodate the wedge-shaped end of the scion (see 4). Using two blades, carefully angle one blade down towards the centre of the root top and leave it there. Using the second blade, make another angled cut down to the first blade, which is there to stop you cutting too deeply. Having a number of roots helps with this tricky process.

4. Make a two-sided slanting cut on the bottom end of the scion to form a wedge then slot this vertically into the V-shaped incision on the rootstock aligned the bark of the scion with that of the rootstock. The scion should fit snuggly, with no gaps, so that in time the two parts can form a seal (the graft union). Bind them tightly with grafting tape so there is no movement and no water can enter the scion.

5. Plant out the grafts in a prepared bed with well-drained soil that is not too dry. A raised bed is a good idea. Sink the grafts deeply into the soil about 10–15cm above the graft union so that rootstock and scion can produce roots underground. Label.

Leave untouched for two years. Good luck!

## TROUBLESHOOTING

Peonies have few ailments. Below I have listed the most common ones.

**Peony Wilt** (*Botrytis paeoniae*) is a fungal disease that can occur when the weather is wet and relatively warm. The stem, and sometimes the flower buds, turn brown and mouldy, and the stem will topple over. Remove and destroy the entire stem. To prevent it happening again spray the whole plant with a systemic fungicide – we use one suitable for roses. You can also clear away dead leaves in autumn, then in spring re-spray the emerging leaves and the surrounding soil with the same fungicide.

**Leaf Blotch** (*Cladosporium paeoniae*) appears after the plant has bloomed. Reddish-brown, irregularly shaped spots of this fungus mark otherwise healthy leaves. These don't damage the plant, but you can always remove them and spray the plant with a systemic fungicide.

**Waterlogging** causes the roots to rot, and the plant to die. If you discover that the soil is far too wet, especially during winter, the only option is to move the plant as soon as possible.

**Frost** can damage the early shoots, which keel over. This causes no permanent damage as peonies can produce further shoots if the first ones are damaged.

## ANTS

Ants don't harm a peony. They are simply collecting the sugary substance that exudes from the flower bud. As soon as the bud opens, the ants disappear.

Leaf blotches won't harm the plant

Overly dry soil has stopped the growth of the flower bud on the left

### TREE PEONY ROGUE LEAVES

A tree peony can produce two different types of leaf, especially in the early years. The rogue leaves, which are often red and less divided than the true leaves, will spring from the base of the peony and are produced from the grafted rootstock. Remove them by pulling or cutting off as they will weaken the growing tree peony.

### FAILURE TO FLOWER

Peony growers are always asked about a plant's failure to flower and below are the most likely reasons for this. But remember that peonies can take up to three years to bloom after planting.

**Planting too deeply** can prevent the formation of flowering shoots. This can easily be resolved by lifting the plant in autumn and replanting it at the correct depth (see p.12).

**Not enough moisture** in the soil will stop the buds from swelling. If the soil is usually moist, but the spring weather is unusually dry, normal flowering should resume the following year. If the soil is permanently dry, move the peony to a spot where the soil gets good rainfall in autumn. Growing peonies in too much shade where overhanging foliage reduces moisture levels can also inhibit flowering. A more open spot is preferable.

**Wet conditions** can cause problems. Flower stems can collapse and flower buds can turn brown and fail to open. This happens with roses and is called 'balling'. Side buds tend to be affected most but it will not cause lasting damage to the plant.

Ants collecting a sugary substance will not damage the peony bud

Early emerging peony shoots can suffer from frost damage in April or May

Flower buds can be spoiled by rain

Growing Peonies | 15

# PEONIES IN THE GARDEN

The majority of peonies are easy to grow in a border among other perennials and shrubs. Whether your border is small and narrow, or large and wide there is a peony to suit every situation, even areas with some shade. But before you rush ahead to plant your peony, there are a few rules to consider for each peony type.

## PLANTING DISTANCE

**Herbaceous peonies** need plenty of space around them in the first few years after planting. Their roots will eventually spread far wider than the clump of leaves extends above ground. To avoid competition from surrounding plants, a peony needs to be planted with half a metre or so of space on either side. During these early years other, smaller plants with shallow roots can be grown near or between the peonies. A list of plant companions can be found on p.29.

**Intersectional peonies** create a densely packed mound of leaves. This is likely to shade out any smaller plants growing nearby as the peony increases in size. Ensure a clear space of at least a metre around these peonies in the early years.

**Tree peonies** make ideal statement plants. When fully mature these can tower above other plants, especially when growing in a border. They do have large roots that don't seem to crowd out those of neighbouring plants, but the canopy of tree peonies may overshadow plants that grow beneath them.

*Paeonia wittmaniana* subsp. 'Rosea' flowers early

*Paeonia* 'First Arrival' is the first intersectional peony to bloom

*Paeonia* 'Angelet' blooms at the same time as *Geum* 'Mai Tai'

*Paeonia* 'Madame Emile Debatène' blooms in late midseason

## FLOWERING SEASON

Although most peonies bloom in June, the earliest can be in flower as early as April. Below is a list of my favourite show-stoppers by bloom season. Choose just 4 varieties from the list below and you can have peonies flowering in the garden for as long as 3 months.

**KEY** to letters in brackets
**Shape**: S - single, SD - semi-double
J - Japanese, D - double
**Type**: L - lactiflora, H - hybrid,
I - intersectional

### Very early: April to mid-May
'Avant Garde' (S, H)
'Early Windflower' (S, H)
'Honor' (S, H)
'Picotee' (S, H)

### Early: mid-May to early June
'Claire de Lune' (S, H)
'Cytherea' (SD, H)
'Eliza Lundy' (D, H)
'First Arrival' (SD, I)
'Krinkled White' (S, L)
'Lemon Chiffon' (D, H)
'Moonrise' (S, H)
'Red Charm' (D, H)
'Roselette' (S, H)

### Midseason: early to mid-June
'Alexander Fleming' (D, L)
'Bartzella' (SD, I)
'Bowl of Beauty' (J, L)
'Bouquet Perfect' (D, L)
'Doreen' (J, L)
'Félix Crousse' (D, L)
'Honey Gold' (J, L)
'Late Windflower' (S, H)
'Midnight Sun' (J, L)
'Myrtle Gentry' (D, L)
'Nancy Nicholls' (D, L)
'Nymphe' (S, L)
'Paul M. Wild' (D, L)
'Pillow Talk' (D, L)
'Sea Shell' (S, L)
'White Wings' (S, L)

### Late season: mid- to late June
'Dinner Plate' (D, L)
'Elsa Sass' (D, L)
'Emma Klehm' (D, L)
'Glory Hallelujah' (D, L)
'Jan Van Leeuwen' (J, L)
'Lady Orchid' (D, L)
'Marie Lemoine' (D, L)
'Pink Parfait' (D, L)

## VERY EARLY TO EARLY SPRING

Spring is one of the most joyous times in the gardening year and April is the first month when flowers make an impact. Although the number of plants in bloom is still limited, newly emerging leaves will create a green, heavily textured carpet. The red leaves of peonies, which in my garden erupt at regular intervals, contrast beautifully with this green tapestry.

The colour of the young leaves is not always red. Those of *Paeonia* 'Lovebirds' are very dark purple and they gradually turn green as the flower buds fatten. At its base I grow an *Epimedium* with fairy-like sprays of little flowers. It won't be troubled by the shade cast over it by the canopy of peony leaves.

One of the loveliest very early flowering peonies is *Paeonia* 'Early Windflower' with gently nodding pure white flowers that grace an upright clump of deeply divided leaves. Coming into bloom slightly later is cream-flowered *Paeonia* 'Claire de Lune'. This earliest large-flowered single peony produces so many side buds that it will still be in flower at the end of May. For a while both peonies bloom together. When the flowers come to an end, the leafy mound of *P.* 'Early Windflower' adds structure to the border, while the leaves of *P.* 'Claire de Lune' simply fade into the pattern of other perennial foliage that surrounds the plant.

The buds of later-blooming hybrids are now starting to fatten. Set on red stems, these look simply lovely when grown among perennials with different leaf colours and shapes.

White Hopton Garden in April when the young red leaves of all types of peonies are scattered through the border

*Paeonia* 'Lovebirds' with flowering *Epimedium pubigerum*

Rounded buds of *Paeonia* 'Lemon Chiffon' contrast with spears of iris foliage

*Paeonia* 'Claire de Lune' and *P.* 'Early Windflower' with blue *Centaurea*

*Paeonia* 'Early Windflower' towers elegantly over its neighbours

Hybrid peony *Paeonia* 'Moonrise' sits in the middle of a large border surrounded by the young foliage of summer-flowering perennials, spring-blooming *Aquilegia vulgaris* 'Ruby Port' and *Euphorbia palustris* with lime flowerheads at the back

## EARLY SUMMER

Towards the end of May very early flowering hybrid and species peonies are nearing the end of their blooming period. Early season lactiflora peonies, later-blooming hybrid peonies and a few tree peonies then continue the show. Big and vividly coloured, the flowers of the latter two are likely to dominate a border. They may also clash with other flowers that are softly coloured or of a similarly large size.

To avoid competition between peonies and other flowers, select perennials that produce a generous display of small flowers. Airy dots of colour will add lightness and contrast with the big peony flowers, avoiding a 'blocky' look. *Aquilegia* (Granny's bonnet), *Astrantia* (Masterwort), *Potentilla rupestris* (Cinquefoil) and tall hardy geraniums are the perfect companions. Their delicate sprays of small blooms sit on upright slender stems at around the same height as the peony.

For balance at the level below the peony foliage, go for mounding perennials with handsome leaves such as *Polemonium* 'Lambrook Mauve' (Jacob's ladder), *Brunnera* (Siberian bugloss) and *Centaurea* (Perennial cornflower). All flower at the same time as peonies and their blooms are much more subtle.

Try to avoid growing plants with large flowers next to peonies if both bloom at the same time. Oriental poppies (*Papaver orientalis*) and flamboyant bearded irises can fight with peonies for attention, although soft-blue irises are an exception. Iris foliage, however, does add excellent upright structure. Choose Siberian and shorter bearded irises that flower well before peonies and you'll avoid colour clashes and competition. Short early irises will also sit neatly in front of the peony.

To create a soft, billowing effect around peonies, use perennials that carry their gently coloured flowers in frothy clouds. *Alchemilla mollis* (Lady's mantle), *Gillenia trifoliata* (Bowman's root), *Chaerophyllum hirsutum* 'Roseum' (Hairy chervil) and *Nepeta* (Catmint) are ideal and their shapes and colours complement peonies in the early summer border.

For colour later in the season and to ensure the border isn't devoid of flowers, plant hardy geraniums and hardy salvias next to early flowering peonies.

*Paeonia* 'Honor' with *Euphorbia polychroma* and *Stachys byzantina* in front, *Geum* 'Prinses Juliana' and *Geranium maculatum* 'Vicki Lynn' on the left

Fluffy, white mound of *Gillenia trifoliata* and purple *Aquilegia vulgaris* 'Ruby Port' add contrast and symmetry to early June blooms of *Paeonia* 'Kansas'

*Paeonia* 'Westerner' with the upright blooms of *Digitalis purpurea* (wild foxglove)

*Chaerophyllum hirsutum* 'Roseum' with *Paeonia* 'Picotee'

Self-supporting *Paeonia* 'Myrtle Gentry' with delicate *Aquilegia vulgaris* 'Alba' (right), *Achillea* 'Moonshine' (front right) and maroon *Sanguisorba menziesii* (front left)

Late-flowering *Paeonia* 'Elsa Sass' blends perfectly with *Geranium clarkei* 'Kashmir Blue' (front), grey *Stachys byzantina* (behind) and greenish-yellow *Alchemilla mollis* (rear left)

## MIDSUMMER

The majority of peonies bloom in mid-June and almost all are lactiflora types, although some tree peonies and a few hybrid peonies are still in flower. Lactiflora peonies grow into glorious large clumps and many bear flowers in colours that blend harmoniously with other perennials in bloom at the same time.

Perennials with flowers in tall spires add a graceful touch to a border where peonies bloom. Summer-flowering *Aconitum* (Monkshood), *Campanula* (Bellflower), lupins and delphiniums are ideal, while *Centranthus ruber* (Valerian) and upright white- or pink-flowered *Lychnis coronaria* will complement the bold, rounded peony flowers.

Add a horizontal dimension to the border with plants such as *Achillea* (Yarrow). The flat plates of small flowers will create lines of colour. Placed in front of the peony, shorter plants like *Dianthus* will provide colour around the base of the plant and fill any gaps. Short hardy geraniums belonging to the *Geranium sanguineum* group do much the same job.

Indeed, hardy geraniums may be the perfect companions for peonies. Small and disc-like, the flowers dispense continuous colour at a lower level for months after peony flowers have faded.

Bold peony foliage is less dominant when broken up by the short, upright flower spikes of hardy salvias and tall *Digitalis grandiflora* (Foxglove) blooms. The iris-like spears of *Sisyrinchium striatum* foliage also work well.

Orange *Geum* 'Totally Tangerine' and *P.* 'Auguste Dessert' are strongly coloured

*P.* 'Shirley Temple' with pink *Astrantia* 'Roma' and red *Heuchera sanguinea*

Tall *Aruncus*, *P.* 'Shirley Temple' and magenta *Geranium psilostemon*

Adding contrast to the bowl-shaped blooms of *Paeonia* 'Surugu' are the spires of grey-leaved *Stachys byzantina* (rear) and pale-yellow spikes of *Sisyrinchium striatum*. The deep-pink divided heads of *Dianthus carthusianorum* blend in beautifully

The white flowers of *Paeonia* 'Bridal Icing' with blue *Centaurea* and *Geranium*

*Paeonia* 'Auguste Dessert' with lilac-pink *Salvia nemorosa* 'Amethyst'

## CONSIDERING COLOUR

Big, showy peony flowers with solid colour can so easily dominate a border unless you give careful consideration to the colour balance between the peony bloom and those of its neighbours.

**Red** is not a very common colour among garden plants and peony blooms oblige with a range of red tones according to type. Lactiflora peonies bloom in tones from soft crimson to dark burgundy – colours that sit on the blue side of the spectrum. These combine well with any blue-flowered plant. Hybrid and intersectional peonies, on the other-hand, drift towards the yellow end of red, in tones that don't sit well with blue but look good with yellow. Eye-catching red hybrid peonies can make a lovely focal point in an early spring border.

**Pink** peony flowers can be a very pale, mid- or a vivid lipstick shade. The softer-toned flowers blend easily in a border with almost any colour of flower, while the harsher pinks of some hybrid peonies look well with lilac and soft-pink flowers. Like red hybrid peonies, when grown as a focal point in a spring border they can look stunning.

**Coral** flowers are almost unknown in the plant world. Found in hybrid and intersectional peonies, the underlying colour of the petal is yellow overlaid with pink. As the flower ages the pink fades and the flower becomes more yellow. I find these extremely difficult to blend in a border so my solution is to grow them where nothing else is blooming.

*Paeonia* 'America' sits on the corner of a border where the early blooms stand out

*P.* 'Magical Mystery Tour' with pale-pink *Geranium*, backed by *Stachys* and *Heuchera*

**Yellow** flowers, until recently, were only seen on species and tree peonies, but over recent decades breeders have produced herbaceous and intersectional peonies in different shades of yellow. Herbaceous peony flowers are pale yellow, almost cream, the flowers of tree and intersectional peony can be a brighter shade. Like daffodils, these look great with orange or blue-coloured spring flowers.

**White** is an easy option as it combines with almost any colour. White peonies can also display a boss of yellow stamens or cream/yellow tints when the petaloids expand. An occasional streak of red might also taint a white petal on lactiflora peonies. The purest white flowers are found amongst hybrid peonies.

Violet-blue hardy *Geranium* 'Brookside' tones with the rich-red of *P.* 'Paul M. Wild'

Soft yellow *Paeonia* 'Lemon Chiffon' with bright orange *Geum* 'Prinses Juliana'

*Paeonia* 'Paula Fay' next to *Aquilegia vulgaris* with the short lilac spires of *Veronica* 'Ellen Mae', nodding white blooms of *Potentilla rupestris* and silver *Stachys byzantina* at the front

**A blend of colours** is a feature of Japanese peony flowers. The central staminodes are always yellow (although they may change with age) but the guard petals display the principal colour. Always focus on this colour when thinking how to blend these peonies into the border.

**Roses and peonies** don't usually make good companions. Big peony flowers, although similar in shape, will just compete with roses. Their habits are also very different. Rose bushes are tall, rigid and lush with leaves while peonies carry their foliage further down the flower stems. The only successful pairing is perhaps a single or semi-double peony next to a rose with small blooms.

*Paeonia* 'Petite Porcelain' in front of English rose *Rosa* 'Boscobel'

### BEST PEONIES FOR COLOUR

Lactiflora peonies range in tone from white to pink and dark red. Hybrid peonies bloom in shades of yellow, hot pink or true red as do tree and intersectional peonies. Below is a short list of recommended peonies by colour

**KEY** to letters in brackets
**Shape**: S - single, SD - semi-double
J - Japanese, D - double
**Type**: L - lactiflora, H - hybrid, I - intersectional, SP - species

#### White
'Bridal Icing' (D, L)
'Elsa Sass' (D, L)
'Honey Gold' (D L)
'Jan Van Leeuwen' (J, L)
'Krinkled White' (S, L)

#### Soft Pink
'Angel Cheeks' (D, L)
'Lady Orchid' (D, L)
'Myrtle Gentry' (D, L)
'Pillow Talk' (D, L)
'Pink Princess' (S, L)

#### Mid-Pink
'Bowl of Beauty' (J, L)
'First Arrival' (SD, I)
'Honor' (S, H)
*officinalis* 'Anemoniflora Rosea' (J, SP)
'The Fawn' (D, L)

#### Hot Pink
'Cytherea' (SD, H)
'Paula Fay' (SD, H)
'Tom Eckhardt' (J, L)

#### Deep Pink
'Barbara' (D, L)
'Gay Paree' (J, L)
'Helen Hayes' (D, L)
'Nice Gal' (D, L)
'Queen of Sheba' (D, L)

#### Cerise Pink to Dark Red
'Buckeye Belle' (SD, H)
'Inspecteur Lavergne' (D, L)
'Paul M. Wild' (D, L)
'Walter Mains' (J, H)

#### True Red
'Eliza Lundy' (D, H)
'Red Charm' (D, H)
'Scarlet O'Hara' (S, H)

#### Coral
'Coral Charm' (SD, H)

#### Yellow
'Bartzella' (SD, I)
'Goldilocks' (D, H)
'Lemon Chiffon (D, H)
'Moonrise' (S, H)

Peonies in the garden | 23

Four Intersectional peony varieties sit at regular intervals in this long, broad border with clumps of *Aster*, *Astrantia* (Masterwort) and hardy geraniums in-between. At the far end, golden-leaved *Paeonia* 'Golden Frolic' is backed by tall *Stipa gigantea* and purple-leaved *Sambucus*

*Astrantia major* and *Geranium renardii* add lightness to *Paeonia* 'Morning Lilac'

*Paeonia* 'First Arrival' with toning *Aquilegia vulgaris* 'Ruby Port' and *Veronica* 'Ellen Mae'

## INTERSECTIONALS IN THE BORDER

These sturdy plants can require some thought when placing in a border. Not only are the flowers large and voluptuous, the foliage grows into a prominent mound that changes little throughout summer.

If you have space for more than one intersectional peony they can be planted at intervals down a long, wide border with perennials that don't grow much higher than the peony. Upright *Geum* (Avens), mounding hardy geranium and bushy *Salvia* or *Veronica* (Speedwell) are good choices. Later-blooming perennials that rise higher than the peonies can be planted a little further away. These will punctuate the summer and early autumn picture as the peonies recede into the background. To soften the green wall of leaves, place plants with small leaves in front. Asters and *Calamintha* (Calamint) as well as plants with sword-like leaves such as irises and *Kniphofia* will help the vista and yield colour from late summer well into autumn.

Intersectional peonies need no support which makes them ideal for growing in a narrow border, even one with some shade such as one along the north side of a drive way. Spring-flowering plants that thrive in shade, such as *Primula* can fill the gaps. For the same reason they are perfect on corner of borders. Shorter perennials like *Persicaria affinis* (Bistort) and *Centaurea* (Perennial cornflower) will allow the peony to stand proud of the border and provide continuous colour throughout the season.

The same border (see left) in September when the peony flowers have been replaced by red *Sedum* (front), *Kniphofia* and *Sanguisorba* (middle) and dark-leaved *Aster* 'Glow in the Dark'

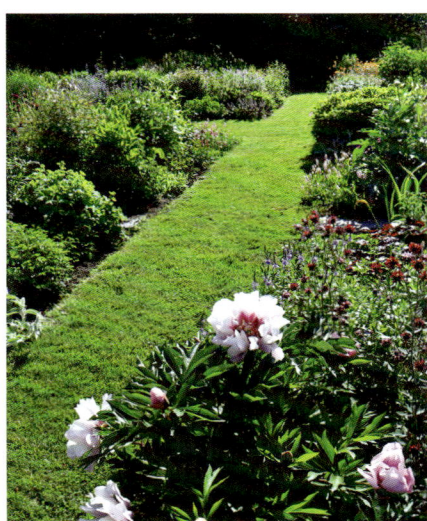

*P.* 'Cora Louise' stands out on the corner of this border edged by a long grass path

Peonies in the garden | 25

## TREE PEONIES IN THE BORDER

With flowers of spectacular beauty and attractive divided leaves, a tree peony always creates a statement in the garden. Grow this woody shrub in a border with other complementary plants, or alone in a lawn where its elegance can be admired.

Generally speaking, peonies look most at home in cottage-style gardens rather than in 'modern perennial' schemes that mix tall grasses and autumn-flowering plants. Their open shape harmonises with informal styles and allows shorter plants and grasses enough light to thrive.

The species types, *Paeonia delavayi* and *P. ludlowii*, form bulky shrubs with copious amounts of leaves. They are most suitable for bigger gardens, placed at the back of a generously sized border. Shorter tree peonies work well in a mixed border with low-growing perennials, such as *Galium odoratum* (Sweet woodruff) and *Pulmonaria* (Lungwort). These are short enough to allow the handsome structure of the woody peony stems to be seen but will cover the bare ground beneath.

Most tree peonies have large, showy blooms in white to yellow and orange to red tones. Purple and orange-flowered perennials will complement the yellows while blue, white and pink ones look good with the reds.

The tree peony's framework of woody stems is a particularly valuable asset in the garden. It will remain visible all winter and provide much-needed structure.

## FOR WINDY GARDENS

Peonies, especially tall herbaceous varieties with heavy blooms, will struggle in gardens exposed to strong gusts of wind. If you cannot find a spot that is sheltered from high winds, don't worry – there are varieties that are suitable for such locations. Intersectional and tree peonies are rigid enough to withstand wind, while single and Japanese herbaceous peonies, will stay upright because their flowers are light in weight. Some semi-double and double peonies with short, stocky stems are also unlikely to fall over. Here is a brief list of double peonies that tend to withstand high winds and heavy rain. Those marked with an * are also short:

**KEY** to letters in brackets:
L - lactiflora, H - hybrid

- 'Adolphe Rousseau' (L)
- 'Bouquet Perfect' (L)
- 'Cutie' (H) *
- 'Eliza Lundy' (H)
- 'Emma Klehm' (L)
- 'Glory Hallelujah' (L)
- 'Helen Hayes' (L)
- 'Joker' (L)
- 'Lancaster Imp' (L) *
- 'Margeret Truman' (L)
- 'Martha Reed' (L)
- 'Myrtle Gentry' (L)
- 'Nancy Nora' ( L)
- 'Petite Elegance' (L) *
- 'Serene Pastel' (L) *
- 'Super Gal' (L) *
- 'The Fawn' (L)
- 'Victorian Blush' (L) *

Apricot-flowered *Paeonia delavayi* blends with the early leaves of *Rosa* 'James Galway'

*Paeonia* 'Shimane Chojuraku' with short, tufted grass *Anemanthele lessoniana*

*Geum* 'Mai Tai' flowers don't mind the shade from the leaves of *Paeonia* 'Gauguin'

The flowers of *Paeonia* 'Surugu' are light enough not to be blown over in wind

*Paeonia delavayi* hybrid with apricot flowers at the end of a border at White Hopton Farm that also features mounding, brown-leaved *Euphorbia dulcis* 'Chameleon', orange *Geum* 'Prinses Juliana', dark-blue *Aquilegia vulgaris* and *Astrantia* 'Roma' (front)

## FOR THE SHADY GARDEN

Peonies grow naturally in semi-arid steppe or scrubland in regions where summers can be dry and winters very cold. A few, such as *Paeonia emodi*, can be found in the dappled shade of forests. Given their natural habitat, it's not surprising that lactiflora and intersectional peonies don't mind a certain amount of shade during the day in summer – up to six hours or so. In winter it doesn't matter if the sun does not reach the planting spot as the peony foliage will have died back and the plant is snug below ground.

I have had great success growing *Paeonia wittmaniana* subsp. 'Rosea', *P. veitchii* and *P. veitchii* var. *woodwardii* along the edges of a wooded area. Here, the peonies are shaded by tree foliage for much of the day. Indeed, in China, tree peonies are grown beneath large trees, as is the practice at RHS Wisley in Surrey. Camellias tend to thrive in similar positions.

## SMALL GARDENS & POTS

If you have a very small garden and dream of growing peonies, choose short, upright varieties (see p.26) or neat-growing intersectional peonies.

When it comes to container planting, I almost never recommend peonies. The roots are very likely to fill a pot that is on the small side within nine months. The plant won't be able to take up enough water, which in turn stops the flowers forming.

However, if there is no alternative choose a pot that is at least 60cm high and 60cm wide, or a wooden barrel with drainage holes. Loam-based compost is the best growing medium, but a peat-free mix is acceptable. Remember to water daily in hot weather and apply a single dose of a balanced fertiliser early in spring before the leaves start growing. You will also need to repot the peony every year or growth and flowering may suffer.

## HELPING BEES

Every wildlife garden should include a peony. The single-flowered types of lactiflora, hybrid and tree peonies produce lots of pollen that will feed bees and other flying insects. Any dead foliage left on the plant will also offer shelter to the myriad of small creatures that overwinter in the garden.

*Paeonia wittmaniana* subsp. 'Rosea' in near shade with other shade loving plants

*P. rockii* photographed at RHS Wisley many years ago growing in the shade of trees

*P. veitchii* var. *woodwardii* with *Corydalis flexuosa* and *Aquilegia v.* 'William Guiness'

Single-flowered peonies display their copious, pollen-filled centre to attract feeding bees

*Paeonia* 'Auguste Dessert' with *Campanula persicifolia* 'Blue Bloomers' (left), *Iris* 'Fond Kiss', *Geranium* 'Brookside' (behind), *Gillenia trifoliata* (back left), *Paeonia* 'Paul M. Wild' and swathes of blue *Nepeta* 'Six Hills Giant'

White Hopton Farm back garden on an early June evening: *Paeonia* 'First Arrival' (front), *P.* 'Moonrise' (right), *P.* 'Cora Stubbs' (left), *Aquilegia*, hardy geraniums and *Veronica*

The front garden in mid-June: *Paeonia* 'Surugu' (centre), *P.* 'Coral Charm' (behind), *P.* 'Myrtle Gentry' (top left). In front (R to L), *Stachys*, *Sisyrinchium*, hardy geraniums, *Gillenia*, *Dianthus*

**COMPANION PLANTS**

Peonies look stunning among plants that don't compete with them for attention. My preference is to grow them among perennials with flowers and leaves that contrast with those of the peony. By choosing plants that bloom before and after peonies, your garden can be filled with colour for almost the whole year. Here is a list of perennials I recommend to grow with peonies.

*Achillea* (Yarrow)
*Alchemilla* (Lady's mantle)
*Aquilegia* (Granny's bonnet)
*Astrantia* (Masterwort)
*Bergenia* (Elephant ears)
*Campanula* (Bellflower)
*Centaurea* (Perennial cornflower)
*Centranthus* (Valerian)
*Dianthus* (Hardy pinks)
*Digitalis* (Foxglove)
*Epimedium* (Bishop's mitre)
*Euphorbia* (Spurge)
*Geranium* (Hardy geranium)
*Geum* (Avens)
*Gillenia* (Bowman's root)
*Iris* particularly *sibirica* types
*Lychnis* (Dusty miller)
*Lupinus* (Lupin)
*Nepeta* (Catmint)
*Persicaria affinis* types (Bistort)
*Polemonium* (Jacob's ladder)
*Potentilla* (Cinquefoil)
*Pulmonaria* (Lungwort)
*Salvia* (Hardy sage)
*Sisyrinchium*
*Stachys* (Lamb's ears)
*Veronica* (Speedwell)

# PEONIES IN HISTORY

## THE GREEK INFLUENCE

According to classical mythology, the peony was named after a physician to the gods during the Trojan Wars. Philip Miller, writing in 1731 sums up the story: "Paeonia; [so call'd of Paeon the Physician, because he is said to have cured Pluto being wounded by Hercules, with this Herb]".

We know peonies grew in the wild in Greece, as they still do. Pliny, the Roman naturalist writing in the 1st century, referred to the medicinal use of roots and seeds by both Greek and Roman herbalists. He describes peony seeds being used to stop the flow of blood from the nose, the stomach and after childbirth. The seeds were probably taken in the form of a powder, in water sweetened with honey. Pliny's contemporary, the Roman physician Galen, describes the taste of peony roots as "a kind of sweetenesse: and hath also joined with a certaine bitter sharpness: it is in temperature not very hot, little more than meanly hot but it is dry and of subtle partes".

In Britain, during the Middle Ages peony seeds were used as a culinary spice, as indicated in these lines from the celebrated late-4th century poem *The Visions of Piers Plowman* by William Langland :"I have pepper and peony," quoth she, "and a pound of garlic, A farthingworth of fennel seed for fasting days."

I feel sure that peonies continued to be used medicinally because the roots and seeds easily survive long journeys. They were certainly cultivated in monastic herb gardens because wild peonies can be found near the sites of ancient monasteries. *Paeonia mascula*, for example, still grows on Steep Holm, an island in the Bristol Channel, close to where a 6th century Christian monastery once stood.

Peonies, like all medicinal plants, were exclusively grown by monks. When Henry VIII ordered the dissolution of the English monasteries from 1536, many of these valuable plants found homes in the gardens of herbalists and apothecaries.

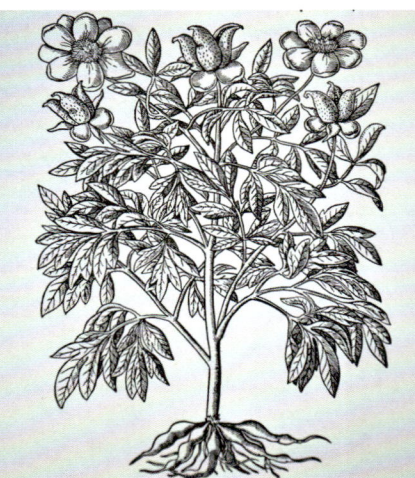

A 16th century engraving of the Female Peony, *Paeonia officinalis*

*Paeonia mascula* was known in medieval times as the Male Peony

*Paeonia officinalis* 'Rubra Plena' has been cultivated since the Middle Ages

## PEONIES IN HERBALS

Herbals, usually written in Latin, contained valuable information about the properties of medicinal herbs and their use in treating a wide range of ailments.

The earliest herbal written in English appeared in 1568 and was the work of William Turner, a physician and botanist. In common with herbalists up until the 18th century, Turner simply reproduced information about peonies gained from the writings of Pliny and Galen. By 1597, however, John Gerard in *The Herball or Generall Historie of Plantes* (revised 1633) was advising that "the roote of the male Peionie being dried, is given to women that bee not well clensed after their deliveries, being drunke in Meade or honied water to the quantitie of a beane; for it scowrth those parts, appeareth the griping throwes and torments of the belly, and bringeth downe the desired sickries." Later, 17th century herbalist John Parkinson advocated peony root as a remedy and in 1651 Nicholas Culpeper advised that: "The root helps women not sufficiently purged after travail, it provokes the menses, and helps pains in the belly, as also in the reins (the kidneys) and bladder, falling sickness, and convulsions in children, being either taken inwardly, or hung about their necks." At that time, childbirth was fraught with danger and the 'falling sickness' was epilepsy.

## THE MALE AND THE FEMALE PEONY

From the Middle Ages to the Victorian era, plants were generally known by common names. The two peonies grown at the time were listed as the Male Peony and the Female Peony. In his *Herball* Gerard recounts that in "ancient times: there were four different types of 'Peionie'", yet he lists only three. One is the Male Peony, which we know today as *Paeonia mascula*, the second he says is too well known to describe, but must be the Female Peony, *Paeonia officinalis*, and the third has flowers "exceeding double, of a very deep red colour, in shape and fashion very like the great double rose of Provance". To my mind, there is no doubt this is *Paecnia officinalis* 'Rubra Plena'.

*Paeonia* illustration from Emanuel Sweert's *Florilegium* (1612)

A page from Philip Miller's *The Gardeners Dictionary* (1733)

A painting by Clara Maria Pope of various types of *Paeonia officinalis* (1824)

## 17th & 18th CENTURIES

Although peonies continued to be cultivated for medicine until the 17th century, evidence suggests that in the early part of the century they were also being grown in gardens as an ornamental.

In 1612, a Dutch nurseryman Emanuel Sweerts published his *Florilegium*, a catalogue featuring 560 engravings of different plants for sale and available at the Frankfurt Fair, a famous international trading market of the time. No prices were mentioned and only one peony was listed: *Paeonia foem: maxim*, otherwise known as *Paeonia officinalis* 'Rubra Plena'.

In the early 18th century, at the start of the British Industrial Revolution, the popularity of ornamental gardens was rapidly increasing among the new, wealthy gentry. Publications such as Philip Miller's *The Gardeners Dictionary* (first published in 1731) offered advice on growing plants. In it, he lists the peony as a medicinal plant as well as recommending it for pleasure gardens. Only the rarest peonies were grown in the large gardens of estate owners – rarity being an indication of wealth.

Miller includes seven commonly available peonies, two of them forms of the Male Peony (*Paeonia mascula*). The first he described as "chiefly propagated for the Roots, which are used in Medicine: the flowers being single, do not afford near so much Pleasure as those of the double Flowers." The second "Sort hath larger single Flowers than the first, but they are of a paler Colour: This is preserv'd by Persons who are curious in collecting the various Kinds of Flowers." Miller also lists three types of the Female Peony (*Paeonia officinalis*). Two of these had double flowers and are "for curious gardens for the beauty of the flowers: which, when intermix'd with other large growing plants in the border of large gardens, do add in the variety, and the flowers are very ornamental in basons and flower-pots, when plac'd in rooms". He also mentions 'The Portugal Peony', which I assume is *P. broteri*, and noted it to be sweetly scented. Amazingly, the cultivation notes given by Miller are in essence no different to those given today.

*Paeonia lactiflora* revolutionised the breeding of garden peonies

## NEW PLANT SPECIES

Until the Victorian era, most of the peonies grown in Europe were of Mediterranean origin. As the Industrial Revolution got underway, however, it offered manufacturers the opportunity to venture further afield and open up new overseas trading routes for their goods.

On their travels they came across new plants, which were collected and sent back to botanic gardens such as Kew in London, as well as to the gardens of private collectors or nurserymen.

For centuries, *Paeonia lactiflora* was highly valued in China and cultivated principally for its medicinal properties. The species, which is native to an area stretching roughly from northern China to Siberia, first arrived in Europe late in the 18th century. This one species was to be the single greatest influence on peony breeding. Prior to its introduction, peonies produced just one, unscented flower on each stem. *Paeonia lactiflora* (known then as *Paeonia albiflora*) had two, scented blooms per stem. This was a cause for celebration by collectors and plant breeders alike, especially in France, where peony lovers and nurserymen set about improving the garden peony beyond recognition. By the end of the century, hundreds of what became known as lactiflora peonies had been bred and introduced.

Peonies in history | 31

## THE FRENCH LEGACY

France soon became the hub for new peony introductions and large collections of plants were assembled, often by the French nobility. When collection holders died, or plants were displaced on account of revolution, peonies were acquired by keen nurserymen who worked to increase the number of varieties available to gardeners. In the early years, new plants were largely raised from seed rather than directly pollinated.

New varieties were often named after wealthy people, members of the hybridisers family, or given names that were approximations of Latin. A fine example of the latter is *Paeonia* 'Edulis Superba', introduced in 1824 by Nicholas Lemon who was the first breeder to accurately record new peony varieties.

France also became the leading importer, probably via Holland, of peonies from China. Working in Charonne, now a suburb of Paris, Modeste Guérin is said to have imported the first plants, registering 45 varieties between 1830 and 1863. His contribution to peonies was so significant that in 1853 the French National Horticultural Society honoured him.

When Guérin died in 1866 his nursery was sold and the peony collection bought by Etienne Méchin, a nurseryman. Méchin, who had amassed a collection of peonies dating back to 1840, worked with his grandson Auguste Dessert. They imported as well as introduced herbaceous and tree peonies right through to the end of the 19th century.

The oldest named peony, *P.* 'Edulis Superba', raised by Nicolas Lemon (1824)

*Paeonia* 'Duchesse De Nemours' introduced by Jacques Calot (1856)

One of the most significant breeders of this time was Jacques Calot from Nancy. Calot inherited his collection of imported Chinese peonies in 1850, and in the 20 years before his death in 1872 introduced a raft of new varieties. Alice Harding, a noted American peony specialist writing in 1917, considered him to have "rare imagination and diligence".

By the time Félix Crousse took on Calot's collection in 1872, peonies had reached such a level of excellence that it was difficult not to produce a beautiful plant. As well as his own seedlings, Crousse continued to introduce Calot's seedlings into cultivation, many of which achieved accolades and awards.

The most celebrated peony breeder of the Victorian era was Victor Lemoine, who, like Calot, lived in Nancy. Lemoine had been trained by Auguste Miellez who bred the celebrated *Paeonia* 'Festiva Maxima'. Working closely with Félix Crousse, who was 17 years younger, the two produced peonies that won accolades. Lemoine actively crossed all types of peonies, and with the assistance of his wife and son Émile, his introductions totalled more than 80. As new peony imports into Europe increased, the talented Lemoine registered some of the first hybrid peonies. He is the only peony breeder to have been awarded, in 1894, the prestigious Veitch Medal by the Royal Horticultural Society, and not just for peonies but also for lilacs. After Lemoine's death in 1911, Émile went on to introduce and breed excellent tree peonies as well as herbaceous types.

*P.* 'Madame Ducel' by Etienne Méchin, introduced by A. Dessert (1880)

*Paeonia* 'Félix Crousse' by Félix Crousse (1881)

French peony and lilac breeder Victor Lemoine

## VICTORIAN BRITAIN

In Britain, unlike in France, peonies did not become go-to plants. Perhaps the austere Victorian style was unsuited to their glamorous and opulent appearance. Even so, peonies were being grown in Britain on nurseries in the early years of Queen Victoria's reign.

Conrad Loddiges & Son, based in Hackney, operated one of the largest nurseries of the time. Their 1814 catalogue lists 13 peonies, all were species and most had been grown for centuries. By the time the 14th edition of the catalogue appeared in 1826, the peony section had increased significantly and included nine different varieties of *Paeonia lactiflora* along with an impressive 29 species, including *Paeonia peregrina*, the 'Balkan' peony.

The boom in railway construction during the mid-19th century brought cross-country travel within the reach of many people. Increasing numbers of gardeners were now able to visit a range of plant nurseries, while growers found rail transport convenient for sending deliveries to customers. Gardeners soon desired to know more about the plants they could grow and gardening books and magazines began to flourish. Highly illustrated and beautifully designed, these publications were aimed at wealthier garden owners who could employ a trained head gardener and a team of under-gardeners.

One such publication, although modest, was the *Handy Book of The Flower Garden*, 1865, by David Thomson who was head gardener at Archerfield gardens in East Lothian. He tells us that the peonies found in nurseries and old gardens can be found in "a great number of varieties of the species - many of which must be regarded as merely botanical curiosities". Thomson's book lists over 20 *Paeonia albiflora* (*P. lactiflora*) varieties, but goes on to suggest: "For a fuller list of these most showy plants we must refer to Mr. Salter's catalogue".

In terms of peonies, John Salter bridges the gap between France and Britain. Salter's early horticulture career was spent in Versailles, France. When the revolution of 1848 forced his return home, he established 'The Versailles Nursery' in Hammersmith. Although he gained fame as a chrysanthemum breeder, Salter assembled a notable peony collection from plants brought over to Britain from Belgium, as well as France.

Like Salter other nurserymen imported plants from Europe purely to sell. Thomas S. Ware of Tottenham offered an extraordinary range of florists' flowers and their catalogues in the 1890s included over seven pages of imported herbaceous and tree peonies.

By the 1860s, new nurseries were opening up in great numbers. Born and raised near Glasglow, Peter Barr opened his nursery in south London. Although celebrated as the 'Daffodil King of Tooting', Barr was an avid collector and grew large numbers of peonies. Each spring his nursery opened its doors to an enthusiastic public. Whether he hybridised peonies or simply selected good versions of seed-raised plants is not known, but in 1898 he registered three varieties of *Paeonia peregrina*. All are still grown.

## KELWAY & SONS

James Kelway was, and still is, the most famous British peony breeder. Having trained as a gardener, he established his nursery in Somerset in 1851. His initial focus was on growing florists' flowers and in particular gladioli, but around 1863 he began importing peonies from France and was soon raising his own varieties. By the end of the century Kelway was registering peonies, concentrating his early efforts on two common species, *Paeonia mascula* and *P. officinalis*. He soon moved on to *Paeonia lactiflora*.

In 1885 Kelway raised 'Snowflake', the first peony to receive a floral certificate. Sadly, it no longer exists. By 1886 *The Garden* reported Kelway & Son listing over 200 varieties of herbaceous and tree peonies, many of them Kelway's own introductions.

James Kelway died in 1899 and his obituary in *The Gardeners' Magazine* is quoted on Kelway's website: "With perfect justification, therefore, was the late Mr. Kelway described some years since as 'one of the great horticultural lights of the Victorian era'."

*Paeonia peregrina* 'Otto Froebel' raised by Peter Barr (1898)

*Paeonia* 'Avant Garde' bred by Victor Lemoine (1907)

*Paeonia* 'Gay Ladye' introduced by Kelways Nurseries (date not recorded)

## 1900 TO 1930

As the new century dawned, peonies were still popular both in Europe and America, but the Great War of 1914–1918 changed everything. As men enlisted in their thousands, the war robbed gardens not just of labour, but owners. Adverts for 'lady gardeners' began to fill the pages of *The Gardener's Chronicle* and vegetables took the place of flowers. Horticultural shows were cancelled, although the older generation of nurserymen still grew peonies, hopeful that the shows would eventually return.

The writings of celebrated American horticulturalist and landscape architect, John C. Wister, provide an insight into peony cultivation immediately after the First World War. Having enlisted in the

*The Book of the Peony* by Mrs. Edward Harding published in 1917

US army at the age of 30, he served in Europe, particularly in France. When he was discharged in 1919, Wister visited French nurseries including those of Émile Lemoine and Auguste Dessert, where he was captivated by new tree peonies, including *Paeonia* 'L'Espérance'. Introduced before the war, it heralded a new generation of tree peonies.

From France, Wister attended the Royal Horticultural Society's (RHS) show in London. It was June 1919 and the shows had only just restarted. Kelway & Sons were amongst the exhibitors and Wister noted that the nurseries showing peonies "possess more of the newer French varieties than the French do themselves".

For a short time after the First World War, new peonies were being raised in Britain and France. Doriat & Son, having purchased the nursery of Auguste Dessert, introduced 50 new peonies between 1920 and 1936. The Dutch firm of L. Van Leeuwen listed six new varieties, three of which are still available. Although peonies were still grown in gardens, this owed more to their longevity than their popularity. Few peonies were mentioned in gardening magazines of the time, apart from the occasional tree peony.

As the 1930s unfolded, many of the old nurseries disappeared, their owners either bankrupt or dying of old age. Kelway & Sons filed for insolvency in 1933, following the decline in sales of plants to large gardens – the nursery's principal market. Fortunately, the nursery was soon rescued by a local syndicate.

In America, where the war had a less devastating effect than in Europe, it was a different story. Peonies were becoming more popular and the link between American and British growers had been maintained. In 1921 a wealthy American peony lover, Mrs. Edward Harding, donated funds to the RHS in respect of a cup, which was to be awarded for the best amateur exhibit of peonies. Alice Harding, as she was also known, set down her knowledge and expertise in *The Book of the Peony* (1917), the first publication dedicated to growing, caring for and selecting peonies. It is still quoted today.

American specialists didn't just grow peonies, they also bred them. Of the new varieties introduced post 1930, the vast majority were raised by breeders such as Vories, Brand, Franklin, Sass, Nichols and Rosenfield. Almost all were types of *Paeonia lactiflora*, but some hybridisers experimented with species peonies.

## PROFESSOR A. P. SAUNDERS

Edward Auten and Lyman Glasscock, who also introduced lactiflora peonies, started crossing species peonies, but the most successful hybridiser was Canadian-born Professor Arthur Percy Saunders. His work with species peony crosses gained the widest recognition.

A professor of chemistry, Saunders began collecting peonies in 1900 simply because they were the only plants that seemed to thrive in his New York garden. In 1905 he started importing species peonies from European nurseries and began systematically crossing them. Each cross was carefully recorded, and in the results he saw opportunities for improvement. He subsequently focused his attention on creating peonies that would flower earlier and in brighter colours.

Over 30 years Saunders made more than a thousand crosses, selecting just 163 plants to be named cultivars. Not content with these achievements, Saunders was deeply frustrated by his failure to cross a tree peony with a herbaceous peony. His aim was the creation of a yellow herbaceous/ tree peony – a goal achieved 11 years after Saunders' death in 1953, when the seedling peonies raised by Japanese breeder Toichi Itoh eventually bloomed.

Professor A. P. Saunders (1869–1953) with *Paeonia* 'White Innocence'

## BRITAIN 1939 TO 1990

Although gardening increased in popularity during the inter-war period, nurseries trying to keep afloat during the Second World War faced many challenges. Bakers of Codsall – famous for introducing the Russell Lupins – clearly asked for their customers' understanding in their autumn 1945 catalogue:

"It is clear many people have little idea of the difficulties under which Nurserymen are working. Apart from restrictions making it necessary to give up the greater part of the land to food crops, little or no skilled labour has been available for propagating and even many of the commoner plants have almost disappeared or stocks have reached a point where it is essential the few in the Nursery should be retained, otherwise we shall have nothing to work on when conditions make it possible to start building up again."

The availability of plants was indeed limited and those that took up more space and time – including peonies – were quickly discarded. Bakers listed just 8 peony varieties, while only 26 were advertised by Bees of Chester. All of these were raised prior to 1900 in France.

From the 1940s, plants on sale to the public tended to be those that could be propagated quickly and in large numbers, such as carnations, roses and irises. Peonies, which are slow to multiply, were offered by just a handful of nurseries.

## BOTANISTS AT WORK

Naming new peony introductions was becoming an issue and not just with cultivars but also with species peonies. Confusion arose because names already in use were often applied to new plants – a problem that had existed and been recognised for many years. Indeed, in 1886 Richard Lynch, the curator of Cambridge Botanic Gardens, made a plea for clarification around peony names. Seven years later in a letter printed in *The Gardener's Chronicle* he asked readers to send popular, named cultivars and those peonies known to be of wild origin to him in Cambridge so they could be properly identified and catalogued. The results were published in *The Journal of the Royal Horticultural Society* in 1890.

## F.C. STERN

Born into a wealthy merchant-banking family, Stern enjoyed the traditional 'gentleman's pursuits' of shooting wild animals and horse racing. Called up to fight in the First World War, he saw military action in the Middle East. At the end of the war, Stern supported the then prime minister, David Lloyd George, as Private Secretary at the Paris Peace Conference. On returning to England in 1919, he married Sybil Lucas and began to collect species peonies. Responding to a suggestion to study them more closely, Stern was sent wild plants as well as seeds to grow in his large garden at Highdown, Sussex. He gleaned additional information from dried herbarium specimens kept at botanical gardens in London, Edinburgh

An article from the magazine *Good Gardening*, June 1938

Lilian Snelling's painting of *Paeonia bakeri* in Stern's *A Study of the Genus Paeonia*

Sir Frederick Stern (1884–1967)

The advent of garden centres during the mid-1960s did nothing to help the popularity of peonies. Garden centres led to a steady decline in plants being purchased from mail-order companies. Eventually, by the 1990s, the traditional way of buying bare-rooted plants in autumn was replaced with pot-grown plants that could be bought throughout the year, a way of growing and selling that does not favour short-blooming peonies.

Of course peonies were still available by mail-order, but the choice was largely, but not exclusively, limited to pre-1940 varieties. Until, that is, newer varieties, often raised in America, reached our shores sometime after 1980.

The same problem concerned American growers and some years later John Coit compiled a list of over 2,700 peonies, which was published in 1907 by Cornell University. Coit had scoured every catalogue for named peonies, including those supplied by Kelways, in an attempt "to bring order out of the confusion which exists in regards to the names of varieties". Largely made up of cultivars, this became the basis of the American Peony Society registration list, which is still in use today.

Species peonies presented more of a challenge. George Anderson made a start in 1817 and after three more attempts over the next hundred years, Frederick Claude Stern made a breakthrough.

and Manchester, as well as from further afield – France, India, Austria and Russia.

On receipt of two £500 donations and the support of the RHS, Stern wrote down his observations. They were published in 1946 in *A Study of the Genus Paeonia,* a book beautifully illustrated by Lilian Snelling. Offering a comprehensive survey of where peonies originated in the wild, Stern's work was to represent the standard view of the genus for the next 80 years. Indeed, his taxonomy is largely followed today. Among Stern's many other gardening achievements, was an in-depth study of snowdrops. For his services to horticulture, Frederick Stern was awarded a knighthood in 1956.

# MY PEONIES

**THE FAMILY BUSINESS**

After more than 20 years of rose breeding, my father, David Austin, had all but given up thinking that his roses would make him a living. So, in 1980, like any good farmer, he decided to diversify and expand the range of plants sold by the nursery. Having produced a catalogue of roses for a number of years, his idea was to create a similar list featuring other plants, particularly perennials. A wide range was considered with specialist collections of irises, hemerocallis and peonies – all of them plants he felt had largely been neglected by British nurseries.

Peony catalogue from 1984 written by David Austin, cover drawing by Pat Austin

Some European and American nurseries had been fortunate enough to buy existing peony collections, but my father had to start from scratch. First, he needed to learn about the best peonies to grow and where and how to source them. In those pre-internet days, books, magazines and journals were the first port of call. His initial purchases were James Kelway's book on peonies and *The Book of the Peony* by Mrs. Edward Harding (see p.34), which in 1980 cost him an eye-watering £25.

With the help of Doreen Pyke, his secretary, my father set to work contacting nurseries around the world by letter. Initially, peonies were bought from UK nurseries. Kelways supplied 11 varieties, a further 17 came from John Waterer, Sons & Crisp Ltd, and 11 from Scotts of Merriot. At the time, Scotts were famous for their beautifully illustrated catalogue. More peonies came from Blooms of Bressingham, the UK's leading wholesale perennial nursery. Although their stock was similar to that of other growers, Blooms were able to supply *Paeonia* 'Whitleyi Major', a very old cultivar that is rarely offered today.

More letters were typed and posted to nurseries in the Netherlands, Japan and America. As in the UK, Dutch wholesalers generally offered peonies introduced

A page from the peony section, David Austin *Handbook of Hardy Plants*, 1985

before 1930. Named Japanese tree peonies were also available but expensive: over 20 years ago they cost the same price wholesale as they do today.

In an attempt to find cheaper tree peonies my father wrote to Japan's trade centre in London. He also wrote to the Japanese Embassy in Tanzania, where I was working for the Ambassador while his permanent secretary was on maternity leave. However, buying tree peonies directly from Japan proved impractical as they were sold by colour and not by name, a practice that still exists.

Unbeknown to my father, his initial forays brought him into contact with individuals who were to become celebrities in the world of peonies, such as Louis Smirnow. Some years later Smirnow was applauded for introducing the unique intersectional peonies raised by Toichi Itoh in Tokyo.

Smirnow advertised his catalogue in the back pages of the RHS magazine *The Garden*. It included tree peonies from Japan and also from China – a country not known for exporting to the West. The handwritten replies from Smirnow to my father's typed order chronicle its progress, or lack of it. Indeed, the order was never released from quarantine by customs officers at Heathrow airport because the American paperwork was not correct. In

The 1988 catalogue with my illustration on the cover

the last of the letters, Smirnow suggested my father became a member of the American Peony Society, which he joined in 1982. Subsequently, catalogues arrived from Al and Dot Rogers in Oregon, David Reath and Gilbert Wild in Missouri, and Charles Klehm & Son in Illinois.

By the time I joined my father's rose nursery at Albrighton in 1983, he had assembled a collection of around a hundred peonies, a catalogue had been printed and a garden planted up with peonies. However, so many plants grown in the peony garden had lost their names, they were soon discarded and replaced by other perennials, which he sold alongside roses.

Perennials in the Lion Garden, Albrighton, 1995, with lion sculpture by Pat Austin

My two children Ellen (6) and Robert (4) with *Paeonia* 'Black Monarch' in 1992

Peonies and irises growing in a field at David Austin Roses, 1991

## MY PEONY STORY BEGINS

When I took over the perennial collection I had no idea that I would still be involved with plants nearly 40 years later. Back then, although I liked plants and my father had been a farmer throughout my childhood, my mother, who carved stone, was also a strong influence. At the age of 24 I knew I wanted to write a book and have children – both objectives since achieved – yet over the years, plants began to grow on (and for) me. Making a living from selling them seemed a good plan and in the pre-internet days of the 1980s the only option was to produce a mail-order catalogue.

The first catalogue was advertised in gardening magazines – potential customers could request a copy by post or telephone. Fortunately, I'd studied graphic design and illustration at Bristol, so was able to create an enticing-looking booklet. At that time, however, colour printing was prohibitively expensive and many catalogues were simply a list of plants, perhaps with a brief description.

The photographs in the first peony catalogues were black and white. Later, a few pages displaying colour photos were inserted among the printed pages. Finally, in 1994 an all-colour catalogue was produced.

### Describing peonies

Photography is a great way of getting to know a plant, particularly when cultivars are similar in colour. My photographic records have been invaluable, especially when identifying peonies whose labels have gone missing or been mixed up. One year a member of the rose nursery staff was working near the peony crop with a machine designed to loosen and break up the soil to a depth of 60cm. He forgot about the peonies and ploughed straight through them. It took me three years of painstaking work to sort out the plants and I realised along the way that written descriptions are also vital. Photographs are ideal for conveying a plant's colour but they don't always show the precise shape of a leaf, or how the flower ages.

Writing plant descriptions truly is an art. Inspiration came from *Perennial Garden Plants* by Graham Thomas, an old friend of my father. I grew up knowing him, and for many years I sent Graham the new catalogue. He always returned it, corrected throughout with beautifully handwritten notes. From Graham, I learnt to describe plants in my own words and make careful notes on every part of them.

The 1997 Hardy Plant catalogue featuring a photograph of *P.* 'Mister Ed' from Klehms

The peony field in full bloom in a field at Albrighton, 1996

## NEW PEONIES FROM AMERICA

In the early years, the range of peonies on offer at David Austin Roses was limited to old varieties grown in Europe. If I wanted to stock new and exciting varieties, America was the place to go.

The Midwestern states have long been home to many famous peony nurseries including Gilbert H. Wild & Son based in Missouri – the first American nursery I ordered peonies from. Up until the late 1980s, Wild's grew many varieties including those raised by family members.

Over in Oregon, Al and Dot Rogers opened Caprice Farm Nursery, selling a good range of peonies including intersectionals and cultivars raised by Walter Marx. In 1995, Al published a book on peonies, which included one of my photographs.

Don Hollingsworth, another Missouri resident, also sent me plants. Before his retirement Don raised peonies, including his most famous cultivar, *Paeonia* 'Garden Treasure', which he sent me as a gift in 2000. On arrival, the peony resembled a stick and I planted it with some misgivings. Two years later the same plant was covered with numerous, beautiful, large yellow blooms and I was star-struck. Visiting Don some years later I appreciated what an authority on peonies he was.

Perhaps the most successful 20th century grower was Klehm Peony Nurseries, originally based in Illinois. For over a hundred years and going back three generations, they raised and sold a mouth-watering range of cultivars. Between 1983 and 2018, we regularly bought plants from Roy Klehm, who had followed his father Carl into the business. Roy introduced over 418 new cultivars, most of them lactifloras. Having also purchased the entire stock of William Krekler peonies in 1977, Klehm's can lay claim to populating the entire peony world with hybrid varieties. Later re-named Song Sparrow and relocated to Wisconsin in 2000, the nursery sadly closed its doors for good in December 2020.

Owing to the popularity of peonies as cut flowers all around the world, the number of specialist nurseries in America and Europe has grown. Oregon-based Adelman Peony Gardens, currently one of the leading American growers, sell bare-rooted plants as well as cut flowers. Their inspirational gardens, which open in May, include stunning varieties raised by peony breeders from across the globe.

Gilbert H. Wild 1983 catalogue cover

Klehm's peony catalogue, 1995

Blooms in vases on show at Adelman Peony Gardens

Don Hollingsworth and myself at his home in Kansas in 2012

Plants in full bloom at Adelman Peony Gardens, May 2018

## DISCOVERING PEONIES IN CHINA

In 1996, the search for new peony varieties took me far afield. I had been buying tree peonies from China for several years but dreamed of seeing the plants in situ. Having asked Mrs. Zhang, the sales representative, if it would be possible to see peonies in flower, I was delighted to hear that every April the city of Heze in Shangdong province hosted a peony festival with hundreds of plants in bloom.

China had not long opened to overseas visitors, so with great excitement I travelled with my companion from Hong Kong to China, visiting the Terracotta Warriors and the Great Wall on the way. Although a seasoned traveller, nothing quite prepared me for the China of 1996. Beijing was smog-bound, despite thousands riding bicycles, and the trains we travelled on had their own tea carriage for passengers. In it, a giant kettle boiled water to fill jam jars containing tea leaves. The hotels were reserved exclusively for foreigners and the standard of cleanliness was so high that the guide, our constant companion, seemed to live in the toilets. We met only two other foreigners on our journey – an American selling computer software and a Dutchman selling tulip bulbs. When we finally arrived at Heze airport, Mrs. Zhang and translator Sue greeted us with great joy, banners with our names held aloft.

Across the northern hemisphere, spring was late and, sadly, no peony flowers were open in Heze. Anxious not to disappoint visitors, organisers had decorated each bush with red, yellow and white paper flowers. In Heze, where peonies are grown on a huge scale, a banquet was held in our honour at the city's best hotel. In truth it was more of a knees-up for city council members and very enjoyable, although I don't think I will ever eat sea slug again. On asking where the toilets were, I was told there were no facilities for women in the hotel. Instead, Mrs. Zhang took me down the street where, to my dismay, I encountered the open-air toilets used by the whole community.

Our next stop was to be the Luoyang Peony Festival but a train ticket for this 24-hour journey was only handed over once the sales agreement had been signed. In Luoyang, south of Heze, the peonies were in full bloom. Mission accomplished, but as we couldn't translate the peony labels, it was impossible to know what they were.

## AUSTRALIAN TREASURES

My husband Ric was raised in Melbourne, Australia, and on one visit early in the new millennium we toured gardens and took photographs. Several featured tree peonies but these were no ordinary plants. We realised we were looking at the cultivars originally raised by Professor A. P. Saunders (see p.34). Each time we asked the owners where they bought their plants, the answer was: "from Ronnie".

Having tracked down Ron Boekel's wholesale nursery, we discovered Ron had gone on a fishing trip. Luckily, he arrived back a day before our return to the UK. During a long, memorable and fascinating encounter, Ron – still in his fishing clothes and holding a "tinny" – showed us around. A true nurseryman and a brilliant propagator, Ron had gathered over 40 varieties, some from Louis Smirnow, when his New York nursery closed. During our visit, Ron gave us the benefit of his considerable knowledge, even explaining how to graft tree peonies. We decided to import them into the UK.

In Australia, plants for export had to be dosed with methyl bromide, a highly toxic pesticide, and placed in quarantine before being flown to the UK. This wasn't ideal, neither was the disruption caused by the seasons in our different hemispheres being out of kilter. Yet in spite of these drawbacks, the plants always grew well. In the end, Australian plant export requirements proved too arduous, but because of Ron I still have Saunders tree peonies growing in my garden.

Paper flowers decorate non-flowering peonies in 1996

Mrs. Zhang (far right) with family, translator Sue (left) and peony breeder in Heze, 1996

Tree peonies in bloom, Luoyang

Australian peony grower, Ron Boekel

## PASSING ON KNOWLEDGE

Where there is a plant lover, there is often a thirst for knowledge. Over the years I have been asked time and time again about growing peonies, including specific questions on which peonies are best for cutting, for scent or for a windy spot. With a bit of searching, information can be found in books, magazines and online or you can seek out other enthusiasts.

### The Peony Society

Joining a local gardening group – or a society if you wanted specialist information – was once an infallible way of gaining plant knowledge. Within the Hardy Plant Society, a peony group already existed, but in 2000, following a proposal by enthusiastic peony experts, a dedicated Peony Society was formed.

Meetings were fun, the people were a truly lovely bunch, and sharing a love of a particular plant with like-minded gardeners felt special. We assembled in venues filled with peonies, arranged an annual peony show at the RHS gardens at Wisley, and also discussed, debated and wrote articles about our favourite plant. It was a sad day, 16 years later, when the society folded – not so much owing to falling numbers but because we were all very busy with no time to organise and run the society. Like other small specialist groups, plant societies have declined in popularity in recent years.

### The Chelsea Flower Show

Visiting garden shows is a great way to learn about plants and the face-to-face contact with experts that they offer is invaluable. For nurseries, they are the perfect opportunity to display plants looking their very best. In the UK, the majority tend to take place at a time of year when, unfortunately, peonies are not in bloom. We first exhibited our peonies at the inauguration of 'The Gardener's World Live' show in 1992, when Geoff Hamilton was front of camera. Since then we have managed to incorporate peonies into our exhibits at the Chelsea Flower Show in May, even though the event is a good month before many peonies come into bloom on the nursery.

Showing peonies is very time consuming. The plants need to have been potted up the previous autumn, then six weeks before the show they are brought into the polytunnel to encourage the buds to plump up. If the weather is very warm, the buds can open too far ahead of the show; it can also result in very small flowers. Including new peony varieties is also very hit-and-miss – they may not bloom at all.

Choosing the right varieties helps, but experience is the key. Eventually we discovered that peonies don't grow any quicker in a heated greenhouse. What they require is lots of natural light, which is not always available in April and May.

The last time I exhibited at Chelsea was in 2016. To say I was disappointed by the silver medal we were awarded is an understatement. It was the moment I realised that the show judges really didn't see plants in the same way I did.

### Garden-worthiness

To help gardeners choose the right plant the RHS gives the best plants in a group an Award of Garden Merit (AGM). After some considerable time, in 2015 the RHS decided to review the AGMs given to peonies. I duly made the long journey to Wisley in Surrey to judge the trials along with a group of knowledgeable peony growers. The trials were to last five years. An interesting project, it not only allowed me to meet like-minded folk, but also to see and study peonies close-up that I had not grown before.

The final year of judging was abandoned owing to the Coronavirus pandemic, but by then all ten Peony Forum members had agreed which cultivars were the most garden-worthy. In the book, the letters AGM are included at the end of the description.

The Peony Society Show at Wisley, 2014

Charlie Dimmock at the nursery, filming a piece on peonies for the BBC, 2014

Chelsea Flower Show exhibit, 1996

*Paeonia* 'Coral Charm' on our stand at the Chelsea Flower Show, 2016

## GROWING A CROP OF PEONIES

We moved the nursery from David Austin Roses down the road to Shifnal in 2001, where we stayed for five years. Unable to convert a barn into a venue for hosting talks we moved again to north Shropshire. Finally, in 2010 the nursery relocated to Montgomeryshire, a mile from the border with Shropshire.

From a practical point of view, growing peonies has been different in each nursery. At Albrighton, sharing land with roses proved problematic because each new rose crop needed to be grown in soil where no roses had been planted for seven years. With limited land, the peonies rarely stayed in the same place long enough for them to establish and multiply.

At Albrighton and the next two nurseries the ground was so sandy that nutrients quickly leached out of the soil, which wasn't ideal for peonies. Fortunately, in Montgomeryshire we have the right soil combination – a good clay-loam that drains well – plus lots of space for the next crop. We can now leave our peonies in place for four or five years at a time, which is long enough for some of the rarer, more demanding cultivars to multiply.

### Lifting and Dividing Peonies

When plants are required to fulfil specific orders, they are simply dug up using a fork. Lifting a whole crop of peonies to divide because they have been growing in the same spot for years, however, is a different proposition. By now, the size and spread of the roots usually calls for a bigger piece of kit – a mini-digger.

Once lifted, the plants are taken into the shed for dividing. The roots are cut back to the minimum of a hand's length and then carefully divided into sections, each with at least three eyes (see p.13) if we are dividing plants to send out by mail-order. Any smaller divisions are kept and replanted so they can grow on. When moving the whole crop, the perceived wisdom is that – like roses – peonies should be planted in a patch of ground where none have grown before. In an ideal world, that is what we aim to do, although it is not always possible. Once divided, the peonies are returned to the soil, either by machine or by hand, depending on the quantities. Once planted, they are labelled and their position mapped so we know exactly where each variety is.

Digging up four-year-old peonies in 2014

Planting peonies in September 2012

### Weeds

Keeping a few acres of land weed-free is no easy task, especially in fertile soil that stays moist. Given that our peonies remain for quite some time in an area that is surrounded by wild plants, it is inevitable that weeds will spring up among them at some point.

To reduce the competition from weeds we use several methods. Taller weeds are cut back several times a year with a hand-held strimmer. Although this is the most environmentally friendly solution, it doesn't prevent perennial weeds such as creeping thistle and nettles from spreading. To eradicate them we resort to a herbicide, which we apply when the plants are dormant in winter. We don't fertilise as peonies grow easily for us.

Peonies after one growing season, 2017

Planted in 2014, the Peony Field seen from White Hopton garden in June 2020

My peonies | 41

*Paeonia* 'Auguste Dessert' in full bloom in the field

## SELLING PEONIES

Many gardeners are unfamiliar with how commercial growers produce and sell plants. The bigger wholesale nurseries, where plants are grown from seeds or plugs, are more like factories and rely on sowing and potting machines. Peonies, are very labour intensive to cultivate and slow growing – and that makes them expensive.

In common with all nurseries, we buy stock from wholesalers as well as selling our own field-grown plants. However, when a whole crop is replanted we must ensure that every plant flowers true to its name. Peonies can be slow to bloom, so this process may take a number of years. Once we are satisfied and have sufficient numbers, the plants are put on sale.

Keeping track of stock numbers is vital. In the days before computers, we recorded individual peony sales on large sheets of paper using tally marks (see below). At that time, peonies were ordered through the catalogue and always sent out as bare-root plants from late October to early spring – never in pots. With the advent of the Internet, we launched our website in 1999 and dispensed with stock sheets. Like many nurseries, our focus has also shifted from bare-rooted autumn sales to supplying container-grown perennials all year round. Not all peonies, however, can be grown in pots so plants continue to be despatched when dormant, bagged in compost, and packed in a cardboard box with straw.

## THE FUTURE OF PEONIES

By default, nurserymen and women tend to be plant collectors. Adding new varieties to the already crowded list of plants is also a good way to keep gardeners interested. As a result, I too have become a plant hoarder, unable to resist buying new peonies from around the world. Given that the majority of cultivars grown in quantity were raised before the 1960s, new introductions have, until recently, been few and far between.

Over the past few years, peony-breeding has undergone something of a resurgence, and a good number of the newly registered cultivars are hybrid peonies. This, I suspect, is due to the increasing number of peonies grown for the cut-flower market. Although exciting, such varieties can be a mixed blessing for gardeners. As with roses, plants grown for cutting are not always good in the garden.

Luckily, the tradition among peony specialists of selling on their collection to younger nurserymen has borne fruit and the American Peony Society's register is filling up with new varieties. Redistribution of plants from retiring growers such as Roy Klehm and Don Hollingsworth has also resulted in many more varieties being grown in Europe. Breeders such as Roger Anderson (see p.143) are still active and an increasing number of new peonies are being registered from countries around the world. While these may be expensive and difficult to source initially, some very exciting new introductions will be making their way into our gardens.

In the 1990s, intersectionals were considered the future of peonies

The Peony Field at White Hopton Farm, June 2019

Stock sheets showing sales, from 1983

A small selection of peonies are grown on the nursery in containers

*Paeonia* 'Auguste Dessert' (front) in White Hopton garden with orange *Geum* 'Totally Tangerine', lilac spears of *Veronicastrum virginicum* 'Lavendelturm' and frothy white *Gillenia trifoliata*

# LACTIFLORA PEONIES

**IT'S ALL IN THE NAME**

The way plants are named has always changed and always will. Peonies are no different. During the 19th century, the peonies growing in Victorian gardens went under a variety of names. Many in the group we now call lactiflora were listed as *Paeonia sinensis* or *P. chinensis* and commonly known as Chinese peonies – a name still used by some today.

These peonies with their big, luscious blooms were first imported into Europe from northern China. Their definitive parentage is unknown, but botanists consider them to be the offspring of *Paeonia lactiflora,* a species that grows over a huge area of East Asia from Japan to Siberia. For two centuries this plant was known as *Paeonia albiflora*, but the name changed to *P. lactiflora* in 1949. This caused uproar among some growers and enthusiasts who saw little justification for the new name.

Until the latter part of the 20th century, horticulturalists listed cultivars of *Paeonia lactiflora* simply as *Paeonia*. In the 1990s the RHS added *lactiflora* to plants raised from this species in order to differentiate them from other peony types. As a result, *Paeonia* 'Top Brass' is now listed by the RHS as *Paeonia lactiflora* 'Top Brass'.

In the US, the American Peony Society decided to create an additional category, the lactiflora group, for these plants. Like most nursery owners, I keep it simple and omit *lactiflora*. Nevertheless, it provides gardeners with useful information on how to cultivate these lovely peonies.

**TWO CENTURIES OF NEW PEONIES**

The decorative cultivars raised from *Paeonia lactiflora,* a single-flowered species, are thought to have arrived from China around the mid-18th century, a little earlier than the species itself which was first imported around the end of the century. There is nothing to indicate that names accompanied the early peonies when they arrived in Europe, therefore it is quite likely that they were 'christened' by growers.

19th-century growers and head gardeners began collecting and sowing seeds of imported peonies and some were deliberately crossed to create new varieties. The resulting plants produced flowers not dissimilar to those on plants imported from China. They were double or single and in shades of pink, white and crimson.

After 1868, when the country was more stable following civil war, Japan started to export plants and a new peony flower shape hit the horticultural market. Grown for centuries, these cultivars with "disorderly petaloids" (petal-like stamens) were greatly admired in Japan where they were known, and still are, as Higo peonies.

The number of lactiflora cultivars has continued to increase. While the flower shape and colours have changed little, the need for plants that are easier to maintain in the garden has led to peonies with shorter and stronger flower stems. The popularity of peonies for the cut-flower trade has also driven new introductions, ushering in a range of peonies with enormous blooms on very thick stems. As with many plants raised commercially for cut flowers, they tend to need staking and can be disappointing in the garden.

For over a century, most new cultivars have come from America but this is changing. In recent years breeders from Canada, the Czech Republic, Belgium, Austria and Lithuania, as well as China, have bred new varieties. All of them have been registered with the American Peony Society, the internationally recognised authority for peony cultivars since 1974.

Chinese-raised *Paeonia* 'Lian Tia' is being sold in the UK as *P.* 'Lady Liberty'

*Paeonia* 'Little Medicine Man' was formerly known as 'Dancing Butterflies'

'Cactus style', *Paeonia* 'Sweet Marjorie' was introduced by Roy Klehm in 1999

*Paeonia* 'Edulis Superba' from 1824 is one of the oldest lactiflora peonies still grown

## THE LACTIFLORA PLANT

Lactiflora peonies are so long-lived that varieties grown since the early 19th century are still in cultivation. They are also extremely hardy, surviving temperatures as low as -40°C. In fact, without an extended period of cold they will not grow or bloom well. They are all herbaceous, dying back in autumn with top growth re-emerging in spring. The thick, brown roots, which provide the plant with sustenance, extend to more than 60cm around the plant, fanning out from a central crown that increases in size over the years. In my garden *Paeonia* 'Shirley Temple', which must be 20 years old, produces up to 25 flower stems each year. Most of these rise from the outer edges of the crown and have up to two side buds. Not all the buds will open.

**The flowers** of lactiflora peonies are big, extravagant and very recognisable. Peony growers group them according to their different shapes: double, semi-double, single and Japanese. Depending on the number of petals on a flower, a plant can bloom for up to 10 days in the garden.

Curiously – and this is possibly due to the highly hybridised nature of lactifloras – the shape of double and Japanese peonies can differ from one year to the next, especially when a plant is not fully established. A recently planted double-flowered cultivar often has fewer petals than a fully mature one, yet some Japanese-type blooms may gain extra petals in the centre. This changeability makes it very difficult to identify a peony once the name is lost.

**Colour** is what makes the peony flower so attractive. Petals that can be so soft they feel like silk, come in tones of white, pink and red and their colour often changes over the flower's lifetime. White forms may open soft-pink then fade to white as the bloom ages. On pink flowers, the colour is sometimes washed unevenly across the petals or may fade to create a silvery edge. In a particular light, some dark red flowers will look almost purple. There are, however, no true red cultivars among lactiflora peonies. Red tones range from pink-red to crimson, magenta to purple-red. Yellow is rare in lactifloras and the colour comes from the yellow petaloids which, through selective breeding, have become as large as the true petals.

Subtle shades of cream and white on the petals of *Paeonia* 'Raspberry Sundae'

Some years the blooms of *Paeonia* 'Bowl of Beauty' may produce extra petals

In 2018 our *Paeonia* 'Krekler's Red' produced more petaloids than petals

The buds of white *Paeonia* 'Elsa Sass' are tinted with green and pink

The early flowers of *Paeonia* 'Nancy Nora' are soft-pink before fading to white

The same *P.* 'Krekler's Red' in 2020, when the number of petals increased

**The flower stems** of peonies with *P. lactiflora* heritage produce side buds, a feature not often found on cultivars raised from other peony species. The number of buds on each side stem also varies. Some cultivars can produce up to three buds per stem, while others on the same plant may have none.

Often tinged with red, peony stems also vary in width. Those of many double varieties raised a hundred years ago are so thin and wiry they are unable to hold the heavy flowers upright. Regarding this as a drawback, breeders began to introduce plants with thicker stems. Fortunately, single, semi-double and Japanese-shaped peony flowers are much lighter and don't suffer from this problem.

**The leaves** are similar in shape and form in all lactiflora peonies. The stems produce up to three separate leaves that are further divided into five fully formed leaflets. Each leaflet is pointed, hairless, often glossy and generally mid-green in colour. The leaves and stems emerge red in spring, a striking and attractive colour that fades as the flower buds develop. The foliage of the few plants with very deep red flowers can be very dark green, although in some it is strongly tinted with red. When the leaves are fully mature they often, but not always, create a neat clump.

The autumn colour of most lactiflora leaves is fleeting, and not always attractive. Where we garden, the leaves of many varieties have shrivelled and become dull brown by late August.

### A–Z of Lactifloras: Terms (pp. 48–103)

**GUARD PETALS** Sit at the base of those blooms with lots of petals. On single flowers they are the main petals.

**PETALOIDS** Look like the petals but are much slimmer and often shorter.

**STAMINODES** Very thin, yellow central stamens on Japanese-type flowers.

**AGM** The Award of Garden Merit given to the most garden-worthy peonies. Updated in 2021 after five-year trials at RHS Wisley.

**BREEDER NAME AND DATE,** where known. When two names appear, the second is the person who acquired the peony (as part of a collection) and the date it was registered.

**FLOWERS** i) the flower form (see p.9)
ii) the period in June when the peonies are in bloom on our nursery:
**Early season** week 2; **Midseason** week 3; **Late season** week 4

The long stems of *Paeonia* 'Barrington Belle' are good for cutting

Red foliage, flower stems and early buds of *Paeonia* 'Better Times'

The red tints on young *Paeonia* 'Shirley Temple' foliage will fade over the season

The attractive coral-tinted pods of *Paeonia* 'Nippon Beauty'

*Paeonia* 'Honey Gold' is a Japanese lactiflora with pink-tinted, white guard petals, soft-yellow staminodes, an inner flute of white petaloids and long side buds

Lactiflora peonies | 47

*Paeonia* 'Adolphe Rousseau'

### 'ADOLPHE ROUSSEAU'

This vigorous, free-flowering, neat-growing plant has shaggy, deep magenta-red flowers. The silky petals open from a ball into an unruly, low dome allowing a ring of golden stamens to be revealed in and around a further cluster of inner petals. The medium-sized blooms are carried on slender, red stems well above the glossy, dark green leaves that may produce a few side buds.

**Breeder:** Dessert & Méchin, 1890
**Height:** 90cm
**Flowers:** semi-double, early to midseason
**Scent:** light
**Staking:** no

### 'ALBERT CROUSSE'

When the flower first opens the fringed, petals, which are entirely soft-pink, arrange themselves into a flat bloom. With age, the petals lose much of the pink colouration along the edges and the flower becomes a big, frilly near-white dome, with soft-pink highlights radiating from the base of the petals. The leaves are dark green and carried on long stems with a few side buds.

**Breeder:** Crousse, 1893
**Height:** 90cm
**Flowers:** double, late season
**Scent:** light
**Staking:** yes

*Paeonia* 'Albert Crousse'

### 'ALEXANDER FLEMING'

A reliable and free-flowering plant with rich-pink blooms. On first opening, the petals rise into a shallow dome, but as they enlarge, the petals become curly, paler at the edges and evolve into a high mound. Thanks to a funnel-like central dip formed by shorter inner petals, the gold stamens are visible. Great for cutting, the blooms are carried on strong stems with plenty of side buds. Often incorrectly listed as 'Dr. Alexander Fleming'.

**Breeder:** Blonk, pre-1950
**Height:** 85cm
**Flowers:** double, early to midseason
**Scent:** heavy
**Staking:** no

*Paeonia* 'Alice Harding'

### 'ALICE HARDING'

The buds are heavily stained with rose-pink, a colour that persists on the round, satiny guard petals as the inner petals unfurl into an elegant dome. Gold stamens are dispersed through the petals, giving the flower a cream glow. When fully open, the stamens are revealed. A good cut flower with thick stems carrying mid-green leaves and side buds. Not to be confused with a yellow tree peony of the same name, also introduced by Lemoine.

**Breeder:** Lemoine, 1922
**Height:** 90cm
**Flowers:** double, midseason
**Scent:** medium
**Staking:** no

*Paeonia* 'Alexander Fleming'

*Paeonia* 'Amabilis'

## 'AMABILIS'

The large, spoon-shaped guard petals are deep pink. On opening, they form a saucer around a frilly centre of long, jagged-edged petaloids that start out the same colour as the guard petals then pale to soft-pink as they age. Hints of yellow can be detected at the base of the petaloids. Carried on slender stems, the flowers are borne just above a lush mound of mid-green foliage.

**Breeder:** Calot, 1856
**Height:** 90cm
**Flowers:** double, midseason
**Scent:** medium
**Staking:** no

*Paeonia* 'Ama-no-Sode'

## 'AMALIA OLSON'

When fully open the flower forms a loose ball that is dipped in the centre. The white petals mingle with slender, cream petaloids giving the bloom a flush of cream, and the guard petals are tinged pink. Considered a good cut flower, the plant has red stems with one to three side buds and dark green leaves. Named after his mother by Christian Olson who raised this cultivar from a seedling given to him.

**Breeder:** Olson, 1959
**Height:** 90cm
**Flowers:** double, midseason
**Scent:** heavy
**Staking:** no

*Paeonia* 'Amalia Olson'

## 'AMA-NO-SODE'

The large, rich-pink guard petals are crinkled along the edges and open to create a shallow cup around a big centre of soft-yellow staminodes. These enclose soft-green carpels that are tipped with pink. Some flowers may also produce a further cluster of pink petals inside the mound of staminodes. The blooms are carried aloft on straight stems with typical lactiflora leaves.

**Breeder:** unknown, pre-1928
**Height:** 90cm
**Flowers:** Japanese, midseason
**Scent:** heavy
**Staking:** no

## 'ANGEL CHEEKS'

This flower is sculpted from tiers of petals that vary in shape and colour. A saucer of pale-pink guard petals, which are laced around the edges, surrounds the first ring of loose, fluffy, pink-tinged, cream petaloids. Next comes a layer of pale-pink petals and finally in the middle a further layer of cream petaloids. The stems bear a few side buds and very thick, dark green leaves. Makes a good cut flower.

**Breeder:** Klehm, 1970
**Height:** 85cm
**Flowers:** double, early to midseason
**Scent:** light
**Staking:** no

*Paeonia* 'Angel Cheeks'

Lactiflora peonies | 49

### 'ANN COUSINS'

Opening into a large, creamy-white, domed flower, the evenly sized petals are wavy and notched along the edges. As the bloom ages, a hollow featuring very short petaloids forms in the middle. Sitting at the base of the inner petals are golden stamens. These suffuse each petal with a cream glow. The rather lax, red-tinted stems have long side stems and large, dark green leaves.

**Breeder:** Cousins, 1946
**Height:** 85cm
**Flowers:** double, mid to late season
**Scent:** heavy
**Staking:** yes

*Paeonia* 'Ann Cousins'

### 'ARGENTINE'

Smooth-petalled and white, when fully open the flower forms a frilly towering globe that is surrounded by two layers of lace-edged guard petals. A tinge of cream can be detected deep in the centre, otherwise the blooms are pure white. Rose-scented flowers are borne on strong stems, with extra buds carried on long side stems, and slightly glossy, mid-green leaves.

**Breeder:** Lemoine, 1924
**Height:** 75cm
**Flowers:** double, late midseason
**Scent:** medium
**Staking:** yes

### 'AUGUSTE DESSERT'

Medium-sized and rich-pink, this bloom's distinguishing feature is the silver rim that edges the lightly undulating petals. As the flower opens, a small bunch of rich-yellow stamens is uncovered. Sometimes this is semi-double, but usually a further cluster of inner petals appears to create a broad domed flower. Free-flowering and with slender, red stems bearing up to two side buds and slightly glossy, mid-green leaves.

**Breeder:** Dessert, 1920
**Height:** 90cm
**Flowers:** double, midseason
**Scent:** none
**Staking:** no

*Paeonia* 'Auguste Dessert'

*Paeonia* 'Argentine'

### 'BARBARA'

The rich-pink flowers of this lovely plant open into a tight ball of curling petals, all interwoven. Between the lower petals, a ring of fruity-pink petaloids is visible. At the base sits a ruff of big guard petals. Although large, the blooms are kept upright on very strong stems with grey-green leaves and some side buds. The blooms last very well in water. AGM

**Breeder:** from Poland, pre-1980
**Height:** 90cm
**Flowers:** double, midseason
**Scent:** none
**Staking:** no

*Paeonia* 'Barbara'

*Paeonia* 'Auguste Dessert' with *Iris* 'Fond Kiss', purple-flowered *Centaurea montana* 'Purpurea' and blue *Geranium* 'Brookside' (behind)

### 'BARONESS SCHROEDER'

The big, white guard petals are very slightly tinged with pink. They form a saucer around a frilly ball of slender, fringed white petals that glow with soft-yellow from the stamens sitting deep within the flower. In the centre, the petals form what the breeder described as a 'deep funnel'. It produces some side buds and mid-green leaves. Once a popular bloom in the cut-flower trade.

**Breeder:** Kelway, 1889
**Height:** 90cm
**Flowers:** double, midseason
**Scent:** heavy
**Staking:** sometimes

*Paeonia* 'Baroness Schroeder'

### 'BEST MAN'

Shiny and purplish-red, the flowers have large guard petals and many inner petals that are lighter in colour at the base and along the deeply notched edges. As the bloom opens, a layer of cream-tipped, pink petaloids can be seen, only to be hidden when the curving petals form a ball around the dipped centre of shorter petals. The dark green leaves are glossy, and a few side stems are present.

**Breeder:** Klehm, 1970
**Height:** 85cm
**Flowers:** double, midseason
**Scent:** heavy
**Staking:** when first planted

### 'BARRINGTON BELLE'

Bright purple-cerise guard petals open into a cup around a tight ball of curling, dark cream staminodes that are cerise at the base. As this handsome flower opens further, the petals get bigger while the centre briefly remains largely curled, until the staminodes eventually sit upright and turn cerise with pretty gold edging. The flower stems are reddish and the leaves are mid-green. AGM

**Breeder:** Klehm, 1972
**Height:** 90cm
**Flowers:** Japanese, late season
**Scent:** medium
**Staking:** no

*Paeonia* 'Best Man'

*Paeonia* 'Barrington Belle'

### 'BETTER TIMES'

An impressive, neat plant with large, rich-pink flowers that initially form a shallow dome with long, lightly fringed petals, paler along the edges. As the flower develops, the petals overlap each other to create a high, loose-petalled frilly bloom. These are carried on thick, upright stems with mid-green leaves and the occasional side branch bearing more buds.

**Breeder:** Franklin, 1941
**Height:** 70cm
**Flowers:** double, late midseason
**Scent:** medium
**Staking:** no

*Paeonia* 'Better Times'

### 'BLUSH QUEEN'

When young, the rings of neat smooth petals are soft-pink. As they open, the pink fades, and continues to do so until the high ball of petals flattens out into a compact, shallow dome. Short, frilly cream petaloids produce a yellow glow at the base of the petals and eventually the whole flower turns creamy-white except for the pink guard petals. A robust, free-flowering plant with strong stems and some side buds.

**Breeder:** Hoogendoorn, 1949
**Height:** 90cm
**Flowers:** double, midseason
**Scent:** medium
**Staking:** no

*Paeonia* 'Blush Queen'

### 'BOUQUET PERFECT'

A peony that always pleases, especially when cut and put in a vase where it will last for well over a week. The medium-sized blooms with large, mid-pink guard petals are serrated along the edges. On top of these sits a ball of swirled, deeply notched petals of the same colour yet slightly yellow at the base. The strong red stems carry a few side stems and small, narrow, mid-green leaves. Forms a tidy clump. AGM

**Breeder:** Tischler, 1987
**Height:** 60cm
**Flowers:** double, midseason
**Scent:** heavy
**Staking:** no

### 'BORDER GEM'

When first registered, the flowers were described as follows: 'Outer petals shrimp red. Inner petals chartreuse green'. The plant sold today is very different and definitely white. It opens into a dome of loose petals with a ring of golden stamens visible in the centre. The guard petals are soft-pink and the outer ones sometimes display a wire-thin edge of red. I do wonder if, over the years, this has been mixed up with *P*. 'Blush Queen'.

**Breeder:** Hoogendoorn, 1949
**Height:** 70cm
**Flowers:** double, midseason
**Scent:** slight
**Staking:** no

*Paeonia* 'Bouquet Perfect'

### 'BOWL OF BEAUTY'

One of the most popular peonies with large, bright-pink guard petals and an inner dome of cream staminodes. As the flower ages these change to milky white and the guard petals also fade in colour. In some years, the flowers may produce a further cluster of petals in the middle. When fully open, dark pink-edged, wing-like tips to the carpels can be seen. Slender, strong stems carry two to three side buds. A good cut flower. AGM

**Breeder:** Hoogendoorn, 1949
**Height:** 90cm
**Flowers:** Japanese, midseason
**Scent:** none
**Staking:** no

*Paeonia* 'Border Gem'

*Paeonia* 'Bowl Of Beauty'

### 'BOWL OF CREAM'

The many, evenly layered petals of this perfectly shaped, creamy-white bloom curl inwards at the edges and create a big ball. At the top, the central petals part to create a narrow, deep bowl filled with short, golden-yellow stamens. Among these emerge a few short, slim petaloids. The blooms are carried on strong stems with some side branches and mid-green leaves. Like many Klehm-raised peonies, this lasts well as a cut flower.

**Breeder:** Klehm, 1963
**Height:** 80cm
**Flowers:** double, early midseason
**Scent:** light
**Staking:** possibly, in windy locations

*Paeonia* 'Bowl Of Cream'

### 'BREAK O' DAY'

When the guard petals, which are the colour of crushed raspberries, first open they are neatly cupped around a tight mound of slender, rich-red, flame-like staminodes. As the flower develops, the staminodes straighten up and loosen to reveal gold stains at the base and tips. The colour fades as it reaches the petal edges, forming a silvery line along the tops. The slender, red stems have a few side buds and mid-green leaves.

**Breeder:** Murawska, 1947
**Height:** 90cm
**Flowers:** Japanese, midseason
**Scent:** none
**Staking:** no

*Paeonia* 'Break o' Day'

### 'BRIDAL ICING'

(opposite) A flower that changes with age. The large, ivory-white guard petals are deeply notched and the soft-cream petaloids, which open into a shallow dome, are long, ruffled and serrated at the top. As the bloom matures, rings of deep yellow stamens appear in between the petaloids and eventually the whole flower turns into a white pompom. The strong stems carry big, light green leaves. Good for cutting.

**Breeder:** Klehm, 1959
**Height:** 80cm
**Flowers:** double, early season
**Scent:** heavy
**Staking:** in windy locations

### 'BUNKER HILL'

Big, cerise-red flower petals are evenly sized, deeply notched and fringed at the edges. As these unfurl and curl outwards they reveal a small central cluster of yellow stamens, with more stamens showing among other petals. The deep red stems carry mid-green leaves and side stems that can get congested if all the flowers open at once. Unlike many 'red' lactiflora blooms, the petals don't deteriorate quickly when the flower is cut.

**Breeder:** Hollis, 1906
**Height:** 90cm
**Flowers:** double, midseason
**Scent:** none
**Staking:** no

*Paeonia* 'Bunker Hill'

Lactiflora peonies

The white flowers of *Paeonia* 'Bridal Icing' with silver-leaved *Stachys byzantina* and orange *Geum* 'Borisii'

*Paeonia* 'Butch'

### 'BUTCH'

A bowl-shaped flower with overlapping, deep red petals, opens into a perfect, shallow rose shape. The tips of the petals pale to silvery-pink as the blooms enlarge and a central ring of golden stamens can be seen. The blooms are borne on slender, but stiff, red stems along with leathery, shiny, mid-green leaves. Some of the stems produce side buds, but not all.

**Breeder:** Krekler, 1959
**Height:** 90cm
**Flowers:** semi-double, midseason
**Scent:** medium
**Staking:** no

*Paeonia* 'Butter Bowl'

### 'BUTTER BOWL'

The large guard petals, which at first curl upwards around the edges, open mid-pink and in time pale unevenly to very soft-pink. The low central cushion of soft butter-yellow, ribbon-like staminodes remains fairly constant in colour. Bearing some similarity to 'Bowl Of Beauty', the flowers of 'Butter Bowl' are much smaller. The blooms are borne high on long, slender stems with lots of side buds.

**Breeder:** Rosenfield, 1955
**Height:** 90cm
**Flowers:** Japanese, midseason
**Scent:** heavy
**Staking:** no

*Paeonia* 'Catharina Fontijn'

### 'CATHARINA FONTIJN'

Opening soft-pink, the petals fade to white and form a loose, low dome with a palest pink tinge on the guard petals. The petals reduce in size towards an inner ring of gold stamens, with further petals sprouting among them to create a full-looking bloom. Red stems produce long-stemmed side buds. Named after the wife of the Dutch breeder and grown in the Netherlands as a cut flower.

**Breeder:** Van der Valk/Van der Zwet, 1952
**Height:** 90cm
**Flowers:** Double, midseason
**Scent:** medium
**Staking:** no

### 'CHARLIE'S WHITE'

When the large flowers open, the centre creates a frilly, creamy-white ball, like a scoop of vanilla ice-cream, surrounded by large, white guard petals. Just visible above the guard petals is a ring of pointed, cream petaloids. The stems, which are long, bear mid-green leaves and the blooms are good for cutting, but flowers are abundant only in summers that are warm and dry. Sometimes incorrectly listed as 'Charles White'.

**Breeder:** Klehm, 1951
**Height:** 90cm
**Flowers:** Double, early season
**Scent:** none
**Staking:** yes

*Paeonia* 'Charlie's White'

*Paeonia* 'Charles Burgess'

### 'CHARLES BURGESS'

Not a particularly vigorous plant, but nevertheless a handsome one. The two rows of wavy, dark red guard petals have a matt appearance so the colour remains unaffected by changes in light levels. Cupped at first, the petals open to reveal a low, wide dome of crinkled, red, gold-edged staminodes. The sharp-scented flowers are carried on matching red stems with dark green leaves.

**Breeder:** Krekler, 1963
**Height:** 90cm
**Flowers:** Japanese, midseason
**Scent:** medium
**Staking:** no

*Paeonia* 'Charm'

### 'CHARM'

Once readily available, this attractive, fragrant plant is now scarce. The large, satiny, dark red guard petals are deeply notched in the centre. They surround a neat inner boss of lacy-edged, cerise staminodes that are lined with gold and stand upright as the flower ages. Sometimes extra tufts of red petals may appear in the centre. The upright stems are green and bear dark green leaves.

**Breeder:** Franklin, 1931
**Height:** 85cm
**Flowers:** Japanese, late season
**Scent:** heavy
**Staking:** no

*Paeonia* 'Cheddar Charm'

### 'CHEDDAR CHARM'

Two rows of ivory-white guard petals encase the dome of slim, twisted, egg-yellow staminodes. These add a yellow glow to the guard petals, which enlarge and become wavy as the yellow staminodes collapse sideways. Each scented flower is carried on upright stems, some have side buds with matt, dark green leaves. This is one of ten peonies introduced by Klehm Nursery of Wisconsin with the prefix 'Cheddar'.

**Breeder:** Klehm, 1985
**Height:** 85cm
**Flowers:** Japanese, midseason
**Scent:** heavy
**Staking:** no

*Paeonia* 'Cheddar Cheese'

### 'CHEDDAR CHEESE'

Set around the base of this rather untidy flower is a ragged layer of white guard petals. Above these is a thick ring of cream, laced-edged petaloids then a flurry of long, twisting white petals completes the effect. At first opening into a low dome, the petals develop and unfurl into a tall, shaggy flower. The slender, green stems bear mid-green leaves and carry one or two side buds.

**Breeder:** Klehm, 1973
**Height:** 90cm
**Flowers:** double, midseason
**Scent:** medium
**Staking:** possibly

## 'CHEDDAR GOLD'

Although varying greatly in size and shape, all flowers have two rows of big, ruffled, ivory-white guard petals and a mound of slender, deeply toothed, soft-yellow petaloids that start out gold. Sometimes more white petals appear so the flower looks double. Carried on upright stems, later flowers can become squashed against earlier blooms. The leaves are dark green.

**Breeder:** Klehm, 1959
**Height:** 75cm
**Flowers:** Japanese, midseason
**Scent:** medium
**Staking:** no

*Paeonia* 'Cheddar Gold'

## 'CHERRY HILL'

A free-flowering peony that bears glistening, dark crimson flowers with unevenly sized, fringed petals. Initially creating a big globe, the blooms open up into a loose ball as they age, revealing a small centre of little, gold stamens around scarlet-tipped carpels. The flowers are carried on slender, dark red stems with lots of side buds just above the mid-green leaves.

**Breeder:** Thurlow, 1915
**Height:** 75cm
**Flowers:** double, midseason
**Scent:** light
**Staking:** no

*Paeonia* 'Chiffon Clouds'

*Paeonia* 'Cherry Hill'

## 'CHIFFON CLOUDS'

Strongly tinted with pink as they open, the single flowers have three rows of near-white petals. At first these are cupped around the central, domed boss of thick, golden stamens which remains short even as the petals become more wavy with age. The flower is distinctly pollen scented. Creates a neat, upright clump with usually only one side bud and dark green leaves.

**Breeder:** Klehm, 1995
**Height:** 90cm
**Flowers:** single, midseason
**Scent:** medium
**Staking:** no

## 'CINCINNATI'

On opening, the shape of the big, dark pink blooms is broad and flat-topped. The large petals are unevenly textured with nicked top edges that pale significantly to silver-pink. Becoming much looser as they develop, the flowers appear almost semi-double and reveal a few golden stamens or, with some flowers, a complete clump of stamens. The blooms are borne on red-tinted stems with the occasional side bud and slightly glossy, mid-green leaves.

**Breeder:** Krekler, 1962
**Height:** 100cm
**Flowers:** double, midseason
**Scent:** heavy
**Staking:** sometimes

*Paeonia* 'Cincinnati'

### 'CLAIRE DUBOIS'

As the flower opens, the petals loosen into a big powder-puff with silvery rose-pink petals that pale along the edges. Each petal curls inwardly, overlapping the next to form a compact, slightly scented, dome-shaped bloom. A collar of slim petaloids shows just above the guard petals. The long arching stems produce deep green leaves that are tinted with grey.

**Breeder:** Crousse, 1886
**Height:** 90cm
**Flowers:** double, late season
**Scent:** light
**Staking:** yes

*Paeonia* 'Claire Dubois'

### 'CORA STUBBS'

Opening lavender-pink the guard petals quickly fade to pale-pink along the notched edges. In the centre is a big mound of creamy, round-topped petaloids that turn almost white as the flower ages. A few extra petals may emerge from the middle of the mound. Nicely scented flowers are borne on upright stems with one or two side buds. Named after the breeder's mother-in-law.

**Breeder:** Krekler, 1985
**Height:** 80cm
**Flowers:** Japanese, midseason
**Scent:** medium
**Staking:** no

### 'CORNELIA SHAYLOR'

Round, green buds open into a lightly fragrant, softly coloured bloom. The blush-pink guard petals create a frilly rim around the tight ball of inner petals. Tiers of almost-white petals and short, cream petaloids lend hints of yellow. The ball loosens and dips in the centre as the petals age and turn completely white. Strong stems carry mid-green leaves and one to five side buds.

**Breeder:** Shaylor, 1919
**Height:** 90cm
**Flowers:** double, late season
**Scent:** light
**Staking:** yes

*Paeonia* 'Cornelia Shaylor'

*Paeonia* 'Cora Stubbs'

### 'CUCKOO'S NEST'

Two rows of large, raspberry-red petals, nicked at the top, encase a massive dome of soft gold-tipped, red staminodes with curled tops. Some flowers produce a cluster of tall, creased petals in the centre. Slender, strong, reddish stems bear some long-stemmed side buds and glossy, mid-green leaves with lightly rippled edges.

**Breeder:** Krekler, 1977
**Height:** 80cm
**Flowers:** Japanese, midseason
**Scent:** none
**Staking:** no

*Paeonia* 'Cuckoo's Nest'

### 'COURONNE D'OR'

An old variety, this bears neatly shaped white flowers with equal sized petals. These are sometimes flecked crimson along the edges, and the guard petals are notched. The centre, which is encircled by larger petals, is dipped with a ring of gold stamens that highlights the base of the central petals. Although the flower stems, some of which bear side stems, are strong, the plant may need supporting.

**Breeder:** Calot, 1873
**Height:** 90cm
**Flowers:** double, midseason
**Scent:** medium
**Staking:** sometimes

*Paeonia* 'Couronne d'Or'

### 'CREAM PUFF'

When first open, the small flowers have rich-pink guard petals that quickly and unevenly fade to very pale-pink, then to near-white. The big, cushion-like centre of slim, cream staminodes takes on pink tinges and becomes crinkled with age. It also loosens to reveal red-tipped carpels. Not a particularly free-flowering plant. Dark red, upright stems carry the flowers just above the dark green, wrinkled-edged leaves with no side buds.

**Breeder:** Marx/Rogers, 1981
**Height:** 80cm
**Flowers:** Japanese, midseason
**Scent:** none
**Staking:** no

### 'DAWN PINK'

The petals of the glowing pink blooms are deeply crimped along the uneven edges and fade almost to white at the base. They surround a thick ring of dark yellow stamens and dark pink-tipped, soft-green carpels. Not prone to fading, the flowers are borne on strong, upright stems. Not to be confused with *Paeonia* 'Pink Dawn', now called *P.* 'Pink Princess', with palest pink petals.

**Breeder:** Sass, 1946
**Height:** 90cm
**Flowers:** single, early to midseason
**Scent:** none
**Staking:** no

*Paeonia* 'Dawn Pink'

*Paeonia* 'Cream Puff'

### 'DAYTON'

A lovely upright plant with deep pink flowers that open into a loose, flat-topped rose shape. Each petal pales along its edges and is deeply notched. As the bloom matures, the petals extend upwards and a few golden stamens are visible throughout. The flowers are borne on slender, red stems with mid-green leaves and the occasional side bud. Named after the city of Dayton, Ohio.

**Breeder:** Krekler, 1962
**Height:** 90cm
**Flowers:** double, late season
**Scent:** medium
**Staking:** no

*Paeonia* 'Dayton'

## 'DINNER PLATE'

The enormous, very lightly scented, soft-pink flowers feature inner petals that are shorter than the outer ones. These pale at the edges and bleached white in strong sun, they become interwoven towards the middle where a few cream petaloids are visible. Despite strong, thick stems that carry thick, leathery, dark green leaves, this plant does need staking. I find it good for cutting.

**Breeder:** Klehm, 1968
**Height:** 100cm
**Flowers:** double, late season
**Scent:** light
**Staking:** yes

*Paeonia* 'Dinner Plate'

## 'DO TELL'

Although the flowers are striking, this peony is shy to bloom in areas of Britain that are cool and damp. Unevenly edged, and soft shell-pink, the guard petals initially form a shallow dish around a high domed centre that is a mixture of slender, vivid-pink staminodes and wavy, softest pink petaloids. As the flower matures, the petaloids enlarge and turn the centre a paler colour. The blooms are borne on stiff stems with a few side buds.

**Breeder:** Auten, 1946
**Height:** 85cm
**Flowers:** Japanese, midseason
**Scent:** light
**Staking:** no

## 'DON RICHARDSON'

Large garnet-red guard petals open into a cup around a tight mound of soft-yellow staminodes that unfurl and then turn the same red as the petals, but with wrinkled gold edges. Sometimes a slim inner flute of garnet petals pops up. The flowers are borne on narrow stems, with dark green leaves and small side buds that may not open. Although beautiful, not a vigorous or free-flowering plant.

**Breeder:** Krekler, 1976
**Height:** 90cm
**Flowers:** Japanese, late season
**Scent:** light
**Staking:** no

*Paeonia* 'Don Richardson'

*Paeonia* 'Do Tell'

## 'DOREEN'

The blooms are large and have two rows of loosely held, bright-pink guard petals, which fade a little with age. In the middle is a low ball of deep yellow staminodes that are slightly wider and ruffled towards the tips and tinged with pink. They loosen as the flower opens to show pink-tipped carpels. On this vigorous, free-flowering plant the blooms are held not far above the glossy, dark green leaves on red stems with some side buds. AGM

**Breeder:** Sass, 1949
**Height:** 90cm
**Flowers:** Japanese, mid to late season
**Scent:** medium
**Staking:** no

*Paeonia* 'Doreen'

Lactiflora peonies | 61

*Paeonia* 'Duchesse de Nemours'

### 'DORIS COOPER'

Opening soft-pink, the large flowers fade to near white and form a big, flat rosette with some pink retained on the guard petals. Interspersed between the short, fringed central petals are a few cream petaloids and gold stamens – all giving the dipped middle a cream glow. The long, lax, red-tinted stems produce lots of side buds and dark green leaves.

### 'DUCHESSE DE NEMOURS'

(opposite) Most popular among the white varieties, largely owing to its reputation as a good cut flower. Opening from greenish buds, at first the large guard petals are cupped around the centre of frilly inner petals. These open into a gently domed flower that has pure white petals, tinted cream at the base because of the short, soft-yellow petaloids. AGM

t, 1856

ɔle, late midseason

n

wer, this opens from a pure
ito a large, shallow bowl
tly creamy, interlaced
nes they may display a
gs. The blooms start out
ɔund, greenish buds,
experience it is rare for
pen. The flower stems
well-branched and carry
een leaves. Good for

930

e, very late season

**The Irish Gardener Store**
Carrigaline, Douglas, Carrigaline, Cork, P43 EC96, Ireland
info@theirishgardener.com
theirishgardener.com

'Emma Klehm'

## 'FAIRBANKS'

The large guard petals are so deeply indented they look like big hearts and are faintest pink at first. On opening, the bloom is bowl-shaped but as it matures the petals flare outwards and turn soft-white. The neat central ring of deep cream staminodes, which don't enlarge as the flower ages, sits around soft-green carpels. Carried on slender stems with a few side buds and very dark green leaves that are wrinkled along the edges.

**Breeder:** Auten, 1945
**Height:** 120cm
**Flowers:** Japanese, late season
**Scent:** light
**Staking:** no

*Paeonia* 'Fairbanks'

*Paeonia* 'Fairy's Petticoat'

## 'FAIRY'S PETTICOAT'

A bomb-shaped bloom that opens in a blend of different shades ranging from palest pink to cream. As it ages the serrated petals become entirely white. The flowers are carried on upright stems with mid-green leaves, some of which bear long side branches. This pretty, short plant is typical of the peonies introduced by American Klehm during the latter half of the 20th century.

**Breeder:** Klehm, 1963
**Height:** 75cm
**Flowers:** double, early season
**Scent:** none
**Staking:** no

*Paeonia* 'Félix Crousse'

## 'FÉLIX CROUSSE'

A softly perfumed cerise-red ball of inward curling petals is encircled by large guard petals creating a neat saucer. All the petals are notched and pale at edges. When fully open, yellow stamens are revealed amongst a centre of smaller petals. Of the many double cerise-red peonies, several are difficult to tell apart. This is similar in style to *Paeonia* 'Inspecteur Lavergne', but blooms slightly later. The red flower stems carry side buds on well-branched stems. AGM

**Breeder:** Crousse, 1881
**Height:** 85cm
**Flowers:** double, late midseason
**Scent:** medium
**Staking:** yes

## 'FESTIVA MAXIMA'

A handsome plant producing pure white flowers that open from a shallow mound into a high dome. As the petals loosen, hints of yellow emanate from soft-yellow petaloids seated deep within the bloom. Occasional red streaks that mark the odd petal along the edges make this cultivar easy to recognise. As the flower grows the shorter inner petals create a dipped centre. Long, branched stems, which are ideal for cutting, bear lush, dark green leaves. AGM

**Breeder:** Miellez, 1851
**Height:** 90cm
**Flowers:** double, early season
**Scent:** medium
**Staking:** yes

*Paeonia* 'Festiva Maxima'

*Paeonia* 'Fiona'

### 'FIONA'

Evenly sized cerise-red petals, much paler along the edges, open into a loose crown-like bloom on dark red stems just above the waxy, very dark green leaves. Acquired under this name some years ago, according to a Dutch source, it is also sold as *P* 'Red Sarah Bernhardt', a red version of *P*. 'Sarah Bernhardt', a plant it in no way resembles. Imported from China into the Netherlands, the plant was re-named for the cut flower industry in 1980.

**Breeder:** unknown, 1980
**Height:** 90cm
**Flowers:** double, midseason
**Scent:** light
**Staking:** no

*Paeonia* 'Florence Nicholls'

### 'FLORENCE NICHOLLS'

Although not large, this ball-shaped flower is beautifully perfumed. Hidden between the creamy petals are slender yellow petaloids that produce a yellow glow deep within. Towards the centre of the bloom the petals gradually shorten to create a dip. The flowers are carried on strong stems with dark green leaves and a few side buds. Good for cutting. AGM

**Breeder:** Nicholls, 1938
**Height:** 90cm
**Flowers:** double, early midseason
**Scent:** heavy
**Staking:** no

*Paeonia* 'Gardenia'

### 'GARDENIA'

This very pretty plant produces clusters of white flowers that resemble the blooms of a rose. On opening, the guard petals are very lightly tinted with pink. Each curling petal loosely overlaps the next and in the middle, shorter petals form a cup around the gold stamens and tiny, red-tipped, dark green carpels. The blooms are carried on red stems with large, dark green leaves. This is favoured by professional cut-flower growers.

**Breeder:** Lins, 1955
**Height:** 90cm
**Flowers:** double, midseason
**Scent:** medium
**Staking:** no

### 'GAYBORDER JUNE'

On first opening, this rich-pink flower with equal sized petals, is a perfect rose shape. Later, as the petals loosen, the pink colouration fades around the deeply notched edges to pale-pink. Eventually as the flower ages further, small yellow stamens interspersed with short petaloids become visible. Some side buds are borne on the slender stems with dull, mid-green leaves.

**Breeder:** Hoogendoorn, 1949
**Height:** 80cm
**Flowers:** double, early season
**Scent:** medium
**Staking:** sometimes

*Paeonia* 'Gayborder June'

### 'GAY PAREE'

A free-flowering plant with blooms that are not over large. Round, bright magenta-pink, good-sized guard petals surround a mound of broad, pale-cream staminodes that are washed with pink. In time, the petals pale almost to white along the edges. Sometimes a further flurry of bright-pink petals pops up in the centre. The blooms, which last well in a vase when cut, are borne on upright stems, some of which have side buds. AGM

**Breeder:** Auten, 1933
**Height:** 90cm
**Flowers:** Japanese, midseason
**Scent:** medium
**Staking:** no

*Paeonia* 'Gay Paree'

### 'GILBERT BARTHELOT'

This plant has what I consider 'classic' lactiflora-shaped flowers. The loose, soft-pink petals are all the same size but darker at the base and serrated around the edges. When fully mature, the centre of the bloom becomes funnel-shaped, allowing golden stamens to be revealed between the layers of petals. The stems bear dark green foliage with one to three side buds.

**Breeder:** Doriat, 1931
**Height:** 90cm
**Flowers:** double, midseason
**Scent:** heavy
**Staking:** yes

*Paeonia* 'Gilbert Barthelot'

### 'GERMAINE BIGOT'

This old, well-scented variety has large, rather shaggy, white flowers that are tinged with pink at the base. Sometimes little flecks of red can be seen along the edges. As the bloom opens into a flat-topped crown, the guard petals stay blush-pink while the remainder fade to white. A few stamens can be viewed in the dipped centre. The long, lax stems carry dull green leaves and one or two side buds.

**Breeder:** Dessert, 1902
**Height:** 90cm
**Flowers:** double, midseason
**Scent:** heavy
**Staking:** yes

*Paeonia* 'Germaine Bigot'

### 'GOLDEN FROLIC'

An unusual peony owing to the unique golden-green colour of the large, rough-surfaced young leaves. As the flowers unfurl from conical buds, the leaves are shaded with green then eventually turn a striking bright green. The pale-pink flower has thick, wavy, ragged-edged petals with broad flares of magenta and a thick ring of stamens. Carried on stiff stems, the blooms can vary in quality from year to year. Produces seed very easily.

**Breeder:** Klehm, 2003
**Height:** 90cm
**Flowers:** single, midseason
**Scent:** heavy
**Staking:** no

*Paeonia* 'Golden Frolic'

*Paeonia* 'Glory Hallelujah'

## 'GLORY HALLELUJAH'

Big and sweetly scented, the mid-pink flowers with layers of unevenly sized, frilly petals open to form a squat crown. The large guard petals are silver along the edges while the inner petals are interlaced with ribbon-like petaloids. These are gold at the base and also create a thick, fringed ruff just above the guard petals. Strong stems carry shiny, dark green leaves and some side buds.

**Breeder:** Klehm, 1970
**Height:** 85cm
**Flowers:** double, very late season
**Scent:** heavy
**Staking:** no

## 'GLOWING CANDLES'

Thick white petals, lightly brushed with very pale-pink, form a ruffled collar around the tight mound of thick cream staminodes. When the guard petals unfurl they are short and curly. As the flower evolves, white petaloids erupt and flare among the staminodes. The green carpels are tipped with cream. Well-branched stems bear bright mid-green leaves.

**Breeder:** Wild, 1966
**Height:** 90cm
**Flowers:** Japanese, early to midseason
**Scent:** medium
**Staking:** no

## 'GUIDON'

At first the outer petals, which are wavy along the tops, open into a shallow, rich rose-pink, flat-topped cup that is unevenly filled with shorter petals. As the flower ages, the petals become uniform in size and pale slightly along the edges as they loosen into a big, ruffled, tobacco scented flower. The blooms are borne in clusters on straight, red stems with two to three side buds and very large, leathery, dull, dark green leaves.

**Breeder:** Nicholls, 1941
**Height:** 90cm
**Flowers:** double, midseason
**Scent:** medium
**Staking:** yes

*Paeonia* 'Glowing Candles'

## 'HELEN HAYES'

Forming a high crown, the flowers have ruffled, dark pink petals that curl inwards and are deeply notched and serrated along the silver-pink edges. The central petals are much shorter and open into a bowl interlaced with pink petaloids, with no trace of yellow is visible. The flowers are not dissimilar to the those of 'Glory Hallelujah' but are smaller in size. Strong stems produce two or three long, side buds and glossy, dark green leaves.

**Breeder:** Murawska, 1943
**Height:** 90cm
**Flowers:** double, midseason
**Scent:** medium
**Staking:** no

*Paeonia* 'Guidon'

*Paeonia* 'Helen Hayes'

Lactiflora peonies | 67

*Paeonia* 'Henry Sass'

### 'HENRY SASS'

Hints of lemon radiate from the small, yellow petaloids that are seated deep within the ball of pure white petals. When fully open, the flower creates a large pompom. As the central petals get shorter, a dip is created. The blooms are carried on strong, brick-red stems with dark green leaves some of which bear side buds but not all. When cut, the flowers last well in water.

**Breeder:** Sass, 1949
**Height:** 85cm
**Flowers:** double, midseason
**Scent:** medium
**Staking:** no

*Paeonia* 'Hermione'

### 'HERMIONE'

The petals of the very large, fluffy, soft-pink flowers are notched around the edges and a darker pink towards the base. Like the guard petals they are consequently paler at the tips. In the middle, a yellow glow emanates from the short gold stamens that sit between similarly short, central petals. The long stems make the flowers suitable for cutting.

**Breeder:** Sass, 1932
**Height:** 90cm
**Flowers:** double, late midseason
**Scent:** medium
**Staking:** yes

*Paeonia* 'Hit Parade'

### 'HIT PARADE'

Two rows of magenta guard petals, which fade in hot sun, frame a low ball of flame-like, pointed, cream staminodes. These are pink at the base and can be deeper pink in some years. A further flute of deep pink petals may also arise in the very centre of the flower. The upright stems have long, side branches and mid-green leaves that are slightly crimped along the edges and bright-green underneath. The scent is difficult to describe but interesting.

**Breeder:** Nicholls, 1965
**Height:** 90cm
**Flowers:** Japanese, midseason
**Scent:** medium
**Staking:** no

### 'HONEY GOLD'

Fluttering around a broad bright-yellow centre of staminodes are two layers of white guard petals. The staminodes, which are fringed at the top, bring a golden glow to the base of the guard petals. As the centre enlarges, the middle turns into a high ball while the guard petals relax. Some blooms produce more white petals right in the middle. Side buds appear towards the top of the strong, thick stems with mid-green leaves.

**Breeder:** Klehm, 1970
**Height:** 90cm
**Flowers:** Japanese, midseason
**Scent:** medium
**Staking:** no

*Paeonia* 'Honey Gold'

*Paeonia* 'Hot Chocolate'

### 'HOT CHOCOLATE'

Not very vigorous but unique in colour, this peony produces very dark red, almost mahogany, guard petals. These curl gently along the edges to form a cup around a tight boss of silver-tipped staminodes that are the same colour as the petals. As these age, they loosen and become slimmer. The slender stems and leaves are almost chocolate in colour.

**Breeder:** Sass/Reynolds, 1971
**Height:** 95cm
**Flowers:** Japanese, mid to late season
**Scent:** light
**Staking:** no

### 'INSPECTEUR LAVERGNE'

A free-flowering, strong-growing plant that produces mid-sized, rich crimson-red flowers. When cut and put in water, these don't immediately shrivel, as is the case with some red peonies. In time, as the blooms grow bigger, the silver-tipped, frilled petaloids become visible and the whole bloom turns into a neat dome. The flowers are carried on tall upright stems with many side buds and mid-green leaves.

**Breeder:** Doriat, 1924
**Height:** 90cm
**Flowers:** double, mid to late season
**Scent:** none
**Staking:** no

### 'INSTITUTEUR DORIAT'

Although classed as a Japanese-type lactiflora because the whole bloom is a uniform colour, it looks more like a double peony. Large, rich carmine-red guard petals sit unevenly around a ball of frilly, white-lined, pointed carmine-red staminodes. The flowers are held nicely on upright stems with mid-green leaves. I have not found this to be a particularly strong-growing plant, but the flowers are unusual and brightly coloured.

**Breeder:** Doriat, 1925
**Height:** 85cm
**Flowers:** Japanese, midseason
**Scent:** none
**Staking:** no

*Paeonia* 'Inspecteur Lavergne'

*Paeonia* 'Instituteur Doriat'

### 'JAMES PILLOW'

Opening pale-pink, the ruffled petals, which have a thick, satiny texture, lighten further along the deeply scalloped edges. As the flower ages, the petals loosen and rings of long, pointed, cream petaloids are revealed. The blooms are carried on tall stems with some side buds and the typical mid-green leaves of a lactiflora peony. This makes a good cut flower, lasting for up to 7 days in a vase.

**Breeder:** Pillow/Christman, 1936
**Height:** 95cm
**Flowers:** double, late season
**Scent:** none
**Staking:** yes

*Paeonia* 'James Pillow'

*Paeonia* 'Jan van Leeuwen' enhanced by a background of dark *Sambucus nigra* f. *porphyrophylla* 'Eva'

*Paeonia* 'Jan van Leeuwen'

### 'JAN VAN LEEUWEN'

For me this is the most consistently perfect peony in terms of flower form and plant shape. Each bloom has two rows of pure white guard petals that form a cup around a low dome of slender, pointed, golden staminodes, which curl towards the top. The flowers are carried on stems that are even in height, have side branches and lightly ruffled, mid-green leaves. A lovely, well-behaved garden plant. AGM

**Breeder:** Van Leeuwen, 1928
**Height:** 90cm
**Flowers:** Japanese, late season
**Scent:** medium
**Staking:** no

*Paeonia* 'Jean Ericksen'

### 'JEAN ERICKSEN'

The big, rich-red guard petals open into a neatly shaped goblet that unfurls further to create an uneven, scooped ruff around the centre of red staminodes. These are so broad they remind me of the tendrils of a sea anemone. Each flower, which opens from a perfectly round bud, sits on a thick stem with leathery, mid-green leaves.

**Breeder:** Ericksen, 1999
**Height:** 90cm
**Flowers:** Japanese, midseason
**Scent:** light
**Staking:** no

*Paeoria* 'Joker'

### 'JOKER'

The flowers change markedly through their life. First, they open into a mid-pink, shallowly domed rosette with frilly petaloids seated amongst the central petals. As the flower ages, all the petals fade to very pale-pink, except for the edges, which stay mid-pink and produce a picotee effect. Obtained by breeder W.S. Bockstoce from Henry Landis, who introduced it, and registered by Al Rogers, Oregon.

**Breeder:** Landis/Rogers, 2004
**Height:** 80cm
**Flowers:** double, early to midseason
**Scent:** none
**Staking:** no

### 'JUNE ROSE'

Magenta petals are woven into the classic form of an 'old rose'. When the shallowly domed bloom opens further, the petals pale to silver-pink along the edges and become slightly shorter in the centre. If you look hard, a few gold stamens can be seen. The red flower stems, which bear a few side buds, are strong and carry handsome dark green leaves. This creates an upright, free-flowering, tidy clump.

**Breeder:** Jones, 1938
**Height:** 85cm
**Flowers:** double, early midseason
**Scent:** mild
**Staking:** no

*Paeonia* 'June Rose'

Lactiflora peonies | 71

*Paeonia* 'Kansas'

## 'KANSAS'

The colour of this big flower is difficult to describe: perhaps dark magenta, although it veers towards pink in tone. The petals, which are large and notched, are woven loosely together to form a compact, frilly dome. This becomes ruffled and shorter in the centre, creating a deep hollow that reveals a few golden stamens. Red stems bear dark green leaves and a few side branches. The blooms last well as a cut flower. AGM

**Breeder:** Bigger, 1940
**Height:** 90cm
**Flowers:** double, midseason
**Scent:** very light
**Staking:** yes

*Paeonia* 'Karen Gray'

## 'KAREN GRAY'

A dish of magenta-red guard petals forms a broad circle around a centre of wrinkle-edged, butter-yellow staminodes carried on red-tinged filaments. Although not the most vigorous or free-flowering variety, it is a nice plant and carries its flowers on straight stems. The lack of side buds allows the flowers to sit very neatly above the clump of dark green leaves. Named after the wife of the breeder's grandson.

**Breeder:** Krekler, 1965
**Height:** 85cm
**Flowers:** Japanese, early season
**Scent:** none
**Staking:** no

*Paeonia* 'Karl Rosenfield'

## 'KARL ROSENFIELD'

Free-flowering and vigorous, this plant produces bright-crimson flowers with inward-curling petals that are notched and slightly paler along the edges. As they open into a flat dome, short yellow stamens can be seen between the petals. The blooms are produced on strong, red stems with dark green leaves and some side buds, and the whole plant forms a neat, self-supporting clump.

**Breeder:** Rosenfield, 1908
**Height:** 85cm
**Flowers:** double, midseason
**Scent:** light
**Staking:** no

## 'KELWAY'S GLORIOUS'

Opening palest pink, the large flower matures into a shaggy almost white bloom with a deep centre and silky petals that are flecked occasionally with red. Shorter inner petals create a central dip and the short cream petaloids sitting between the loose petals give their bases a yellow glow. The mid-green leaves are glossy. AGM

**Breeder:** Kelway, 1909
**Height:** 90cm
**Flowers:** double, midseason
**Scent:** medium
**Staking:** yes

*Paeonia* 'Kelway's Glorious'

72 | Lactiflora peonies

### 'KRINKLED WHITE'

The pristine white flowers have just a single row of crepe-like petals. Initially these are cupped like a tulip around a tight boss of curling, golden-yellow stamens with a centre of white-tipped carpels. A free-flowering plant, the blooms open just above an evenly shaped, very upright clump with shiny, light green leaves. The stiff stems occasionally carry side buds.

**Breeder:** Brand, 1928
**Height:** 80cm
**Flowers:** single, early season
**Scent:** heavy
**Staking:** no

*Paeonia* 'Krinkled White'

### 'LADY ALEXANDRA DUFF'

Opening mid-pink, the petal colour gradually fades to white towards the middle. Shorter inner petals, flecked with red, curl inwards to form a hollow around a loose ring of yellow stamens and prominent dark pink-tipped, red carpels. The breeder states that flowers opening from the side-branches may be single to semi-double. Named after one of Queen Victoria's god-daughters. AGM

**Breeder:** Kelway, 1902
**Height:** 85cm
**Flowers:** double, midseason
**Scent:** medium
**Staking:** sometimes

*Paeonia* 'Lady Orchid'

### 'LADY ORCHID'

A pretty flower with soft-to-the-touch, pale-pink petals that overlap each other, are lightly serrated and paler around the edges. The flat blooms are evenly shaped and held on long red stems with large waxy, grey-green leaves that create a wonderful contrast to the pink flowers. One of the later peonies to flower, this is useful for extending the season and the strong stems ensure the blooms stay upright.

**Breeder:** Bigger, 1942
**Height:** 90cm
**Flowers:** double, late season
**Scent:** none
**Staking:** no

*Paeonia* 'Lady Alexandra Duff'

### 'LANCASTER IMP'

A short plant with slender, fringed, white petals so tightly woven they open from a shallow dome into a white pompom. An inner creamy glow is discernible deep within and the guard petals remain large throughout the flowering period. The blooms, which have a fruity scent, are carried just above a short, compact clump of mid-green leaves on strong stems that have one to three side buds. Good for windy spots.

**Breeder:** unknown, Klehm, 1987
**Height:** 65cm
**Flowers:** double, early season
**Scent:** medium
**Staking:** no

*Paeonia* 'Lancaster Imp'

Lactiflora peonies | 73

### 'LARGO'

As the cup of vivid-pink guard petals opens into a loose ruff their colour fades to pale-pink. They sit around a wide, flat mound of pink-flushed, cream staminodes that are wrinkled towards the ends. More often than not a further flurry of pink petals will erupt from the centre. This free-flowering plant carries the blooms well above the deep green, crinkle-edged foliage on evenly spaced red stems with lots of side stems.

**Breeder:** Vories, 1929
**Height:** 90cm
**Flowers:** Japanese, midseason
**Scent:** heavy
**Staking:** no

*Paeonia* 'Largo'

### 'LAURA DESSERT'

Until recently there were almost no yellow herbaceous peonies. Those that are available are still very expensive, but this more affordable lactiflora produces lovely creamy-yellow blooms. Small, white guard petals enclose a pompom of slim, fringed, soft-lemon petaloids that are interspersed with broader white petals. As the petals get bigger, the flower turns white. The blooms are borne on straight stems with dark green leaves. AGM

**Breeder:** Dessert, 1913
**Height:** 90cm
**Flowers:** double, midseason
**Scent:** light
**Staking:** no

*Paeonia* 'Le Cygne'

### 'LE CYGNE'

It is easy to see why the French breeder named this beauty 'The Swan'. The buds open into a ball of white petals that are fringed and laced around the edges, and tinged with cream. As the flower evolves into a large, creamy-white bloom, the incurving, slightly pink-tinted guard petals encase a centre of petals that curl over each other like feathers. The leaves are dark green.

**Breeder:** Lemoine, 1907
**Height:** 85cm
**Flowers:** double, early season
**Scent:** light
**Staking:** yes

*Paeonia* 'Laura Dessert'

### 'LESLIE PECK'

A dish of slightly wavy, deep pink guard petals frames a central mound of slender, soft-pink ribbons that are heavily tinted with yellow giving the blooms a peachy tone. The flowers are carried well above the foliage on upright stems with lots of side buds that admirably extend the flowering period.

**Breeder:** Niva/Snelson, 1999
**Height:** 90cm
**Flowers:** Japanese, early season
**Scent:** light
**Staking:** yes

*Paeonia* 'Leslie Peck'

*Paeonia* 'Liebchen'

## 'LIEBCHEN'

The big, mid-pink guard petals create a shallow cup around a ring of fine, yellow stamens. Paler pink at the base, these petals loosen and become more wavy over time. The blooms are carried on strong, slender stems above large, mid-green leaves. The name means 'sweetheart' in German, and the breeder chose to stick with this on discovering the English name had already been allocated to a much earlier peony.

**Breeder:** Murawska, 1959
**Height:** 90cm
**Flowers:** single, midseason
**Scent:** medium
**Staking:** no

## 'LILAC TIME'

Two rows of large, round, deep pink guard petals frame a wide centre of slender staminodes. Some of the staminodes are very pointed and the same colour as the guard petals. Others, just tipped with yellow, sit among short pure yellow ones that bring an apricot hue to the centre where the bright-pink carpels are very visible. The rather dainty blooms are carried on long, branched stems with mid-green leaves.

**Breeder:** Lins, 1958
**Height:** 90cm
**Flowers:** Japanese, late season
**Scent:** light
**Staking:** no

## 'LILLIAN WILD'

A beautiful flower that is softest pink when it first opens. As the petals uncurl into a flat-topped dome, the large, gently curved petals fade to white. Sitting between them are rings of short, creamy-white petaloids casting a soft-cream glow that rises from the depths of the bloom. Sometimes the petals are streaked with magenta. The flowers are borne in clusters on long, rather lax stems with large, dark green leaves.

**Breeder:** Wild, 1950
**Height:** 90cm
**Flowers:** double, midseason
**Scent:** light
**Staking:** sometimes

*Paeonia* 'Lilac Time'

## 'LITTLE JOE'

Evenly-sized and bright-magenta, the petals curl inwards along the edges. At first they open into a cup that encompasses a dense ring of little, gold stamens. An inner tuft of magenta petals, shorter than the guard petals, then emerges in the centre of the stamens. Eventually the flower becomes a flat rosette. The petite blooms are borne on red stems with up to three side buds above a clump of mid-green leaves.

**Breeder:** Krekler, 1977
**Height:** 70cm
**Flowers:** semi-double, midseason
**Scent:** medium
**Staking:** no

*Paeonia* 'Lillian Wild'

*Paeonia* 'Little Joe'

Lactiflora peonies | 75

*Paeonia* 'Little Medicine Man'

### 'LITTLE MEDICINE MAN'

The rich-pink guard petals of the single flowers flutter around a dense centre of fine yellow stamens and small red-tipped carpels. Flowers are small but produced in great numbers on stiff red stems with mid-green foliage. Introduced from China around 2000, where it was grown for the roots and known as 'Fen Yu Nu', this peony was called 'Dancing Butterflies' when I first bought it. The name changed again to 'Little Medicine Man' in 2006.

**Breeder:** Unknown, pre-2000
**Height:** 80cm
**Flowers:** single, early to midseason
**Scent:** strong
**Staking:** no

*Paeonia* 'Lois Kelsey'

### 'LOIS KELSEY'

Unique and very recognisable, the pure white flowers are so deeply incised along the edges they look as though they have been cut with scissors. On first opening, the petals form a cup that matures into a flattish flower with a small ring of golden stamens and dark pink-red carpels. Sometimes red streaks mark the white petals. The blooms sit just above the leaves on stiff stems with a few side buds.

**Breeder:** Kelsey, 1934
**Height:** 80cm
**Flowers:** semi-double, midseason
**Scent:** none
**Staking:** no

*Paeonia* 'Lord Kitchener'

### 'LORD KITCHENER'

Among the very few single, red-flowered lactiflora peonies, this may not be the most elegant but it is free-flowering. The small, crimson blooms produce just a single row of shiny petals and a boss of very short golden stamens. The blooms are borne on very slender, well-branched, dark red stems with shiny, dark green leaves. Once known by the name of 'Balliol'.

**Breeder:** Kelway, 1907
**Height:** 90cm
**Flowers:** single, midseason
**Scent:** none
**Staking:** no

### 'LOTUS QUEEN'

Throughout the life of the flower, the large, round, white guard petals, which have lightly nipped edges, remain cupped around a broad ring of staminodes. At first these are gold but grow to resemble upright, white threads. The carpels are greenish-white, tipped with pale-pink. Stiff stems with some side buds and smooth, deep green leaves carry the blooms.

**Breeder:** Murawska, 1947
**Height:** 85cm
**Flowers:** Japanese, midseason
**Scent:** light
**Staking:** no

*Paeonia* 'Lotus Queen'

*Paeonia* 'Louis Barthelot'

### 'LOUIS BARTHELOT'

Curling, lightly fringed, white petals create a feathery ball highlighted with hints of soft-amber radiating from pale-yellow petaloids set deep inside the flower. Sometimes a few of the petals might be streaked with raspberry-red. The blooms sit nicely on red-tinted stems with some side branches and lots of slender, deep green leaves.

**Breeder:** Doriat, 1927
**Height:** 80cm
**Flowers:** double, late season
**Scent:** medium
**Staking:** no

*Paeonia* 'Lowell Thomas'

### 'LOWELL THOMAS'

I have not found this plant easy to grow, but it's worth including in a garden for the velvety, crimson flowers. The unevenly sized blooms display a tight mound of inner petals surrounded by wavy guard petals. They are carried on upright, very dark green stems with side stems, and dark green leaves, which look crumpled on the surface.

**Breeder:** Rosenfield, 1934
**Height:** 90cm
**Flowers:** double, midseason
**Scent:** none
**Staking:** no

*Paeonia* 'Madame Calot'

### 'MADAME CALOT'

When first opening, the flowers may be softest pink, others can be white. As the bloom becomes globe-shaped, just the two rows of large guard petals remain pink. The inner petals, which have deeply notched edges, fade to soft-white, becoming almost translucent. Slender, cream petaloids add an inner yellow glow. In the dipped middle sit red-tipped carpels. A neat plant, the flower stems are strong and well-branched.

**Breeder:** Miellez, 1856
**Height:** 90cm
**Flowers:** double, midseason
**Scent:** medium
**Staking:** no

### 'MADAME DUCEL'

Big, slightly wavy, rose-pink guard petals form a flaring saucer around the ball of smaller petals. These are so interlaced they look like a tight pompom. With age, the bloom softens in colour and a thin collar of apricot petaloids becomes visible just above the guard petals. The flowers are carried on stiff stems with glossy, mid-green leaves.

**Breeder:** Méchin, 1880
**Height:** 85cm
**Flowers:** double, midseason
**Scent:** none
**Staking:** no

*Paeonia* 'Madame Ducel'

Lactiflora peonies | 77

*Paeonia* 'Madame Edouard Doriat'

### 'MADAME EDOUARD DORIAT'

Opening from green-tinged, red-striped buds, the big white ball of flower is created from layers of large petals and short, pale-cream petaloids. Some petals are streaked lightly with crimson. As the bloom evolves further, the petals loosen and the centre becomes dipped. A few yellow stamens can be seen among the surrounding petals. Long, stiff stems make this a good cut flower.

**Breeder:** Dessert/Doriat, 1924
**Height:** 90cm
**Flowers:** double, midseason
**Scent:** light
**Staking:** yes

### 'MADAME EMILE DÉBATÈNE'

When first open, the deep pink blooms form a flat, rose-shaped flower filled with evenly sized petals. As the flower ages, the bright-pink petals, which have serrated edges, loosen enough to show the centre of small petals as well as the cluster of golden stamens. Long, slender, red stems bear one or two side branches and mid-green foliage.

**Breeder:** Dessert/Doriat 1927
**Height:** 90cm
**Flowers:** double, late midseason
**Scent:** medium
**Staking:** yes

### 'MAGENTA MOON'

The vivid-magenta flowers have thick, round petals that are equal in size. The backs of the petals are paler in colour, as are the upper edges which feature a little slit in the middle. The blooms open into a very low dome that gradually flattens as the flower matures. They are carried on strong stems, some of which have side buds, with mid-green leaves.

**Breeder:** Klehm, 1995
**Height:** 85cm
**Flowers:** semi-double, early season
**Scent:** medium
**Staking:** no

*Paeonia* 'Madame Emile Débatène'

### 'MARGARET TRUMAN'

On opening, the deep pink flowers resemble an old rose, then the large outer petals part to reveal a centre of unevenly sized petals. As the bloom ages, these loosen and lighten along the edges. Clusters of gold stamens can be seen between the smaller central petals. The long, slender, red stems bear one or two side branches and shiny dark green leaves. This was named after the daughter of US President Harry Truman.

**Breeder:** Van der Valk, 1953
**Height:** 90cm
**Flowers:** double, midseason
**Scent:** medium
**Staking:** no

*Paeonia* 'Magenta Moon'

*Paeonia* 'Margaret Truman'

### 'MARGARET CLARK'

Layers of pure pink petals pale to silver along the edges. As the bloom matures and creates a loose dome, the occasional yellow stamen sitting deep within the centre is visible. Eventually the centre opens wide, revealing more stamens. The sturdy stems, which sometimes bear side stems, hold the flowers not far above a mound of dark green leaves.

**Breeder:** Mains, 1956
**Height:** 80cm
**Flowers:** double, late season
**Scent:** light
**Staking:** no

*Paeonia* 'Margaret Clark'

### 'MARIE LEMOINE'

Small green buds unfurl into a swirling ball of soft-white that looks like a scoop of ice-cream. This opens further into a small, shallow-domed, nicely perfumed white bloom. Very short, pale cream staminodes produce a lemon glow at the base of the petals, which are crinkled like crêpe paper. The flowers are carried on red stems with between one and three side buds. Sadly, wet weather can spoil the flowers.

**Breeder:** Calot, 1869
**Height:** 75cm
**Flowers:** double, late season
**Scent:** heavy
**Staking:** no

*Paeonia* 'Marietta Sisson'

### 'MARIETTA SISSON'

The colour is described by the breeder as 'magenta rose' although it isn't solid and runs over the petals in fine rivers. The petals are crimped, very finely notched and paler pink along the tops. Opening into a tight, fluffy ball, the form becomes looser with age and a ring of gold stamens between the petals is eventually revealed. The long lax stems tumble from a dense mound of mid-green foliage.

**Breeder:** Sass, 1933
**Height:** 90cm
**Flowers:** double, early to midseason
**Scent:** heavy
**Staking:** yes

*Paeonia* 'Marie Lemoine'

### 'MARTHA REED'

At first, the large, broad petals are blush-pink. As the flower develops the pink tinge disappears, leaving a dome of equal sized, slightly wavy-edged, creamy-white petals. The middle petals part sufficiently to reveal a few gold stamens. The stiffly, upright stems carry the occasional side bud and big, mid-green leaves that form a lush mound. In drier soils, the side buds may dry out. Named by Alice Krekler after an employee.

**Breeder:** Krekler, 1965
**Height:** 70cm
**Flowers:** double, late season
**Scent:** light
**Staking:** no

*Paeonia* 'Martha Reed'

### 'MATILDA LEWIS'

This dark red peony was raised by Professor A. P. Saunders, a peony breeder more famous for hybrid and tree peonies than lactiflora types. The ball-like flower has smooth, evenly sized petals that are uneven along the tops and in certain lights can look almost black. The blooms are borne on stiff stems with a few side stems and dark green leaves. Although not free-flowering, it is garden worthy because the petal colour does not fade.

**Breeder:** Saunders, 1921
**Height:** 90cm
**Flowers:** double, midseason
**Scent:** light
**Staking:** no

*Paeonia* 'Matilda Lewis'

### 'MIDNIGHT SUN'

Two rows of wide, garnet-red guard petals, which have a matt finish, create an upturned circle around a tight come of gold staminodes. With age, these lengthen and become red with soft-yellow edging, while the guard petals remain cupped. This absolutely beautiful flower stays elegantly upright on stiff, dark red stems with a few side buds and shiny, dark green leaves. Consistently one of the best of its kind. AGM

**Breeder:** Murawska, 1954
**Height:** 90cm
**Flowers:** Japanese, midseason
**Scent:** light
**Staking:** no

*Paeonia* 'Minnie Shaylor'

### 'MINNIE SHAYLOR'

White flowers with frilled petals display pretty hints of lemon and a few streaks of light red appear on the small guard petals. The inner petals become slimmer and form a many layered cup around a small ring of gold stamens and carpels that are tipped with red. The rigid red flower stems carry shiny, dark green leaves. AGM

**Breeder:** Shaylor, 1919
**Height:** 80cm
**Flowers:** semi-double, midseason
**Scent:** medium
**Staking:** no

*Paeonia* 'Midnight Sun'

### 'MISCHIEF'

The long, round-ended petals, which number around ten, start deep rose-pink. With time, these gradually fade unevenly to pale-pink inwards from the edges. The gold stamens are carried on fine filaments that allow the red-tipped, dark green carpels to show through. These delightful blooms are borne on red-tinted stems with lots of side buds and mid-green leaves.

**Breeder:** Auten, 1925
**Height:** 90cm
**Flowers:** single, late season
**Scent:** medium
**Staking:** no

*Paeonia* 'Mischief'

*Paeonia* 'Midnight Sun'

*Paeonia* 'Miss America'

### 'MISS AMERICA'

Of the comparatively few semi-double peonies, not many are white. The guard petals of these crisp, pure white flowers are lightly brushed with pale-pink and become smaller towards the centre of deep lemon stamens and lemon-tipped, green carpels. A free-flowering plant with clusters of blooms on straight stems with large, dark green leaves. AGM

**Breeder:** Mann/van Steen, 1936
**Height:** 90cm
**Flowers:** semi-double, early season
**Scent:** very light
**Staking:** no

### 'MISS ECKHART'

Opening from dark pink buds, the bloom's inner petals rise upwards into a loose dome while the guard petals curl downwards. Each petal is deeply cut and in time the colour softens and forms a wide paler pink band at the edges. Eventually the centre opens enough to reveal a small group of golden stamens and red-tipped carpels. The sturdy stems carry soft-green leaves and lots of side buds.

**Breeder:** Van der Meer, 1928
**Height:** 90cm
**Flowers:** double, midseason
**Scent:** medium
**Staking:** yes

*Paeonia* 'Miss Eckhart'

### 'MISTER ED'

Double, high-domed, soft-pink flowers have interwoven, fringed petals. Around them are large guard petals that fade to white. Long flower stems and dark green glossy foliage add to the appeal, making it a good cut flower. This cultivar came about when *P.* 'Monsieur Jules Elie' was treated with colchicine (a chemical used by some breeders to raise stronger plants) and it is likely to produce the occasional deep pink flower typical of its parent.

**Breeder:** Klehm, 1980
**Height:** 90cm
**Flowers:** double, midseason
**Scent:** medium
**Staking:** yes

*Paeonia* 'Monsieur Jules Elie'

### 'MONSIEUR JULES ELIE'

A broad collar of round, soft-pink guard petals surrounds the big centre of slender petals that are deeply serrated and lined with silver. These twine around each other and are interspersed with slim petaloids. In time, the heavily rose-scented blooms turn pale-pink. These are borne on stems that cannot carry the weight of the flowers but despite the need for staking this lovely plant is good for cutting. Often referred to simply as 'Mons. Jules Elie'.

**Breeder:** Crousse, 1888
**Height:** 90cm
**Flowers:** double, early season
**Scent:** heavy
**Staking:** yes

*Paeonia* 'Mister Ed'

*Paeonia* 'Moon of Nippon'

### 'MOON OF NIPPON'

The milk-white guard petals are thick, silky and slightly crinkled along the edges. At first, these are cupped around a tight dome of rich golden-yellow staminodes. As the flower ages, the petals open into a flat, slightly uneven saucer, while the staminodes enlarge, pale slightly and become looser. A free-flowering plant, it produces lots of side buds on the upright stems along with dark green leaves that are greyish-green underneath. AGM

**Breeder:** Auten, 1936
**Height:** 90cm
**Flowers:** Japanese, midseason
**Scent:** light
**Staking:** no

### 'MOON RIVER'

Low dome-shaped flowers display pale-pink petals that are lightly fringed along the edges. These gradually fade to soft-white with touches of pink here and there. In the dipped centre, the petals are highlighted with apricot and pink while a hint of blush-pink stains the guard petals. The long lax stems carry mid-green leaves and some, but not all stems, have up to three side buds. Not a particularly free-flowering variety.

**Breeder:** Klehm, 1972
**Height:** 70cm
**Flowers:** double, midseason
**Scent:** light
**Staking:** yes

*Paeonia* 'Mother's Choice'

### 'MOTHER'S CHOICE'

This perfectly shaped bloom has layers of wavy cream-white petals of varying size, from large to small. When fully mature they open into a flat-topped flower suffused with a yellow glow from deep inside the prettily interwoven central petals. Although good for cutting and in the border, in our experience this does not perform well when lifted and potted up into a container.

**Breeder:** Glasscock, 1950
**Height:** 90cm
**Flowers:** double, late midseason
**Scent:** light
**Staking:** no

### 'MR. G. F. HEMERIK'

At first, the large, mid-pink guard petals form a cup around a swirling centre of wrinkled, butter-yellow staminodes that have darker yellow edges and pink tips. In time, the whole flower fades in tone and gets bigger, although the colour on the guard petals pales unevenly. The red stems bear some side buds and mid-green leaves that are distinctively, crinkled along the edges. This peony was formerly listed as 'originator unknown'.

**Breeder:** Van Leeuwen, pre-1928
**Height:** 90cm
**Flowers:** Japanese, midseason
**Scent:** none
**Staking:** no

*Paeonia* 'Moon River'

*Paeonia* 'Mr G. F. Hemerik'

Silver-grey *Stachys byzantina* complements the soft-pink blooms of *Paeonia* 'Myrtle Gentry'

### 'MRS. EDWARD HARDING'

Large, domed and pure white, this bloom has very big guard petals and a dented centre of fine white petaloids. Short gold stamens are hidden under the inner petals, turning them soft-yellow, and a further small cluster of stamens sits right in the middle of the flower. In hot sun, the petals may be scorched brown. The long flower stems, which are red, carry bright-green foliage.

**Breeder:** Shaylor, 1918
**Height:** 90cm
**Flowers:** double, midseason
**Scent:** light
**Staking:** yes

*Paeonia* 'Mrs. Edward Harding'

### 'MY PAL RUDY'

The petals of this pink bloom are so deeply notched, the flower is positively frilly. As the bloom opens into a flat rosette, the deep pink fades around the top of the petals but remains at the base. When fully opened and the petals have loosened sufficiently, a ring of yellow stamens and small red-tipped, green-red carpels are apparent. The blooms are borne on upright stems that rise above a neat clump of glossy, deep green leaves.

**Breeder:** Klehm, 1953
**Height:** 90cm
**Flowers:** double, late season
**Scent:** medium
**Staking:** no

### 'MRS. FRANKLIN D. ROOSEVELT'

At first the rose-pink guard petals form a pink ball, but on opening their colour, along with that of the inner petal rings, fades to soft pink. When fully open the outer petals surround a broad centre of short, incurving creamy-white petals. Eventually, the whole flower fades to palest pink. Although the long stems, which bear a few side buds, can be rather lax, this makes a good cut flower. Often referred to as 'Mrs. F.D.R'.

**Breeder:** Franklin, 1932
**Height:** 85cm
**Flowers:** double, early to late midseason
**Scent:** medium
**Staking:** yes

*Paeonia* 'Mrs. Franklin D. Roosevelt'

*Paeonia* 'My Pal Rudy'

### 'MYRTLE GENTRY'

Perfectly rose-shaped flowers open pale-pink and fade, from the guard petals first, very nearly to white. When mature, the flowers resemble a large white crown. The guard petals are slightly bigger than the inner petals while those in the centre are short. The upright, self-supporting stems are well-branched and carry matt, mid-green leaves. Named after a female employee of the breeder who went on to own the nursery. AGM

**Breeder:** Brand, 1925
**Height:** 90cm
**Flowers:** double, late midseason
**Scent:** heavy
**Staking:** no

*Paeonia* 'Nancy Nicholls'

### 'NANCY NICHOLLS'

The large fluffy flower ball is composed of perfect layers of creamy-white petals, each deeply notched into short frills. The guard petals are lightly brushed with pale-pink. As the bloom develops, the central petals become shorter, forming a funnel that is filled with ribbon-like white petaloids. The flowers are held just above a neat round clump of big, dark green, satin-like leaves with some side buds. Good for cutting.

**Breeder:** Nicholls, 1941
**Height:** 90cm
**Flowers:** double, midseason
**Scent:** light
**Staking:** no

Paeonia 'Nancy Nora'

### 'NANCY NORA'

This highly scented flower is perfect for cutting. Opening soft-pink, the thick silky, white petals are evenly sized and lightly notched along the tops. As the bloom opens into a perfect old rose shape, it turns almost white, while the short central petals create a funnel-like dip. Strong flower stems bear grey-green leaves with lots of side stems and it grows into an upright plant. AGM

**Breeder:** Bernstein, 1942
**Height:** 90cm
**Flowers:** double, midseason
**Scent:** heavy
**Staking:** no

### 'NELLIE SAYLOR'

Very different in appearance from other Japanese peonies. The deep magenta-pink guard petals sit loosely around a swirling ball of palest magenta-pink petaloids (not staminodes), some heavily stained with magenta. Further drama is created when a flurry of magenta petals emerges from the middle of the ball. This is a slow growing plant, with some side buds and very dark green leaves. The breeder named it after his sister. AGM

**Breeder:** Krekler, 1967
**Height:** 90cm
**Flowers:** Japanese, mid to late season
**Scent:** medium
**Staking:** no

Paeonia 'Neon'

### 'NEON'

Very bright pink, as befits its name, the flowers of this neat plant are surprisingly dainty. Two rows of round guard petals remain cupped around a small dome of long, ribbon-like pink staminodes that are finely edged with gold. An inner cluster of pink petals may arise, but at the same height as the surrounding staminodes. The blooms are borne on tall, slender, pink-tinted stems with one or two side buds and leathery, mid-green leaves

**Breeder:** Nicholls, 1941
**Height:** 90cm
**Flowers:** Japanese, midseason
**Scent:** medium
**Staking:** no

### 'NICE GAL'

The dark pink flower looks more double than semi-double. As it opens, the petals create a flat-topped bloom that loosens enough to expose a few gold stamens. More stamens peek out between the lower petals. The flowers are carried on very upright, reddish stems with mid-green leaves that have a dull sheen, and gently rippled edges. Forming a neat round clump, this is a good plant for windy as well as small gardens.

**Breeder:** Krekler, 1965
**Height:** 80cm
**Flowers:** semi-double, late season
**Scent:** heavy
**Staking:** no

Paeonia 'Nellie Saylor'

Paeonia 'Nice Gal'

*Paeonia* 'Nick Shaylor'

### 'NICK SHAYLOR'

The buds and early flowers of this scented bloom are soft-pink. As they open into a rose-shaped flower, the evenly sized, curling petals pale to white and soft-pink tints remain on the guard petals. Short, creamy-white inner petals form a dip to show off small, golden stamens. Eventually the whole bloom becomes shaggy. Rather lax red stems bear extra buds on long stems and large, dark green leaves. Good for cutting.

**Breeder:** Allison, 1931
**Height:** 90cm
**Flowers:** double, late season
**Scent:** heavy
**Staking:** yes

*Paeonia* 'Nippon Gold'

### 'NIPPON BEAUTY'

A free-flowering plant with smallish blooms. The rich-magenta guard petals are, at first, cupped around a central ball of wrinkled, red staminodes that are tipped with cream. As the flower ages, the guard petals open flat and become somewhat unruly, while the staminodes elongate and loosen, but remain curled around the edges. The blooms are carried well above the dark green leaves on slender, upright stems.

**Breeder:** Auten, 1927
**Height:** 90cm
**Flowers:** Japanese, late season
**Scent:** light
**Staking:** no

*Paeonia* 'Nippon Beauty'

### 'NIPPON GOLD'

A delicate-looking flower with 10 to 12, round, dark pink guard petals that, on opening, form a cup around the ball of crinkled yellow staminodes. Right in the centre, the green carpels are tipped with pale-pink. As the flower develops, the guard petals pale to soft-pink and the staminodes turn creamy. Straight stems carry both the flowers and mid-green leaves.

**Breeder:** Auten, 1929
**Height:** 90cm
**Flowers:** Japanese, late season
**Scent:** medium
**Staking:** no

*Paeonia* 'Norma Volz'

### 'NORMA VOLZ'

On first opening, the thick, round, white petals, which are tinged with pink, form a ball and this soon develops into a neat dome. Sometimes, the pink tints on the petals disappear and the bloom turns almost ivory-white, although a blush of soft-pink remains and a few short red streaks line the tops. When fully open a ring of soft-yellow petaloids is visible. The flowers are carried on upright red stems with dark green leaves.

**Breeder:** Volz, 1962
**Height:** 80cm
**Flowers:** double, late season
**Scent:** medium
**Staking:** no

*Paeonia* 'Nymphe'

### 'NYMPHE'

One of the best free-blooming, single-flowered peonies we grow. The medium-sized, rose-pink, saucer-like flowers open wide to display a centre of small, slender bright-yellow stamens. The soft-green carpels are tipped with red. As the bloom matures, the petal colour fades slightly. Carried on straight stems with dark green leaves, the flowers are loved by bees and produce ample quantities of seeds each year. AGM

**Breeder:** Dessert, 1913
**Height:** 90cm
**Flowers:** single, midseason
**Scent:** light
**Staking:** no

### 'PAUL M. WILD'

In my opinion, this is one of the best red lactiflora peonies with luxurious, deep red flowers that do not fade as they age. As they open, the blooms evolve into a flat-topped dome. The guard petals and most of the inner petals are similar in size, while the inner petals are shorter and interwoven with short petaloids that are faintly tipped with cream. The red-tinged flower stems bear big green, shiny leaves. Lasts well as a cut flower in a vase.

**Breeder:** Wild, 1964
**Height:** 90cm
**Flowers:** double, midseason
**Scent:** light
**Staking:** sometimes needs support

### 'PETITE ELEGANCE'

A short plant with proportionally small flowers. The five rows of incurving petals, which open soft-pink, remain cupped. As the flower ages, the petals become creamy-white with occasional darker pink streaks marking the guard petals. In the middle of the bowl is a ring of gold stamens and short, red-tipped carpels. There is no branching on the stems, just dark green leaves.

**Breeder:** Klehm, 1995
**Height:** 60cm
**Flowers:** semi-double, early season
**Scent:** medium
**Staking:** no

*Paeonia* 'Paul M. Wild'

### 'PETITE PORCELAIN'

The white petals of this small bloom make a thick ruff around a circle of gold stamens. In time, they open flat and curl slightly back to show off the short, gold stamens and small, green, red-tipped carpels. The blooms open just above dark green foliage that forms a short, neat clump. Lots of side branches ensure lots of flowers.

**Breeder:** Klehm, 1998
**Height:** 70cm
**Flowers:** semi-double, midseason
**Scent:** medium
**Staking:** no

*Paeonia* 'Petite Elegance'

*Paeonia* 'Petite Porcelain'

### 'PHILIPPE RIVOIRE'

Deep cerise-red flowers, which are not large, open into a fluffy ball with equal sized petals that are wavy and notched along the edges. In certain lights, the flower takes on purple hues and looks very dark indeed. The guard petals are not much bigger than the inner petals and with time they all soften slightly in colour to a pinkish red. Not very free-flowering, this can be tricky to grow.

**Breeder:** Rivière, 1911
**Height:** 85cm
**Flowers:** double, early season
**Scent:** medium
**Staking:** no

*Paeonia* 'Philippe Rivoire'

### 'PILLOW CASES'

Long, white petals in a wavy row are heavily coated with tiny rich-pink dots. The speckling coats the top half of the petals then fades so they become white around a dense centre of slender, very yellow stamens. In the middle are cream carpels tipped with pink. The flowers are carried in clusters on strong stems with leathery, broad leaves.

**Breeder:** Krekler/Klehm, 1994
**Height:** 90cm
**Flowers:** single, midseason
**Scent:** medium
**Staking:** no

*Paeonia* 'Pillow Cases'

*Paeonia* 'Pillow Talk'

### 'PHILOMÈLE'

A variable flower, the blooms can appear double one year and look like Japanese peonies the next. When double, the large, rose-pink guard petals surround a layered ball of soft-yellow staminodes that pale as the flower opens, and soft-pink, frilly-edged petaloids. In other years, pink petals are not produced and the centre is filled with lots of slender cream staminodes. The strong stems bear dark green leaves.

**Breeder:** Calot, 1861
**Height:** 90cm
**Flowers:** double, midseason
**Scent:** medium
**Staking:** no

*Paeonia* 'Philomèle'

### 'PILLOW TALK'

This lovely soft-pink peony opens into a pure rose-pink ball then, as the flower gets bigger, the petals loosen slightly and soften to pale-pink. At first the edges of the petals are lightly clipped, but become more fringed with age. A layer of short, cream petaloids is eventually revealed in the very centre. The long, branched stems with more flower buds also carry shiny, mid-green leaves. Good for cutting.

**Breeder:** Klehm, 1973
**Height:** 80cm
**Flowers:** double, midseason
**Scent:** medium
**Staking:** no

*Paeonia* 'Pink Delight'

### 'PINK DELIGHT'

Opening into a deep, mid-pink cup, then into a shallow dish, this delicate-looking flower has three or four layers of frilly soft-pink petals. These are finely edged with silver and cut unevenly along the top. The petals decrease slightly in size towards a ring of small, gold stamens and red carpels with paler red tips. The blooms are carried on strong stems with between one and three side buds and mid-green foliage.

**Breeder:** Klehm, 1995
**Height:** 75cm
**Flowers:** semi-double, early season
**Scent:** none
**Staking:** no

### 'PINK GIANT'

A fitting name for a plant with very large flowers. On opening soft-pink, the petals form a perfectly shaped, rose-pink bloom. With age, the guard petals turn almost white, as do the short, jagged-edged inner petaloids, which twist among the larger petals. These stay a soft, if a little washed-out, pink. Eventually the flower grows into a huge flattened dome. The long, arching stems bear leathery, dark green leaves.

**Breeder:** Vurens, 1966
**Height:** 90cm
**Flowers:** double, very late season
**Scent:** none
**Staking:** yes

### 'PINK LEMONADE'

The flowers of this pretty plant are similar to other bomb-shaped peonies raised by Klehm's, although they are smaller in size. When they first open, the petals create a soft-pink dome, and as the flower loosens further a round ball surrounded by large, pink guard petals forms. Around the base of this ball of petals is a thick ring of cream petaloids.

**Breeder:** Klehm, 1951
**Height:** 90cm
**Flowers:** double, midseason
**Scent:** light
**Staking:** no

*Paeonia* 'Pink Giant'

*Paeonia* 'Pink Lemonade'

### 'PINK PARFAIT'

A substantial flower that opens deep rose-pink. The ragged petals then age and pale along the edges, before loosening further to form a shallow dome. The shorter inner petals hollow out into a deep centre with no stamens showing. The very long arching stems carry large, mid-green leaves that have a grey sheen.

**Breeder:** Klehm, 1975
**Height:** 85cm
**Flowers:** double, late season
**Scent:** heavy
**Staking:** yes

*Paeonia* 'Pink Parfait'

*Paeonia* 'Pink Princess'

### 'PINK PRINCESS'

On close inspection, the pink flowers are actually white petals ever so lightly speckled with tiny pink dots. These fade towards a boss of slender, golden stamens and lipstick-pink, red-tipped carpels. The strong stems bear lots of side buds and big dark green leaves. This cultivar, which produces lots of seed, was sold for years as 'Pink Dawn'. The breeder is unknown, but Don Hollingsworth suggests H. P. Sass around 1950 as a possibility.

**Breeder:** Unknown, listed by Klehm, 1985
**Height:** 90cm
**Flowers:** single, midseason
**Scent:** light
**Staking:** no

### 'PRESIDENT LINCOLN'

Deeply cupped at first, the two rings of rich-red petals open loosely into a wavy petalled bloom. At the centre is a tight boss of gold stamens that are carried on red filaments. The soft-green carpels are also red-tipped. Its slender red stems stay upright. Of the very few single, red lactifloras available this cultivar – named after the famous US president – was once considered the best by peony growers.

**Breeder:** Brand, 1928
**Height:** 90cm
**Flowers:** single, late midseason
**Scent:** light
**Staking:** no

### 'PRESIDENT WILSON'

Introduced in the year the First World War ended, this is named after the US president in office at the time. The globular flowers are, at first, pure pink and pale to soft-pink with age as shorter central petals unfold to create a deeply dipped centre. A ring of long, thin, soft-yellow petaloids may be visible between the guard petals and the inner ball of petals when fully open. The flower stems are red, the foliage mid-green.

**Breeder:** Thurlow, 1918
**Height:** 90cm
**Flowers:** double, midseason
**Scent:** heavy
**Staking:** yes

*Paeonia* 'President Lincoln'

*Paeonia* 'President Wilson'

### 'QUEEN OF SHEBA'

Dark pink petals gradually reduce in size as they reach the centre of the frilly, shallowly domed, spicy-scented bloom. The petals are ruffled and notched along the edges with a central dip that allows a few golden stamens to be seen. The blooms are carried in clusters on red stems with long side stems, and the plant forms a neat clump. The greyish leaves have wavy edges.

**Breeder:** Sass, 1937
**Height:** 85cm
**Flowers:** single, very late season
**Scent:** medium
**Staking:** no

*Paeonia* 'Queen of Sheba'

Paeonia 'Raspberry Sundae'

### 'RASPBERRY SUNDAE'

This striking flower is a chameleon. On opening, rings of creamy-yellow petaloids with serrated edges are surrounded by large, pale-pink guard petals. Soft-pink petals then begin to emerge from the middle to conceal the cream petaloids. Eventually the flower evolves into a big ball. The long stems, which make it good for cutting, can arch over with the weight of the blooms causing them to tumble forward.

**Breeder:** Klehm, 1968
**Height:** 90cm
**Flowers:** single, late midseason
**Scent:** medium
**Staking:** yes

### 'RED EMPEROR'

Two rows of flaring, vivid raspberry-pink guard petals are, at first, cupped around a centre of large, wrinkly staminodes, which are tipped with cream. These just about hide the green carpels. As the outer petals age they loose the red tone, turn bright pink and become rather unruly. The blooms are carried on stiff stems with dark green leaves, creating an open, upright clump that is quite delicate in appearance.

**Breeder:** Auten, 1931
**Height:** 90cm
**Flowers:** Japanese, midseason
**Scent:** none
**Staking:** no

Paeonia 'Red Emperor'

### 'RED SATIN'

Heavy, dark red flowers with shiny petals loosen as they open, revealing no stamens. The stems are very lax. Although this cultivar is listed as a lactiflora, the leaves are very similar to those of a hybrid peony, while the flowers resemble cultivars with Paeonia officinalis heritage. There is no evidence that the breeder made a note of the parents and so it is included, like other peonies raised by Sass, in the lactiflora group.

**Breeder:** Sass, 1937
**Height:** 75cm
**Flowers:** double, late midseason
**Scent:** none
**Staking:** yes

Paeonia 'Roland'

### 'ROLAND'

Two rows of brilliant cerise-pink petals – although the shade is on the red side of pink – surround a small, tight boss of golden stamens and red-tipped carpels. The mid-green leaves are thick and carried on stiff stems with one or two long side stems. This was introduced by Roy Klehm in 2003, a year after Krekler's death.

**Breeder:** Krekler/Klehm, 2003
**Height:** 65cm
**Flowers:** single, midseason
**Scent:** none
**Staking:** no

Paeonia 'Red Satin'

*Paeonia* 'Reine Hortense'

### 'REINE HORTENSE'

Starting life soft-pink, this lovely, big, fluffy flower pales in colour as the bloom fills out into a shallow dome. Each petal is so frilly it looks as though it has been chewed. In time, the top half turns almost white and a few red streaks may mark the petals. The flower also loosens enough to reveal some golden stamens. The red-tinged stems produce some side buds and characteristic mid-green lactiflora leaves.

**Breeder:** Calot, 1857
**Height:** 90cm
**Flowers:** double, midseason
**Scent:** light
**Staking:** yes

*Paeonia* 'Renato'

### 'RENATO'

The inner petals of this large, deep cerise-red bloom curve inwards to form a big bomb-shaped ball. As they open further, the petals become lighter at the edges and loosen enough to create a dip in the middle. Around the base of the inner petals sit large guard petals. The blooms are borne on red stems with dark green leaves and a few side stems. Considered an excellent cut flower.

**Breeder:** Murawska, 1949
**Height:** 90cm
**Flowers:** double, midseason
**Scent:** none
**Staking:** yes

*Paeonia* 'Ruth Cobb'

### 'RUTH COBB'

At first the bluish-pink, silver-backed petals curl into each other then open into a mildly spice-scented, ruffled, flat flower. In time, this develops further into a dome with a few cream-edged petaloids showing, then pales to very soft-pink. The glossy dark green leaves are carried on long, rather lax stems that make this peony excellent for cutting.

**Breeder:** Wild, 1963
**Height:** 90cm
**Flowers:** double, late midseason
**Scent:** light
**Staking:** yes

### 'SANTA FE'

A white dome of ragged-edged petaloids lightly touched with pink is encased by mid-pink guard petals that open flat to create a saucer. Not overly large, the flowers are carried on tall, very upright stems with long side branches and big, mid-green leaves. Registered with the American Peony Society as a semi-double, this is better described as a Japanese peony.

**Breeder:** Auten, 1937
**Height:** 90cm
**Flowers:** Japanese, midseason
**Scent:** light
**Staking:** no

*Paeonia* 'Santa Fe'

*Paeonia* 'Shirley Temple' flowering in early June with pink-flowered *Astrantia* 'Roma' and mauve *Thalictrum* 'Black Stockings'

### 'SARAH BERNHARDT'

One of the most recognisable peonies, this is a very popular cut flower and easy to find in supermarket flower buckets. The soft-pink petals are often flecked with red at the top. These pale slightly at the edges and curl over one another before opening from a shallow bloom into a high, fluffy dome. The red-tinted stems are not particularly strong and carry mid-green leaves. AGM

**Breeder:** Lemoine, 1906
**Height:** 90cm
**Flowers:** double, late season
**Scent:** medium
**Staking:** yes

*Paeonia* 'Sarah Bernhardt'

### 'SERENE PASTEL'

Growing into a neat plant, this produces shallowly domed flowers that are not large. Each has seven rows of creamy-white petals that are brushed with soft-magenta and guard petals that are similar in size to the inner petals. As the flower opens, rich-gold stamens can be seen between the central petals. The blooms are carried on stiff stems, some of which have side buds, and dark green leaves.

**Breeder:** Klehm, 2000
**Height:** 70cm
**Flowers:** double, midseason
**Scent:** medium
**Staking:** no

### 'SEA SHELL'

The three rows of large, mid-pink petals are lightly crinkled and paler around the irregularly notched edges. In the middle are short, sunny-yellow stamens making a neat ring around deep pink-tipped, small green carpels. As the flower ages, it pales in colour to soft-pink. The leaves are slim and dark green while the stems are strong, red and branched. Like many single peonies, it produces seeds readily.

**Breeder:** Sass, 1937
**Height:** 95cm
**Flowers:** single, midseason
**Scent:** light
**Staking:** no

*Paeonia* 'Serene Pastel'

### 'SHIRLEY TEMPLE'

Some of the petals of the white, domed flower are tinted very pale-pink and sometimes also marked with thin red streaks. Pale-cream staminodes are interspersed between the petals adding a soft golden glow to the base of them. The blooms are borne just above the large, shiny, mid-green leaves, which are pale-green beneath. I have found that 'Shirley T' blooms freely in a partly shaded spot. It makes an excellent cut flower. AGM

**Breeder:** unknown, pre-1952
**Height:** 90cm
**Flowers:** double, early season
**Scent:** medium
**Staking:** sometimes

*Paeonia* 'Solange'

*Paeonia* 'Sea Shell'

### 'SOLANGE'

A lovely, rose-shaped flower with pale-pink guard petals the same size as the inner petals, which also open softest pink. As the flower grows, each layer of petals is interspersed with rings of very pale amber-pink petaloids. Although the centre dips down, no stamens are revealed. As the flower ages further it turns almost white. The strong stems bear side branches and very dark green leaves. Makes a great cut flower.

**Breeder:** Lemoine, 1907
**Height:** 85cm
**Flowers:** double, late season
**Scent:** light
**Staking:** no

Lactiflora peonies | 95

### 'SORBET'

In 1987, Dutch perennial specialist Luc Klinkhamer discovered this peony in a South Korean orchard, where it was grown for medicinal purposes. The large, rose-pink guard petals form a broad dish around a centre piled with softest apricot petaloids that are touched with pink. A further ring of rich-pink petals encircles the central cream petaloids. As the flower ages, the petals get bigger and pale in colour.

**Breeder:** unknown
**Height:** 75cm
**Flowers:** double, midseason
**Scent:** medium
**Staking:** yes

*Paeonia* 'Sorbet'

### 'SUPER GAL'

If you want a short plant for a windy spot this is worth seeking out. The deep pink flowers open into shallow domes, each petal reducing in size as it reaches the centre. Here, a ring of short, deep yellow stamens sits among the petals, which pale slightly at the edges. There are no side branches on the stiffly upright flower stems.

**Breeder:** Klehm, 2000
**Height:** 65cm
**Flowers:** semi-double, mid to late season
**Scent:** medium
**Staking:** no

*Paeonia* 'Super Gal'

### 'STARDUST'

On first opening, the milk-white petals of this single bloom are tinged with palest pink. The pink tint disappears on the two inner rows of petals, but remains on the outer petals. In the centre gleams a tuft of short golden stamens. This fairly upright plant has red stems and dark green leaves. Although a lactiflora type, this grandchild of *Paeonia* 'Le Cygne' is the parent of white hybrid peonies.

**Breeder:** Glasscock/Falk, 1964
**Height:** 80cm
**Flowers:** single, midseason
**Scent:** medium
**Staking:** no

*Paeonia* 'Stardust'

### 'SURUGU'

This absolutely delightful plant produces smallish purple-red flowers. At first the petals, which curl inwards along the edges, are very cupped, but with age they open out slightly. The central domed boss of curling soft-lemon staminodes, which resemble regular stamens, encircle carpels that are also red. The blooms are carried on stiff, short, branched stems with glossy deep green leaves. An excellent peony for a windy garden.

**Breeder:** Millet, 1917
**Height:** 90cm
**Flowers:** Japanese, midseason
**Scent:** heavy
**Staking:** no

*Paeonia* 'Surugu'

*Paeonia* 'Sweet 16'

### 'SWEET 16'

Soft-cream petaloids of this ball-like flower mingle with pale-pink petals to form a frilly bloom. Larger, soft-pink guard petals make a neat ruff around the base. As the flower ages, the petals fade almost to white. Strong stems carry the full-petalled blooms keeping them nicely upright in a neatly shaped clump.

**Breeder:** Klehm, 1972
**Height:** 85cm
**Flowers:** double, midseason
**Scent:** light
**Staking:** no

### 'SWORD DANCE'

A free-flowering plant that is worthy of a place in any border. The purplish-scarlet guard petals surround a large cushion of staminodes that are streaked with red down the middle. Initially these are curly and dark cream but as the flower loosens with age, they grow longer and turn gold. The blooms are borne on tall, straight stems with no side buds and very dark green leaves. AGM

**Breeder:** Auten, 1933
**Height:** 90cm
**Flowers:** Japanese, midseason
**Scent:** medium
**Staking:** no

### 'TAMATE-BOKU'

A cleanly shaped flower with large, round, soft-pink guard petals that are gently cupped. The colour fades in patches on some petals, while others have darker pink highlights. In the centre, the low mound of thin, rich yellow staminodes stays largely stable. Deep within it are small carpels tipped with red. The blooms are carried aloft on strong stems with leathery, pointed, mid-green leaves with wavy edges.

**Breeder:** from Japan pre-1913
**Height:** 90cm
**Flowers:** Japanese, late season
**Scent:** medium
**Staking:** no

*Paeonia* 'Sword Dance'

*Paeonia* 'Tamate-boku'

### 'THE FAWN'

An intriguing plant with large, white petals that are so heavily brushed with deep pink dots and dashes the whole flower appears mid-pink. At first, the bloom opens into a flat dome that becomes higher with age. The middle dips sufficiently deeply to show off a few golden stamens. The blooms are borne on strong, reddish stems with shiny, round, mid-green leaves. AGM

**Breeder:** Wright, date unknown
**Height:** 90cm
**Flowers:** double, midseason
**Scent:** light
**Staking:** no

*Paeonia* 'The Fawn'

*Paeonia* 'The Mighty Mo'

### 'THE MIGHTY MO'

When this first opens the velvety, bright raspberry-red petals, which are similar in size, reveal a ring of fine deep yellow stamens. In time, a cluster of petals develops in the centre expanding to create a double flower that almost hides the stamens. The straight stems produce a few side buds. Not widely grown, which is a shame because the flower colour is smooth and even.

**Breeder:** Wild, 1950
**Height:** 85cm
**Flowers:** double, midseason
**Scent:** none
**Staking:** no

*Paeonia* 'Tom Eckhardt'

### 'TOM ECKHARDT'

A row of big, cupped, bright-pink guard petals enhances the clump of deep cream staminodes that curl over at the top and are flushed with pink. Sometimes a further flurry of pink petals emerges from the middle. Over time, the staminodes fade in colour and can also be blackened by heavy rain. The stems carry lots of side buds and large, bright-green leaves that have lightly ruffled edges.

**Breeder:** Krekler, 1965
**Height:** 90cm
**Flowers:** Japanese, midseason
**Scent:** light
**Staking:** no

*Paeonia* 'Top Brass'

### 'TOP BRASS'

An unusual flower with two rows of big, white guard petals forming a base for the pompom of butter-yellow petaloids. Out of the top pops a cluster of tall, ruffled, notched white petals. Sometimes these remain small. The stems, which are stiff enough not to collapse, produce a few side branches and mid-green leaves. A free-flowering plant that is easy to grow and, like many Klehm introductions, is recommended for cutting.

**Breeder:** Klehm, 1968
**Height:** 85cm
**Flowers:** double, midseason
**Scent:** light
**Staking:** no

### 'TOPEKA GARNET'

Very few lactiflora peonies produce such red flowers. The colour of the round guard petals is rich-red with lots of creases extending into the petals from the edges. The colour fades a little as the bloom ages. In the centre, a ring of yellow stamens surrounds the dark red-tipped carpels. Slender, red-tinged stems carry dark green leaves and a few side branches. Sadly, this it is not a strong-growing plant for us.

**Breeder:** Bigger, 1975
**Height:** 75cm
**Flowers:** single, midseason
**Scent:** none
**Staking:** no

*Paeonia* 'Topeka Garnet'

*Paeonia* 'Tom Eckhardt'

### 'TORO-NO-MAKI'

The white flowers have two or three rows of thick, wavy petals that open very, very pale-pink and turn white. These surround staminodes that start life pale-yellow then, as the flower ages, elongate to form a loose, fringed, almost-white ball with tints of yellow. In the centre sit greenish-white carpels with pink-tinted tops. The blooms are carried on strong stems with average-sized leaves.

**Breeder:** origin unknown
**Height:** 90cm
**Flowers:** Japanese, midseason
**Scent:** light.
**Staking:** no

*Paeonia* 'Toro-no-maki'

### 'TOUCH OF CLASS'

A broad collar of soft-pink guard petals with slightly silvery edges is the perfect foil for the centre of creamy petaloids. These are interwoven and densely packed into a low dome that, as time passes, rises up into a big, soft-cream ball. The guard petals also relax slightly. The strong stems carry some side buds and dark green leaves. A seedling originally raised by William Krekler.

**Breeder:** Krekler/Klehm 1999
**Height:** 90cm
**Flowers:** Japanese, midseason
**Scent:** medium
**Staking:** no

### 'URSA MINOR'

Slender, fringed petals in a striking mix of dark magenta, soft raspberry-red and almost white form a ball. They open in dense layers above two rows of half-moon shaped, magenta guard petals. Sometimes an extra flute of magenta petals appears in the centre. The blooms are carried on upright stems with side branches and dark green leaves. Not free-flowering, yet extraordinary.

**Breeder:** Klehm, 2000
**Height:** 75cm
**Flowers:** double, mid to late season
**Scent:** none
**Staking:** no

*Paeonia* 'Ursa Minor'

*Paeonia* 'Touch of Class'

### 'VICTORIAN BLUSH'

A short, neat plant with rather shaggy but tightly held milk-white flowers. The inner petals curl and the large guard petals are faintly tinted with pink. In the middle are shorter petaloids and the yellow stamens, visible among the petals, give the flower a creamy glow. The blooms are carried on stiff stems with glossy, deep green leaves.

**Breeder:** Klehm, 1999
**Height:** 70cm
**Flowers:** double, late season
**Scent:** medium
**Staking:** no

*Paeonia* 'Victorian Blush'

*Paeonia* 'Vivid Rose'

### 'VIVID ROSE'

An aptly named plant with large, bright rose-pink flowers that open into a flat rose form. Layers of big petals, interspersed with smaller ones, are curved around each other, becoming shorter and tangled in the centre. With age, the outer petals pale slightly. This is not only a good garden plant but also a strong-stemmed cultivar that is good for cutting.

**Breeder:** Klehm, 1952
**Height:** 85cm
**Flowers:** double, late midseason
**Scent:** heavy
**Staking:** maybe

*Paeonia* 'Vogue'

### 'VOGUE'

A free-flowering plant with sturdy stems bearing large white flowers that are tinged with pink. As the bloom ages, the pink persists on the guard petals. Some petals may appear etched along the top with red. Short stamens add an inner glow and as the central petals part these are revealed. The leaves are dark green and the long stems make it a good flower for cutting.

**Breeder:** Hoogendoorn, 1949
**Height:** 90cm
**Flowers:** double, midseason
**Scent:** heavy
**Staking:** maybe

*Paeonia* 'Westerner'

### 'WESTERNER'

This strong-growing plant has big, perfumed, eye-catching flowers. Opening soft-pink, the two rows of large, round guard petals pale unevenly to palest pink. A central dome of soft-yellow staminodes, curled towards the top, also pale over time to cream. The blooms are borne on strong, red stems with some side branches and dark green leaves.

**Breeder:** Bigger, 1942
**Height:** 90cm
**Flowers:** Japanese, midseason
**Scent:** medium
**Staking:** no

### 'WHITE CAP'

Seen at its best, this peony is a perfect combination of form and colour. Two rows of dark raspberry-red guard petals edge a broad mound of magenta-stained, soft-yellow staminodes. With age, the jagged-edged staminodes turn nearly white. In our wet climate, where the staminodes can be badly damaged by rain, this plant can be a challenge, although the Dutch grow it for cutting. Dark red flower stems carry the occasional side bud. AGM

**Breeder:** Winchell, 1956
**Height:** 90cm
**Flowers:** Japanese, midseason
**Scent:** medium
**Staking:** yes

*Paeonia* 'White Cap'

Lactiflora peonies

*Paeonia* 'White Wings'

### 'WHITE GRACE'

Pure white, semi-double flowers have frilly petals that form a thick, flat ruff. These part in the middle to reveal a small ring of short, golden-yellow stamens and small, white-tipped, green carpels. The guard petals, which are of a similar size to the petals, are brushed with palest pink. The strong stems of this free-flowering plant produce one to three side buds and mid-green leaves.

**Breeder:** Klehm, 2000
**Height:** 70cm
**Flowers:** semi-double, midseason
**Scent:** light
**Staking:** no

*Paeonia* 'White Grace'

### 'WHITE WINGS'

(opposite) A satisfyingly neat plant to grow with simply shaped flowers that have pure white petals. Slightly serrated along the edges, these open into a wide, yet shallow cup around a ring of golden stamens and soft-green carpels with dark pink tops. The flower buds are heavily tinged with pink. The blooms are carried on upright, red stems with between one and six side buds, and thick, mid-green leaves.

**Breeder:** Hoogendoorn, 1949
**Height:** 90cm
**Flowers:** single, midseason
**Scent:** medium
**Staking:** no

### 'WHITE IVORY'

At first, the flower opens into a big ball of soft-white, rendered more yellow by the short stamens sitting at the base of the curled petals. As the flower grows, these loosen to create a perfect rose shape. The shorter, inner petals flatten out to form a broad, dipped centre. Strong stems, which bear lots of side buds and dark green leaves, make this good for cutting.

**Breeder:** Klehm, 1981
**Height:** 85cm
**Flowers:** double, midseason
**Scent:** medium
**Staking:** sometimes

*Paeonia* 'Wiesbaden'

### 'WIESBADEN'

Opening soft-pink, the petals quickly fade to very pale-pink, and turn white in the middle. A few red streaks may appear at the top of the petals. At first the flower is low and domed in shape, but in time the dome turns into a loose rather shaggy bloom with lots of gold stamens on view. The stems are strong and carry a few side branches along with mid-green leaves.

**Breeder:** Goos & Koenemann, 1911
**Height:** 85cm
**Flowers:** double, midseason
**Scent:** light
**Staking:** no

*Paeonia* 'Zuzu'

*Paeonia* 'White Ivory'

### 'ZUZU'

A pretty flower that is the shape of an old-fashioned rose. The white, incurving petals are shaded so delicately with pink that they emphasise the cupped shape of the bloom. A small ring of slender, golden stamens add golden glow to the surrounding petals. The blooms are borne on strong stems with mid-green leaves, but no side stems. This forms a neat plant.

**Breeder:** Krekler, 1955
**Height:** 65cm
**Flowers:** semi-double, midseason
**Scent:** heavy
**Staking:** no

*Paeonia veitchii* var. *woodwardii* thrives in a lightly shaded spot with *Corydalis flexuosa* 'China Blue' (left) and *Aquilegia vulgaris* 'William Guiness' (behind)

# GARDEN-WORTHY SPECIES

**Deviating from Tradition**

The term species can be problematic when it comes to peonies. Technically speaking, to call a plant a species it has to be the same or very similar to its parent when grown from seed. Should there be any marked differences, then the plant in question is likely to be a hybrid of the species. If peonies grow near to one another they can cross-fertilise, as anyone who has tried to grow species peonies from seed will know. When they flower, the resulting seedlings are very unlikely to resemble the desired peony.

Most specialist plant books cover species before cultivars, but I have chosen to break with tradition by placing them between lactiflora and hybrid peonies for three reasons:

Firstly, many of the most garden-worthy species are highly likely to be hybrids of a species or they may even be of garden origin. Secondly, because the next part of this book concerns peonies created by crossing species, it makes more sense to cover species first. Thirdly, many peonies currently listed as species can be very difficult to grow in the average garden.

**Name Changes**

The discovery and documenting of peonies started several centuries ago. A concise list of the taxonomy of the genus *Paeonia* as it currently stands can be found on page 6. However, the names do not necessarily correspond with those given in the following pages because in recent years, botanists have renamed or reclassified certain species into subdivisions. Such is the case with *Paeonia mlokosewitschii* and *P. wittanniana*. These two lovely plants have similar leaves so botanists decided they were closely related to the pink-flowered species *Paeonia daurica* – a plant I have never seen for sale. As many of the recent taxonomy changes are still being debated, it seemed sensible to stick with the names designated by F.C. Stern in 1946.

**Subspecies and Variety Explained**

Two botanical terms that are used to describe some of the peonies in this chapter are subspecies (subsp.) and variety (var.). A peony with a name that includes subsp. is very similar to the main species and is a variant that has occurred naturally, probably because it was found growing in an isolated area away from the species. A variety is also a naturally occurring variant of the plant that has simply popped up when a seed has germinated. *Paeonia veitchii* var. *woodwardii* is a good example.

**What Makes a Species Garden-worthy?**

The peonies described in the following pages are those that I have grown successfully in my various gardens. They are as easy to grow as lactiflora peonies, thriving in an average, well-drained soil in full sun or part shade. They are also, in the main, readily available from peony specialists. Those that are not, such as *Paeonia officinalis* subsp. *banatica* and *P. officinalis* subsp. *villosa*, are so easy to grow that they are worth tracking down.

**Flowers, Flowering Season and Foliage**

Species peonies generally flower early in the season. Their new spring growth is often very beautiful, pushing through the soil as it warms and the days become longer. In our part of the country, this can be as early as mid-February.

The blooms of most species peonies are fleeting, principally because most produce only one simply shaped bloom per flower stem. *Paeonia officinalis* 'Rubra Plena' with its big double blooms is the exception, but even this lovely plant doesn't bloom for long. However, the advantage species peonies have over many lactiflora cultivars is the beauty of their leaves. These can vary in appearance from large and round to so finely divided that they resemble the foliage of ferns.

All peonies owe their longevity to their root systems. In some species peonies, these resemble those of lactiflora types; others are divided into short tubers attached to each other by slim threads. The seeds of lactiflora peonies are an earthy-brown colour while those of many species are deepest blue and shiny.

**FLOWERS** i) the flower form (see p.9)
ii) these peonies bloom on our nursery:
**Very early season** mid May; **Early season** end of May; **Midseason** early June

This pink version of *Paeonia mlokosewitschii* shows it was raised from seed

Shiny, blue-black pearl-like seeds of *Paeonia veitchii*

Emerging leaves of *Paeonia officinalis* 'Rosea Plena' in early April

## EMODI

For some years there has been a debate around this plant and the two hybrids 'Early Windflower' and 'Late Windflower' raised by A.P. Saunders. Although all three are extremely similar, the difference lies in the size of the white flowers. Those of *P. emodi* are larger with rounded, unruly petals and a single carpel in the middle of the gold stamens. Unlike many species peonies, the slender stems, which carry slim, pointed leaves, bear one or two side buds. Its natural habitat is the slopes of the Himalayas. AGM

**Height:** 80cm
**Flowers:** single, very early season
**Scent:** none
**Staking:** no

*Paeonia emodi*

## MLOKOSEWITSCHII

The name of this very desirable plant is pronounced *mloko-se-witch-ii*. Each slender stem bears just one fleeting, single, soft-yellow bloom and the distinctive leaves are oval, slightly wavy edged, thick, and soft- or blue-green.

In the past few years, botanists have disagreed over the correct botanical name for this beauty. Some now consider it a subspecies of *P. daurica*, others stick with the name that celebrates its Polish discoverer, G. Mlokosiewicz, who found it growing on the rocky slopes of the Caucasus mountains in 1900.

Not the easiest peony to grow, it has never thrived in any of my gardens, perhaps because the soil is too wet and cold in spring. Yet in a warm and dry spot, in soil that is very well-drained for most of the year, it should flourish, especially if planted near to a warm wall in the south of the country.

After four years of waiting for my peony to bloom, to my disappointment the flowers were pink. Most plants sold by nurseries are not divisions but seed-raised, and because of this they can be variable. However, the pink flower does match the description given for *P. daurica*, the peony name in dispute. AGM

**Height:** 60cm
**Flowers:** single, early season
**Scent:** light
**Staking:** no
**Synonym:** *P. daurica* subsp. *mlokosewitschii*

*Paeonia mlokosewitschii*

## MOLLIS

Although probably not technically a species, the combination of simply shaped, soft cerise-pink flowers and grey-green, matt leaves together create the effect of a species peony. The crêpe-like petals slightly fade along the edges and surround a big ring of soft-yellow stamens and soft pink-tipped, white carpels. Easy to grow, this seems to adapt well to most garden conditions. I saw a particularly lovely plant growing in a well-drained, sandy soil.

**Height:** 45cm
**Flowers:** single, early season
**Scent:** light
**Staking:** no

*Paeonia mollis*

*Paeonia obovata*

### OBOVATA

Despite being rather fussy as to location, this is a lovely plant. The single, cupped blooms can vary from soft-white to pale or rich pink. They bloom on straight flower stems with broad, oval leaves that maybe purplish-green or plain green. The leaves continue to grow after the blooms have faded. A widespread species, this grows naturally in an area from China to Siberia and extending to Japan and Korea, where it thrives in locations that are shaded for part of the day.

**Height:** 60cm
**Flowers:** single, early season
**Scent:** none
**Staking:** no

*Paeonia officinalis* subsp. 'Anemoniflora Rosea'

### OFFICINALIS SUBSP. 'ANEMONIFLORA ROSEA'

The round, vivid magenta-pink guard petals create a wide saucer around a dome of dark pink staminodes that are edged and tipped with yellow. As the blooms age, the guard petals fade to very pale pink. The leaves, which are totally unlike those of the double forms of *P. officinalis*, are slender, matt grey-green and curl slightly at the edges to reveal pale-green undersides. This useful, short plant carries its flowers just above the leaves. AGM

**Height:** 60cm
**Flowers:** Japanese, early season
**Scent:** light
**Staking:** no

*Paeonia officinalis* subsp. *banatica*

### OFFICINALIS SUBSP. BANATICA

This beautiful plant came to me from the Royal Botanic Gardens, Kew. Its flowers are small with soft-magenta petals that pale as they age and are borne on branchless stems just above a very low, dense mound of foliage. As with all the true *officinalis* types, the leaves are small, wavy and grey-green. Found growing wild in parts of Hungary, Romania and Serbia, this rare plant is rather fleeting yet very easy to grow.

**Height:** 60cm
**Flowers:** single, early season
**Scent:** light
**Staking:** no
**Synonym:** *P. banatica*

### OFFICINALIS SUBSP. VILLOSA

A very short plant with small, vivid-magenta blooms carried on short stems with no side buds. The deeply divided leaves are soft-green and grey underneath. Native to south-eastern France, this species grows happily in our clay-loam soil. A similar form called *P. officinalis* subsp. *humilis* exists but the flowers are more purple in tone.

**Height:** 60cm
**Flowers:** single, early season
**Scent:** light
**Staking:** no
**Synonym:** *P. macrocarpa, humilis* subsp. *villosa*

*Paeonia officinalis* subsp. *villosa*

Garden-worthy species

*Paeonia officinalis* 'Lize Van Veen'

*Paeonia officinalis* 'Rosea Plena'

### OFFICINALIS HYBRIDS

Known as 'cottage' peonies, these double-flowered plants are very hardy, long-lived and easy to grow. In one form or another, they have been cultivated in gardens for centuries. The species *P. officinalis* has just a single row of petals but its hybrids produce a mass of frilly petaloids that unfurl into a shallow dome. As the bloom ages, the petals push up to create a high fluffy ball that is edged by a ring of large, round guard petals. There are several different colour variations ranging from white to red.

The blooms are carried on short stems with no side buds and long, semi-glossy, mid-green leaves. When the flowers are fully open their weight causes the stems to tumble forward. All *P. officinalis* hybrids have tuberous roots, which look like long, thin, slightly ridged potatoes. If any are left in the soil they will eventually sprout again.

In 2018 the RHS changed the name of the double forms of *P. officinalis* to *P. × festiva* after the Swedish Nomenclature and Taxonomy Advisory Group questioned whether these plants should be classified as hybrids rather than species. Whilst I agree that they are probably hybrids and that the leaves are entirely different to those of *P. officinalis* (see p.107 for some subsp. and variants), these plants have been known under this name for so long I feel *officinalis* should remain. Currently the Royal Botanic Gardens, Kew, also list *P. × festiva* as a synonym of *P. officinalis*.

### OFFICINALIS 'LIZE VAN VEEN'

A garden-worthy variant of the red type with flowers that open from round pink buds into a dome of frilly, white petals very lightly flushed with pink. These are surrounded by softest rose-pink flushed guard petals.

### OFFICINALIS 'ROSEA PLENA'

Opening into a rich-pink bloom, the flower colour fades slowly to soft-pink with dark pink still visible in the depths of the frilly petals.

### OFFICINALIS 'RUBRA PLENA'

(Red Cottage Peony) This is so familiar to gardeners it hardly needs describing. Found growing in gardens throughout the country, this is the first peony I can recall, although it may have been the tiny ants crawling over the round flower buds that enthralled my young mind rather than the large brilliant-red blooms.

The short stems, which bear mid-green leaves with a dull gloss, are never straight and fall forward under the weight of the double blooms. Large and true red, the flowers consist of short, intertwined petals and a flat saucer of guard petals that curl back on themselves. These allow the central petaloids to form a large ball that darkens to deep magenta. AGM

(for all the above versions of *Officinalis*)
**Height:** 60cm
**Flowers:** double, very early season
**Scent:** light
**Staking:** yes
**Synonym:** *P. × festiva*

*Paeonia officinalis* 'Rubra Plena'

*Paeonia peregrina* 'Otto Froebel'

### PEREGRINA 'OTTO FROEBEL'

The species, *Paeonia peregrina* which has pure red flowers, is hard to source yet it has been grown in gardens for 400 years and is found in the wild from Greece to Turkey. This variant is more readily available. The cupped, glowing orange-red blooms are borne on thick stems with no side buds and serrated, glossy, bright-green leaves. Inside, wispy golden stamens rise on fine filaments. The long roots, which are divided into short sections, fan out from the centre.

**Height:** 60cm
**Flowers:** single, midseason
**Scent:** light
**Staking:** no
**Synonym:** *P. lobata*

*Paeonia × smouthii*

### × SMOUTHII

This hardy little plant was named after Monsieur Smout, a Belgian chemist. Crimson flowers, which are cupped at first, open wide to show off a ring of slim, gold stamens. The blooms are borne singly just above rich-green leaves that are so finely cut they are almost fern-like. Considered to be a hybrid between *Paeonia lactiflora* and *P. tenuifolia*, this plant was known in gardens years before it was officially recorded in 1843.

**Height:** 45cm
**Flowers:** single, early season
**Scent:** light
**Staking:** no

*Paeonia tenuifolia*

*Paeonia tenuifolia* 'Plena'

### TENUIFOLIA

Finely cut, extremely slender leaflets are what make this plant so distinctive. They are carried so thickly up short stiff flower stems that when viewed from above they resemble a frilly, green skirt. At the top, the single crimson bloom opens into a cup revealing a thick ring of gold stamens.

Known to have been grown in gardens for over two centuries, this peony originates in the unforested flatlands of Hungary, Romania and the Ukraine – harsh environments that account for its short stature and hardiness.

### TENUIFOLIA 'PLENA'

Although the flowers are small they are most attractive, particularly when fully opened into a ruffled shiny, crimson ball that is frilled by fine, mid-green leaves.

### TENUIFOLIA 'ROSEA'

Personally I find the tiny flowers of this pink form rather uninspiring because the petals, which become transparent with age, are covered with little bumps. As easy to grow as other *P. tenuifolia* species.

(for all *Tenuifolia* listings above)
**Height:** 60cm
**Flowers:** early season
**Scent:** none
**Staking:** no

*Paeonia tenuifolia* 'Rosea'

*Paeonia veitchii* var. *woodwardii*

The deeply divided leaves of *Paeonia veitchii* var. *woodwardii*

### VEITCHII VAR. WOODWARDII

The blooms of *Paeonia veitchii*, a Chinese native species, are richer pink than this lovely variety. The gently nodding, small, cupped blooms are carried on short stems with one or two side shoots and lush, deeply cut, mid-green leaves. Found growing in a Chinese monastery in 1912 by G. Fenwick-Owen, its seed was sent to Robert Woodward to germinate and raise. Following Woodward's death in the Second World War, the plant was named after him. It grows well in a semi-shady spot along the edge of trees.

**Height:** 30cm
**Flowers:** single, early season
**Scent:** none
**Staking:** no
**Synonym:** *P. anomala*

### WITTMANNIANA

There are only two yellow-flowered species peonies, *Paeonia mlokosewitschii* and this one. Very pale yellow or creamy-white in colour, the flowers have a ring of rather floppy, yellow stamens with filaments that are red at the base. The straight stems bear large, round, mid-green leaflets that have a slightly glossy surface and long veins that create deep grooves. It can be found growing naturally on rocky slopes and in the beech woods of the west and south Caucasus.

**Height:** 90cm
**Flowers:** single, early season
**Scent:** none
**Staking:** no

### WITTMANNIANA SUBSP. 'ROSEA'

Many years ago I ordered *Paeonia wittmanniana* from a Dutch wholesaler and received this plant. Not unlike hybrid *Paeonia* 'Avant Garde', this too may be a cross between *P. wittmanniana* and *P. lactiflora*. A robust plant, it carries soft-pink flowers that fade with age above a broad clump of large, bright-green leaves. The leaves are less pointed than those of the species, and remain handsome all summer. Happy in a partially shaded spot in well-drained soil.

**Height:** 90cm
**Flowers:** single, early season
**Scent:** none
**Staking:** no
**Synonym:** *P. daurica* subsp. *wittmanniana* 'Rosea'

*Paeonia wittmanniana*

In early spring, the emerging leaves and flower buds of *Paeonia wittmanniana* subsp. 'Rosea' are particularly beautiful

*Paeonia wittmanniana* subsp. 'Rosea'

# HYBRID PEONIES

The plants in this varied group of peonies are the result of breeders crossing two or more species. Extremely useful in the garden, their flower colours are often brighter and clearer than those of their lactiflora cousins. Perhaps more importantly, these lovely plants can bring the start of the peony flowering season forward by up to three weeks. In my garden, a few hybrid peonies will be in bloom early in May, although the majority don't flower until the end of the month, and a few varieties will bloom alongside lactiflora peonies.

### Patience and Tireless Optimism

Most hybrid peonies have lactiflora heritage. By mixing lactifloras with species peonies, the resulting plants can produce side buds – a trait absent in all but three species peonies. Apart from *Paeonia officinalis*, the flowers of species peonies have just a single row of petals yet it is possible to cross them with lactifloras and create hybrids with double, semi-double and Japanese-type flowers. The majority of crosses, however, are single-flowered.

Raising new peonies is not for the faint-hearted. It takes determination and patience, plus a certain amount of vision. Having chosen the two parents, a breeder has to hope the cross produces seeds. The seeds will take at least two years to germinate and, provided they grow, another five years to bloom. After evaluating the whole plant for quality of bloom and growth, it will be another few years before the plant can be multiplied. It is easy to see why there are so few new peonies, and why, when they have been introduced, they are so expensive.

### The Early Pioneers

As new species of peonies were found, peony breeders turned to making crosses between them. A handful of new plants were introduced by Lemoine in France in the first decade of 20th century (see p.32) By the middle of the century, hundreds more were added, many by the visionary Canadian-born Professor A.P. Saunders (see p.34). The majority of the early hybrid peonies came from America, largely because the country was less affected by war, but also because of the North American climate.

A good proportion of species peonies originate in regions where the temperature swings from extremely hot to bitingly cold. So, it is not surprising to discover that many of the early American hybridisers came from Illinois, a state with harsh winters and very hot summers.

Edward Auten, who died in 1974, built a business in Illinois around peonies and expressed a desire to raise red-flowered varieties that did not fade in heat. He succeeded in registering 276, most of them lactiflora types, but among his red hybrids is *Paeonia* 'Chocolate Soldier' an extremely dark red cultivar.

On US Memorial Day in late May, in some states it is traditional to place peonies on the graves of fallen soldiers. Lyman Glasscock, a bricklayer turned building contractor, found the blooms of lactiflora hybrids died very quickly and although *Paeonia officinalis* bloomed early, the flowers did not last when cut. Hoping to create peonies that were good for cutting, in 1918 he began crossing species peonies with great success. Of the 40 hybrids he introduced, 13 are featured in this chapter. When he died in 1952, his daughter Elizabeth Falk took all her father's peonies and planted them at her property. Over the next 35 years she introduced a further 20 varieties.

The blooms of peonies naturally range in colour from white to pink and red. Coral-coloured flowers are unusual on any plant, but it was the aim of Samuel Wissing, another Illinois resident, to raise peonies of this colour. Wissing worked for 29 years to achieve his goal, concentrating on plants with just one bud per flower stem. After collaborating with nursery-owner Carl Klehm, Klehm's introduced a handful of plants. Four of these remain popular today and all are good for cutting.

### The Story of One Peony

The mission to raise a particular form of a plant is often the goal of plant breeders. One of Professor Saunders' aims was to produce a peony with yellow flowers that would be hardy in the US. He crossed *Paeonia mlokosewitschii*, which is not so hardy, with the very hardy *P. lactiflora*, but none of the resulting plants produced any seeds, so he gave up.

The same challenge was taken up decades later by Dr. Earle B. White, a dentist living in Maryland. Notes written in 1949 outline his obsession:

"For eight years I made 500 crosses each season, using pollen of *Paeonia mlokosewitschii* on the Chinese peony 'Mons. Jules Elie', and have had only one plant in all that time which ever reached maturity. I had several others which germinated – perhaps 3 or 4 – but they died in infancy".

The seedling he mentions was named *Paeonia* 'Claire de Lune'. For many years it was the only yellow peony to produce side buds.

*Paeonia* 'Claire de Lune' is a cross between yellow-flowered *Paeonia mlokosewitschii* and the double pink-flowered lactiflora *P.* 'Monsieur Jules Elie'

(Right) *Paeonia* 'Eliza Lundy' is typical of the double hybrid forms of *P. officinalis*

## THE HYBRID PLANT

Like lactifloras, hybrid peonies are very hardy, coping with temperatures that drop to -40°C. During conversations with other peony growers, I discovered that a handful fail to thrive in some gardens, including in one of my own with well-drained sandy soil. Hybrids raised by A. P. Saunders with the complicated parentage of *Paeonia lactiflora*, *P. officinalis*, *P. mlokosewitschii* and *P. macrophylla* seem to be the least hardy. This could be down to either *P. mlokosewitschii*, a plant I find difficult to grow, and/or *P. macrophylla*, which I have yet to see growing in UK gardens. By contrast, peonies with *Paeonia lactiflora* and *P. officinalis* heritage do well in almost all garden situations.

**The flowers** of hybrid peonies are most likely to be single and although there are more semi-double shapes than among lactifloras, there are few double-flowered varieties. Of the 92 peonies in this chapter, just 21 cultivars produce full-petalled blooms.

Single and semi-double flowered hybrids open into a cup or deep goblet before the petals uncurl to form a flat saucer around the stamens and carpels. Both stamens and carpels add further, often unique, colour and shape to the bloom. The stamens are often carried on red-tinged filaments, while the carpels, which are often covered with hairs rendering them furry, usually have brightly coloured tips.

The petals of many hybrids can be so thick and waxy they prevent them scorching in hot sun or losing colour in wet weather. They are certainly more robust than the delicate petals of lactifloras.

**Colour** is the most distinctive aspect of hybrid peonies. Before their arrival, peony flowers were generally pastel shades of white to pink, or rich shades of magenta and crimson. Hybrids have added vivid pinks, coral-pink, yellow and pillar-box red flowers to the palette. On some the petals can fade as the flower ages, but a good proportion of red hybrid blooms stay richly toned. While yellow and coral-pink peonies are particularly rare, the limited number of newer hybrids in these colours have proved to be excellent garden plants. In addition, flares and washes of richer tones can be found at the base of the petals, adding further colour to the bloom and helping to make this peony group not only beautiful, but diverse.

Peonies raised from *Paeonia peregrina*, such as *P.* 'Coral Charm', have similar tuberous roots

Hairy, red-tipped carpels are visible on *Paeonia* 'Early Glow'

The woolly carpels of *Paeonia* 'Nosegay' turn into attractive, furry seed pods

Yellow peonies like double-flowered *Paeonia* 'Sunny Girl' are expensive

*Paeonia* 'Montezuma' bears single blooms closely resembling those of *P. officinalis*

Coral-pink *Paeonia* 'Pink Hawaiian Coral' produces semi-double flowers

Very tightly packed with petals, the bud of *Paeonia* 'Paula Fay' takes ages to open

The leaves of *Paeonia* 'Red Charm' are typical of plants with *P. officinalis* heritage

*Paeonia* 'Scarlet O'Hara' has distinctive deeply incised leaves

**The flower stems** of hybrid peonies generally remain sternly upright. This has less to do with the single or semi-double nature of most flowers, and is down to the thickness of the stems. However, varieties with very large flowers and extra-long stems are still likely to topple over when in full bloom.

Hybrid varieties tend to bloom for around three weeks, but those that produce no side buds will inevitably flower for a shorter period. The lack of competition from other buds allows the solitary bud to grow into a big bloom – a benefit for cut-flower growers who usually have to remove side buds to achieve this goal.

When a hybrid peony emerges from the soil in spring, the structure and form of the flower buds is very handsome. Unlike lactiflora peonies, most buds are not wrapped in leaves and push through the ground like small fists before extending to produce foliage.

**The leaves** of hybrid peonies vary in tones of green, unlike those of lactifloras, which tend to be a similar shade of mid-green. Often leathery, the surface may be glossy or have a light sheen. And some varieties have extremely ornamental foliage. Those with large, round leaves and finely divided foliage often form bushy clumps that blend easily into a border with other perennials. Peonies with thick stems and big leaves also accent a border by injecting strong shape and colour.

### A–Z of Hybrids: Terms (pp.116–141)

**GUARD PETALS** Sit at the base of those blooms with lots of petals. On single flowers they are the main petals.

**PETALOIDS** Look like the petals but are much slimmer and often shorter.

**STAMINODES** Very thin, yellow central stamens on Japanese-type flowers.

**AGM** The Award of Garden Merit given to the most garden-worthy peonies. Updated in 2021 after five-year trials at RHS Wisley.

**BREEDER NAME & DATE,** where known. When two names appear, the second is the person who acquired the peony (as part of a collection) and the date it was registered.

**FLOWERS** i) the flower form (see p.9) ii) the period when the peonies are in bloom on our nursery:
**Very early** early May: **Early** mid-May
**Midseason** late May: **Late** early June

*Paeonia* 'Garden Peace' carries almost black seed pods on long red stems

*Paeonia* 'Lovely Rose' has stems that carry no side buds

The attractive leaves of *Paeonia* 'Early Windflower' create a handsome clump

Hybrid peonies | 115

*Paeonia* 'America'

### 'AMERICA'

Brilliant-red flowers have big, wavy petals that first open into an unevenly shaped cup. As the flower matures, the petals enlarge and become looser, creating a ruffled 'windmill' around a thick ring of yellow stamens and very pale pink-tipped, soft-pink carpels. The strong stems carry dark green leaves and the occasional long-stemmed side bud. One of the parents is *P.* 'Burma Ruby' (p.119).

**Breeder:** Rudolph, 1976
**Height:** 90cm
**Flowers:** single, early season
**Scent:** medium
**Staking:** no

*Paeonia* 'Angelo Cobb Freeborn'

### 'ANGELO COBB FREEBORN'

The colour of the rich coral-red flowers is unique. A mass of pleated, silver-tipped petals weave around each other into a big ball that is surrounded by large guard petals. The thick stems are long and lax and bear shiny *P. officinalis*-type, light green leaves. Sadly, this variety is not widely available, probably because it's slow to multiply.

**Breeder:** Freeborn, 1943
**Height:** 90cm
**Flowers:** double, midseason
**Scent:** none
**Staking:** yes

*Paeonia* 'Athena'

### 'ATHENA'

A fleeting beauty created by crossing four different species. Globular and very pale peach at first, the peach tinge of the petals fades, leaving the blooms palest pink. As the flower evolves into a saucer shape, soft-raspberry flares radiate from a thick ring of yellow stamens and magenta-topped, soft-green carpels. Strong flower stems bear thick, mid-green leaves. AGM

**Breeder:** Saunders, 1949
**Height:** 85cm
**Flowers:** single, early season
**Scent:** light
**Staking:** no

### 'AUTEN'S 1816'

Although not registered with the American Peony Society, this has always been in our peony collection. The handsome ball-shaped flower is composed of rich-red petals that are slightly paler along the edges and emit a faint inner glow of purple. Despite being relatively short, the stems are not strong enough to keep the flowers upright. The leaves are typical of *Paeonia officinalis* 'Rubra Plena'.

**Breeder:** Auten, date not recorded
**Height:** 75cm
**Flowers:** double, early season
**Scent:** none
**Staking:** yes

*Paeonia* 'Auten's 1816'

*Paeonia* 'Avant Garde'

## 'AVANT GARDE'

As they age, the petals of this very soft pink flower become almost transparent and turn near-white. Cupped at first, the flower opens into a small dish with an airy ring of gold stamens carried on slender, magenta-based filaments that elongate. The blooms are borne just above a wide mound of shiny, bright-green leaves that are long, broad and pointed. One of the first hybrid peonies to be registered.

**Breeder:** Lemoine, 1907
**Height:** 70cm
**Flowers:** single, very early season
**Scent:** light
**Staking:** no

*Paeonia* 'Belle Center'

## 'BELLE CENTER'

Spicy-scented and deep ruby-red, the flowers have glossy, round petals that are woven into three rows. In the wide centre sit yellow stamens tinged with red down the middle. Among them arise more red petals, which often enlarge to create a double flower. The stems are stiff, but not sturdy and carry mid-green leaves. Almost identical to *P.* 'Buckeye Belle' (p.118) but blooms slightly earlier.

**Breeder:** Mains, 1956
**Height:** 75cm
**Flowers:** semi-double, early season
**Scent:** medium
**Staking:** no

*Paeonia* 'Bess Bockstoce'

## 'BESS BOCKSTOCE'

A unique, changeable flower. Dark rose-pink when it unfurls into a flat-topped rosette, the outer petals then fade with age to pale salmon-pink with tints of red along the edges. Meanwhile, the central petals remain deep pink. The blooms are carried on lax stems with light green leaves, and no side buds. In Canada the same name applies to a different peony with pink flowers, while in the US this plant is sometimes sold as *P.* 'Rose Heart'.

**Breeder:** Bockstoce, 1955
**Height:** 85cm
**Flowers:** double, early season
**Scent:** light
**Staking:** yes

## 'BLACK MONARCH'

The enormous flowers are a glowing deep red, a colour that leans more towards blue than yellow. Deep within the petals, mahogany tints may appear and all the petals are so tightly interwoven they cannot help but form a tidy, round ball. Poking out from the base are large, round guard petals. The stems are very long and the mid-green leaves are glossy.

**Breeder:** Glasscock, 1939
**Height:** 90cm
**Flowers:** double, early season
**Scent:** none
**Staking:** yes

*Paeonia* 'Black Monarch'

Hybrid peonies | 117

*Paeonia* 'Blaze'

### 'BLAZE'

Although registered as a single, the number of petals creates an almost semi-double bloom. As the cupped, pure red petals extend into a large, loose bloom, they maintain their colour well. A ring of gold stamens with red filaments sits around red-tipped, soft-green carpels. Mid-green leaves are carried on stems that are not very thick. Unlike many red hybrid peonies, I have not found this to be a robust plant. AGM

**Breeder:** Fay, 1973
**Height:** 80cm
**Flowers:** single, early season
**Scent:** none
**Staking:** no

*Paeonia* 'Bright Knight'

### 'BRIGHT KNIGHT'

The flowers produce two rows of spoon-shaped scarlet petals, which are on the orange rather than the blue side of red. The petals remain cupped around a thick ring of mid-yellow stamens and soft-green carpels that are tipped with pale-pink. Each bloom is borne on thick stems with wide, dark green leaves similar to *Paeonia officinalis* 'Rubra Plena'.

**Breeder:** Glasscock, 1939
**Height:** 90cm
**Flowers:** single, very early season
**Scent:** none
**Staking:** no

*Paeonia* 'Buckeye Belle'

### 'BUCKEYE BELLE'

A beautiful plant that produces masses of large, shallowly cupped, glistening, rich dark red flowers. The large guard petals help to create the perfect rosette-shaped bloom. At the centre is a mixture of short, crinkled petals and soft-yellow stamens with red filaments. Thick flowers stems with glossy, dark green leaves make this hybrid a good cut flower.

**Breeder:** Mains, 1956
**Height:** 75cm
**Flowers:** semi-double, early to midseason
**Scent:** none
**Staking:** no

### 'BURMA MIDNIGHT'

The single, fairly small, bright-red flowers have two rows of lightly ruffled petals that fade in colour as they age. Yet unlike some red hybrid peonies, the petals don't grow larger with age. In the centre sits a tight boss of yellow stamens and white-tipped, light green carpels. The flowers are carried high above a clump of glossy, mid-green leaves. This has superseded the beautiful *P.* 'Burma Ruby' (opposite), one of its parents, in popularity.

**Breeder:** Klehm, 1980
**Height:** 80cm
**Flowers:** single, early season
**Scent:** medium
**Staking:** no

*Paeonia* 'Burma Midnight'

*Paeonia* 'Burma Ruby'

### 'BURMA RUBY'

Seen at their best, the flowers are very beautiful. Before they open fully, the bright-red petals create a tulip shape that develops into a broad bowl-shaped flower with touches of purple. In the centre, the yellow stamens with red filaments grow into a broad boss. The leaves are shiny and mid-green.

**Breeder:** Glasscock, 1951
**Height:** 70cm
**Flowers:** single, early season
**Scent:** none
**Staking:** no

### 'CAROL'

Big flower buds uncurl into a perfectly shaped, pure red flower. The petals are evenly sized and arranged into ruffled layers creating a lovely low dome with a slightly dipped middle. The stems are bare of side buds and have big, mid-green leaves. Although ungainly in habit, the long flower stems make this good for cutting.

**Breeder:** Bockstoce, 1955
**Height:** 75cm
**Flowers:** double, early season
**Scent:** none
**Staking:** yes

### 'CHALICE'

On first opening, the two rows of white petals are brushed with soft-yellow and pale-pink, creating an apricot tinge. In the centre, the yellow stamens curl over at the tops and are carried on filaments with red bases. As these unfurl, they loosen into silky threads around deep pink-tipped, green carpels. The petals, which are initially thick and satiny, become thin and nearly transparent. The big, glossy, dark green leaves form a broad clump.

**Breeder:** Saunders, 1929
**Height:** 90cm
**Flowers:** single, early season
**Scent:** none
**Staking:** no

*Paeonia* 'Carol'

*Paeonia* 'Chalice'

### 'CHAMELEON'

Small, bright lilac-pink flowers have a single row of petals. These are cupped around a centre of relaxed gold stamens on red filaments and red-tipped, soft-green carpels. No parents are recorded and this plant has never been registered, but as the slender, grey-green leaves closely resemble those of *Paeonia officinalis* subsp. *banatica*, I wonder if it might be a selected seedling of that peony or even the same plant.

**Breeder:** Krekler/Klehm 2001
**Height:** 35cm
**Flowers:** single, early season
**Scent:** none
**Staking:** no

*Paeonia* 'Chameleon'

Hybrid peonies | 119

### 'CHERRY RUFFLES'

Large, glowing, light red flowers are at first cupped then widen over time to form a nicely shaped, shallow bowl. In the centre sits a narrow ring of fine yellow stamens and pink-tipped, green carpels. The blooms are carried on stiff, thick flower stems with no side buds. The large, shiny, mid-green leaves are similar to those of *Paeonia peregrina*, one of its parents.

**Breeder:** Hollingsworth, 1996
**Height:** 85cm
**Flowers:** semi-double, midseason
**Scent:** none
**Staking:** no

*Paeonia* 'Cherry Ruffles'

### 'CHRISTMAS VELVET'

As they open, the pure red flowers form a shallow dome that is filled with shiny, unevenly edged and deeply interwoven petals. A collar of smaller, fringed petaloids sits between this and the two rows of large, round guard petals. Over time, the dome turns into a gorgeous big ball that is borne on strong stems with fresh green leaves.

**Breeder:** Anderson, 1992
**Height:** 75cm
**Flowers:** double, midseason
**Scent:** light
**Staking:** sometimes

### 'CHOCOLATE SOLDIER'

This is one of the darkest red peonies I have grown, although it is not the most floriferous. Originally registered as a Japanese-type peony, the very dark red flowers open into a goblet that gets bigger with age, although the petals stay largely cupped. In the centre, the thick tuft of cream stamens have red filaments and soft red-tipped, soft-green carpels. The blooms are carried on strong stems with dark green leaves and no side buds.

**Breeder:** Auten, 1939
**Height:** 70cm
**Flowers:** single, very early season
**Scent:** none
**Staking:** no

*Paeonia* 'Christmas Velvet'

*Paeonia* 'Chocolate Soldier'

### 'CLAIRE DE LUNE'

(opposite) Consistently one of the first peonies to bloom, the big, round, soft-lemon petals have a slightly bumpy texture. At first they are ever-so-faintly tinted with pink, but this quickly fades. A wide dome of stamens gives the bloom a dramatic golden centre, with white-tipped carpels just showing. The flowers are carried on red stems with dark green leaves and some side buds. AGM

**Breeder:** White/Wild, 1954
**Height:** 70cm
**Flowers:** single, early season
**Scent:** heavy
**Staking:** no

*Paeonia* 'Claudia'

### 'CLAUDIA'

An upright plant bearing semi-double, rich-pink flowers, which are not overly large. These open from a goblet into a pale-pink saucer with a centre of delicate stamens forming a slender ring around pink-tipped, light green carpels. Strong flower stems bear glossy, mid-green leaves that are relatively small, and no side buds.

**Breeder:** Saunders, 1944
**Height:** 90cm
**Flowers:** single, midseason
**Scent:** none
**Staking:** no

*Paeonia* 'Claire de Lune' in May with furry grey *Stachys byzantina* behind

*Paeonia* 'Color Magnet'

### 'COLOR MAGNET'

The single, rose-pink flowers have ten, large, wavy petals that fade in colour towards the edges. Look closer and the pink colouring is unevenly spread over a background of white. In the centre, a perfect ring of yellow stamens encircles the deep red-tipped, red carpels. Some side stems are produced on the stems along with big, glossy, dark green leaves.

**Breeder:** Hollingsworth, 1994
**Height:** 90cm
**Flowers:** single, midseason
**Scent:** light
**Staking:** no

*Paeonia* 'Command Performance'

### 'COMMAND PERFORMANCE'

Bright pink-red petals, serrated along the top, weave themselves into a densely packed low dome with a broad ruff created by the large guard petals. The flowers are borne singly on very long, lax flower stems with dark green leaves and no side stems. Although I consider this a lovely peony on account of the stunning colour, I have not found it to be free-flowering.

**Breeder:** Hollingsworth, 1996
**Height:** 80cm
**Flowers:** double, midseason
**Scent:** light
**Staking:** yes

*Paeonia* 'Coral Charm'

### 'CORAL CHARM'

As they enlarge, the big, deeply cupped, coral-pink petals pale slightly along the edges. Eventually the blooms turn very soft coral. In the centre, a loose ring of golden stamens surrounds the short, magenta-tipped carpels. I cannot warm to this plant, largely due to the limited number of very thick, unbranched stems that if not staked, topple over. The few big leaves are dark green. Cut flowers will last for up to 10 days in water. AGM

**Breeder:** Wissing, 1964
**Height:** 90cm
**Flowers:** semi-double, early season
**Scent:** none
**Staking:** yes

### 'CORAL FAY'

A delicate plant with small flowers composed of slightly unruly, rich-pink petals. A centre of comparatively large golden stamens is loose enough for the soft pink-tipped, pale-green carpels to show through. Each slender stem rises from the extremely handsome clump of deeply segmented, soft-green leaves that resemble those of *Paeonia veitchii*, one of its parents.

**Breeder:** Fay, 1973
**Height:** 75cm
**Flowers:** semi-double, early season
**Scent:** light
**Staking:** no

*Paeonia* 'Coral Fay'

## 'CORAL 'N GOLD'

Two rows of big, coral-pink petals form a wide cup around a broad centre of long, slender stamens that hang loosely around pale pink-tipped, soft-green carpels. The stems are slim but sturdy and bear light green leaves. Another in the 'Coral' series of peonies introduced by Klehm's of Wisconsin during the 1980s suitable for the cut-flower market.

**Breeder:** Cousins/Klehm, 1981
**Height:** 90cm
**Flowers:** single, early season
**Scent:** none
**Staking:** no

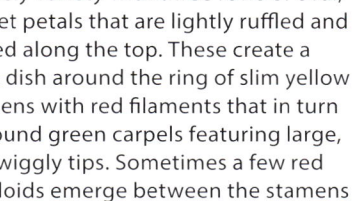
*Paeonia* 'Coral 'n Gold'

## 'CORAL SUNSET'

The petals of the soft-coral, cupped flowers are darker towards the top, fading to very pale coral at the base where they appear almost yellow – a colour reflected from the ring of yellow stamens. As the petals unfurl into a flat saucer, the yellow tints fade leaving the whole flower soft-pink. Strong stems produce slim, dark green leaves but no side buds. The flower shape is inherited from *Paeonia* 'Minnie Shaylor', its lactiflora parent. AGM

**Breeder:** Wissing, 1965
**Height:** 75cm
**Flowers:** semi-double, early season
**Scent:** light
**Staking:** no

## 'CRUSADER'

A lovely variety with three rows of oval, scarlet petals that are lightly ruffled and nicked along the top. These create a wide dish around the ring of slim yellow stamens with red filaments that in turn surround green carpels featuring large, red, wiggly tips. Sometimes a few red petaloids emerge between the stamens and the carpels. The blooms are carried on stiff stems with glossy, bright-green leaves.

**Breeder:** Glasscock, 1940
**Height:** 80cm
**Flowers:** semi-double, early season
**Scent:** none
**Staking:** no

*Paeonia* 'Crusader'

*Paeonia* 'Coral Sunset'

## 'CUTIE'

Appropriately named, the blooms of this pretty, short plant are generally cream. A ring of lightly ruffled, pure white guard petals surrounds the centre of slender, fringed, cream staminodes. In time, further white petals appear among the petaloids creating a creamy-white pompom as they enlarge. The blooms are carried on stiff stems with glossy, dark green leaves and the occasional side bud.

**Breeder:** Glasscock, 1986
**Height:** 65cm
**Flowers:** double, midseason
**Scent:** light
**Staking:** no

*Paeonia* 'Cutie'

### 'CYTHEREA'

Opening into a large, perfectly shaped bowl, the central boss of gold stamens creates a ring around soft pink-tipped, green carpels. The petals remain incurved throughout the life of the fruity-scented flower, although they pale slightly with age. Despite having long stems that tend to splay outwards, these don't collapse entirely but create a neat clump with light green leaves. One of the peonies grown commercially as a cut flower.

**Breeder:** Saunders, 1953
**Height:** 90cm
**Flowers:** semi-double, midseason
**Scent:** light
**Staking:** no

*Paeonia* 'Cytherea'

### 'DANDY DAN'

A rather shaggy flower producing many layers of rich-red petals that are ragged along the edges and slightly ruffled. As the bloom ages, a deep centre is revealed with a small ring of gold stamens and deep pink-topped, soft-green carpels. A few other stamens may be seen among the outer petals. The stiff stems, which carry bright-green leaves, have no side stems.

**Breeder:** Auten, 1946
**Height:** 85cm
**Flowers:** semi-double, midseason
**Scent:** light
**Staking:** no

*Paeonia* 'Defender'

### 'DEFENDER'

The first red peony to bloom with many large, poppy-like, globe-shaped flowers. These have a single row of glossy, dark crimson petals, which are cupped around a cluster of unruly golden stamens. The stems are thick and carry big, glossy, mid-green leaves. One of a series that the breeder A. P. Saunders christened the 'Challenger' strain, after a peony that is no longer available but had dark crimson blooms.

**Breeder:** Saunders, 1929
**Height:** 75cm
**Flowers:** single, midseason
**Scent:** light
**Staking:** no

*Paeonia* 'Dandy Dan'

### 'EARLY GLOW'

The two layers of large, almost translucent petals are lightly crinkled. In colour they are palest lemon, flushed with light pink that combines with soft-yellow to create a pale-buff appearance. Cupped at first, the blooms open to display a broad ring of delicate gold stamens and soft-green carpels that are tipped with raspberry-red. The long stems are flushed with red as far as the three side buds. A bushy plant with long, mid-green, glossy leaves.

**Breeder:** Hollingsworth, 1992
**Height:** 75cm
**Flowers:** single, early season
**Scent:** light
**Staking:** no

*Paeonia* 'Early Glow'

*Paeonia* 'Early Windflower'

## 'EARLY WINDFLOWER'

In my garden this is not only one of the earliest peonies to bloom, it is also one of the nicest perennials. The petals of the small pure white flowers are pinched at the top. As they age, they open wide to show off a tight ring of golden stamens. Long stems carry one to three side buds and handsome, glossy, slender, mid-green leaves. A dense, bushy, upright plant with a long flowering season, it is a cross between *Paeonia emodi* and *P. veitchii*.

**Breeder:** Saunders, 1939
**Height:** 110cm
**Flowers:** single, very early season
**Scent:** none
**Staking:** no

*Paeonia* 'Ellen Cowley'

## 'ELLEN COWLEY'

Bright reddish-pink petals that curl inwards and are notched at the edges open into a goblet shape. Although the petals loosen a little with age, the small blooms remain cupped. In the middle is a ring of slim, gold stamens. Short, slender stems carry the flowers not far above lots of narrow, mid-green leaves.

**Breeder:** Saunders, 1940
**Height:** 80cm
**Flowers:** semi-double, early season
**Scent:** none
**Staking:** no

*Paeonia* 'Eliza Lundy'

## 'ELIZA LUNDY'

This lovely, very free-flowering plant was named after the breeder William Krekler's grandmother. The small, rich-red petals twist around each other to create a tight ball, and a frill of wavy guard petals forms a ruffled plate around the base of the flower. Each reasonably sized flower is balanced neatly just above a clump of slender, mid-green leaves to create an excellent short plant. AGM

**Breeder:** Krekler, 1976
**Height:** 60cm
**Flowers:** double, early season
**Scent:** none
**Staking:** no

## 'ELIZABETH FOSTER'

When this first opens, the large, incurving petals are very crumpled. As they get bigger, the petals become smoother although little ridges remain. Golden stamens form a dense ring around the large, red-tipped, soft-pink carpels. Goblet shaped at first, the blooms open into wide, deep cups that are carried on strong stems with soft-green leaves. The foliage is similar to those of *Paeonia peregrina,* one of its parents.

**Breeder:** Saunders, 1941
**Height:** 90cm
**Flowers:** single, midseason
**Scent:** none
**Staking:** no

*Paeonia* 'Elizabeth Foster'

*Paeonia* 'Etched Salmon'

*Paeonia* 'Eventide'

### 'ETCHED SALMON'

Thick, wavy, scallop-edged, salmon-pink petals open into a shallow, flat-topped cup. As the petals grow larger, the bloom evolves into a shallow dome and displays guard petals that are slightly larger than the inner petals. In strong sun, the top of the flower fades to pale-pink. Thick stems with glossy, mid-green leaves are also bare of side stems, making this excellent for cutting.

**Breeder:** Cousins/Klehm, 1981
**Height:** 90cm
**Flowers:** double, midseason
**Scent:** medium
**Staking:** yes

### 'EVENTIDE'

Three or four rows of large, ruffled, bright-pink petals open into a wide, shallow bowl around a centre of pale pink-tipped, light green carpels and gold stamens. As the flower ages, the petals, which fade to pale-pink along the tops, become rather unruly, two-toned and widen into a shallow cup. The stems are upright and have glossy, light green leaves. Unfortunately, the scent is rather unpleasant and not unlike cat's pee!

**Breeder:** Glasscock, 1945
**Height:** 80cm
**Flowers:** single, early season
**Scent:** medium
**Staking:** no

*Paeonia* 'Fairy Princess'

### 'FAIRY PRINCESS'

Neatly edged by a row of large, round, clear-red petals, the yellow stamens form a thick ring around white-tipped, pale-green carpels. As the stamens age, they flop over to show their red filaments, adding a further ring of colour between the yellow anthers and the carpels.
A short neat plant, the flowers are carried on strong stems with shiny, pure green leaves.

**Breeder:** Glasscock/Falk, 1955
**Height:** 60cm
**Flowers:** single, early season
**Scent:** none
**Staking:** no

### 'FIRELIGHT'

A single layer of soft-pink petals opens evenly to display cerise-pink flares that spread upwards from each petal's base. A ring of yellow stamens sits around pink-tipped, pale-green carpels. Carrying long, slender, mid-green leaves, the tall flower stems splay sideways. This plant is the result of a complex mixture of species that includes *Paeonia lactiflora*, *P. officinalis*, *P. mlokosewitschii* and *P. macrophylla*.

**Breeder:** Saunders, 1950
**Height:** 90cm
**Flowers:** single, early season
**Scent:** slight
**Staking:** no

*Paeonia* 'Firelight'

### 'FLAME'

A free-flowering plant with vivid coral-pink flowers that veer in tone towards crimson rather than pink. A single row of petals, which have white streaks on the reverse, curl inwards to form a cup. In the centre the long, gold stamens surround red-tipped, soft-green carpels that bring further colour to the bloom. As the flower ages, the stamens grow finer and thin out, eventually collapsing sideways. Stiff flower stems carry mid-green leaves.

**Breeder:** Glasscock, 1939
**Height:** 80cm
**Flowers:** single, early season
**Scent:** none
**Staking:** no

*Paeonia* 'Flame'

### 'GARDEN PEACE'

Very beautiful and pure white, the bloom produces a single row of shiny petals. Initially these are flushed with pink but this quickly fades as the flower opens. In the middle sits a neat clump of gold stamens, the filaments pink at the base. Three or four long side buds are produced on the thick, dark red stems with large, dark green leaves. In a good soil the stems can grow so tall they are incapable of standing upright.

**Breeder:** Saunders, 1941
**Height:** 90cm
**Flowers:** single, early season
**Scent:** none
**Staking:** sometimes

### 'GARDEN LACE'

Although a pretty plant, the blooms are rather inconsistent in shape. The large guard petals are washed with soft-pink and on some blooms pale to near white. A central mound of wavy, occasionally divided, twisting staminodes begin deep yellow and fade to cream as they get bigger. The upright stems have one to three side stems and rich-green leaves. Registered as a hybrid but listed by the American Peony Society as a lactiflora.

**Breeder:** Hollingsworth, 1992
**Height:** 80cm
**Flowers:** Japanese, midseason
**Scent:** light
**Staking:** no

*Paeonia* 'Garden Peace'

*Paeonia* 'Goldilocks'

*Paeonia* 'Garden Lace'

### 'GOLDILOCKS'

This peony is the result of crossing the only two yellow herbaceous varieties that existed at the time. Although the blooms can be variable in shape, each produces a loose ring of large, cream guard petals. On top of these sits a thick layer of slender, soft butter-yellow petaloids. Sometimes a further cluster of large cream petals erupts from the top. The blooms are borne on strong stems with the occasional side bud and dark green foliage.

**Breeder:** Gilbertson, 1975
**Height:** 70cm
**Flowers:** double, midseason
**Scent:** none
**Staking:** no

*Paeonia* 'Henry Bockstoce'

### 'HENRY BOCKSTOCE'

An impressive dark rich-red flower with evenly sized, round, ruffled, shiny petals that overlay each other, creating a neat dome. The flower stems are extremely thick, as are the rich-green leaves, but are bare of side buds. Considered to be an excellent cut flower, although this is not a free-flowering plant.

**Breeder:** Bockstoce, 1955
**Height:** 100cm
**Flowers:** double, early season
**Scent:** none
**Staking:** yes

### 'HONOR'

This delightful plant does not bloom for long, but the shade of its delicate mid-pink flowers injects colour into the spring garden. Bright-pink to start with, the slightly crimped petals pale to soft-pink as they enlarge. In the centre are yellow stamens displaying delicate white filaments and pale-green, white-tipped carpels. The slender, fresh green leaves form an attractive loose clump.

**Breeder:** Saunders, 1941
**Height:** 75cm
**Flowers:** single, very early season
**Scent:** light
**Staking:** no

### 'HORIZON'

Very large, oval, soft-pink petals create a ruff around the immense centre of long, loose, deep yellow stamens and red-tipped, soft-green carpels. Quickly fading to palest pink from the top, the base of each petals stays a slightly deeper colour. Strong flower stems produce wavy-edged, dark green leaves but no side buds.

**Breeder:** Saunders, 1943
**Height:** 80cm
**Flowers:** single, early season
**Scent:** light
**Staking:** no

*Paeonia* 'Honor'

### 'ILLINI BELLE'

The rich dark red, rosette-shaped flowers of this peony are fabulous. Some blooms remain entirely semi-double, with just a ring of shiny petals. Others produce a flurry of short inner petals that weave themselves among central yellow stamens with red filaments, to create a fluffy flower. The straight stems, which carry no side buds, produce glossy, mid-green leaves. Not dissimilar to *Paeonia* 'Buckeye Belle' but blooms earlier.

**Breeder:** Glasscock, 1941
**Height:** 75cm
**Flowers:** semi-double, early season
**Scent:** light
**Staking:** no

*Paeonia* 'Horizon'

*Paeonia* 'Illini Belle'

### 'ILLINI WARRIOR'

Opening from a perfect ball-shaped bud, the velvety, rich-red flower forms a neatly shaped goblet. As the spoon-shaped petals grow, the bloom turns into a deep cup. In the centre, upright stamens form such a thick clump they remind me of the tendrils of a sea anemone waving around pale pink-tipped, pale-green carpels. Each flower sits on a thick stem with leathery, mid-green leaves that have a metallic tint.

**Breeder:** Glasscock/Falk, 1955
**Height:** 90cm
**Flowers:** single, early season
**Scent:** medium
**Staking:** no

*Paeonia* 'Illini Warrior'

### 'JOYCE ELLEN'

The rosy-red flowers have two rows of lightly ruffled petals. In the middle, a tight ring of golden stamens is carried on filaments of the same colour as the petals. These, in turn, surround red-tipped, bright-green carpels. The foliage is light green, and there are no side buds on the slender, but strong side stems. Named after one of the breeder's daughters.

**Breeder:** Moots, 1960
**Height:** 75cm
**Flowers:** single, early season
**Scent:** light
**Staking:** no

*Paeonia* 'Joyce Ellen'

*Paeonia* 'Late Windflower'

### 'JOHN HARVARD'

Hard to source, this handsome peony has very dark red flowers that don't fade over time and can look almost black in a certain light. The petals, which have a matt surface, are round and slightly crimped. They create a deep bowl around gold stamens that eventually loosen enough to show soft-green carpels with little pink tips. Stiff flower stems carry thick, dark green leaves, but no extra flower buds.

**Breeder:** Auten, 1939
**Height:** 90cm
**Flowers:** single, early season
**Scent:** none
**Staking:** yes

*Paeonia* 'John Harvard'

### 'LATE WINDFLOWER'

Strong, tall stems carry lots of long, slender, mid-green leaves and up to three pure white flowers. A row of wavy, oval petals forms an uneven saucer around a circle of gold stamens and two soft-green carpels that have white tips. Almost identical to 'Early Windflower', this blooms about a week later. Both plants grow into a magnificent leafy clump that harmonises well with other perennials in a border.

**Breeder:** Saunders, 1939
**Height:** 110cm
**Flowers:** single, midseason
**Scent:** none
**Staking:** no

### 'LADONNA'

This jolly flower resembles neither of its parents – lactiflora *Paeonia* 'Nippon Gold' and the hybrid *P*. 'Cytherea'. Opening mid-pink, the petals unfurl into a flat, saucer-like, fluffy bloom with a ring of slim, yellow staminodes. A flute of soft-pink petals then emerges and later all the pink petals fade unevenly to white. The blooms are borne on branched stems with mid-green leaves that resemble those of *Paeonia lactiflora*.

**Breeder:** Hollingsworth, 1997
**Height:** 80cm
**Flowers:** double, midseason
**Scent:** medium
**Staking:** no

*Paeonia* 'LaDonna'

### 'LEMON CHIFFON'

(opposite) Pale-lemon and crimped along the edges, the many layers of ruffled petals open into a large, very beautiful bloom. A ring of gold stamens and red-tipped, soft-green carpels sits at the centre where, occasionally, extra petals emerge to create a double flower. The stems, which are tinged with red, can be rather lax. They carry up to three side buds and big, reasonably glossy, mid-green leaves. AGM

**Breeder:** Reath, 1981
**Height:** 80cm
**Flowers:** double, early season
**Scent:** none
**Staking:** sometimes

### 'LAVENDER WHISPER'

A delicate-looking flower with one row of ruffled petals that open pale-pink and fade quickly to white, although a hint of pink remains. The yellow stamens, which are carried on pink-tinged filaments, create an airy mound around the small, magenta-tipped, yellow-green carpels. Stiff stems, which have no side buds, produce handsome large, oval, soft-green leaves.

**Breeder:** Klehm, 1999
**Height:** 65cm
**Flowers:** single, early season
**Scent:** light
**Staking:** no

*Paeonia* 'Lovebirds'

### 'LOVEBIRDS'

Not a free-flowering plant, this produces cupped blooms with very pale pink petals. In the centre, a ring of gold stamens surrounds red-tipped, hairy carpels that twist around each other, giving the plant its name. Red stems bear up to two side buds and very large, glossy, dark green leaves that are an asset throughout the summer. From experience this needs a damp soil, otherwise the buds fail to open.

**Breeder:** Goldsmith/Smetana 1994
**Height:** 75cm
**Flowers:** single, early season
**Scent:** light
**Staking:** no

*Paeonia* 'Lovely Rose'

*Paeonia* 'Lavender Whisper'

### 'LOVELY ROSE'

A beautiful big flower bud opens into a perfect deep bowl of bright, salmon-pink petals that are smooth and slightly notched around the edges. A thick central ring of golden stamens surrounds green, pink-tipped carpels. Unbranched flower stems produce big, mid-green leaves that have a dull sheen. Owing to the lack of side buds, all the blooms tend to open together. But don't be put off, this is a really lovely plant.

**Breeder:** Saunders, 1942
**Height:** 80cm
**Flowers:** semi-double, early season
**Scent:** none
**Staking:** no

*Paeonia* 'Lemon Chiffon' with lilac *Geranium maculatum* 'Vickie Lynn' and contrasting orange *Geum* 'Prinses Juliana'

*Paeonia* 'Mackinac Grand'

### 'MACKINAC GRAND'

A plant with big, dark red flowers. The petals display a brownish tint as they open into a full bowl around a ball of fine stamens. Inside the stamens, soft-green, pale pink-tipped carpels are just visible. The long, lax flower stems carry large, glossy leaves. A little confusingly, the American Peony Society lists this peony as 'The Mackinac Grand' although it was registered as 'Machanic Grand'. The name at the top is used by most nurseries. AGM

**Breeder:** Reath, 1992
**Height:** 90cm
**Flowers:** semi-double, midseason
**Scent:** none
**Staking:** yes

### 'MAI FLEURI'

Opening into a deep cup, the slightly lumpy-surfaced, large petals are palest pink around the edges and pastel peach-yellow in the middle. A central ring of gold stamens floats on filaments with maroon bases. Straight stems carry the flowers stiffly above the handsome, broad, bright-green leaves. A beautiful plant and among the earliest peonies to bloom. One of its parents is shade-tolerant *Paeonia wittmanniana*.

**Breeder:** Lemoine, 1905
**Height:** 75cm
**Flowers:** single, very early season
**Scent:** none
**Staking:** no

### 'MANY HAPPY RETURNS'

A loose ball of spiky, bright, rosy-red petals becomes fuller and smoother as the petals grow and age. Around the base the large, round guard petals soon curl downwards, showing off the ball of petals. Borne on strong, upright, unbranched stems, the shiny, wavy, mid-green leaves create a cheerful neat, mounding plant.

**Breeder:** Hollingsworth, 1986
**Height:** 80cm
**Flowers:** double, midseason
**Scent:** none
**Staking:** no

*Paeonia* 'Mai Fleuri'

### 'MAY LILAC'

At first the large, lightly ruffled petals open into a soft lilac-pink goblet. At the base of the petals a faint flush of deep pink is apparent. As the petals age into a wide cup, they fade rapidly to palest pink, but a dark flush remains at the bottom of each. A dense ring of fine gold stamens sits around the furry, soft-pink carpels, which have large red tips. The attractive leaves are very large, fairly round, shiny and light green.

**Breeder:** Saunders, 1950
**Height:** 80cm
**Flowers:** semi-double, early season
**Scent:** none
**Staking:** no

*Paeonia* 'Many Happy Returns'

*Paeonia* 'May Lilac'

*Paeonia* 'Merry Mayshine'

## 'MERRY MAYSHINE'

Eye-catching and rich-red, the petals of the flower are lightly pleated. They open into a wide cup around a thick ring of yellow stamens and soft-green carpels that have tips the same colour as the petals. Slim stems bear the slender, fern-like leaves characteristic of one of its parents *Paeonia tenuifolia*. A short plant, this was originally called 'Zelda' but the name changed when it was introduced.

**Breeder:** Saunders/Hollingsworth/Smetana, 1994
**Height:** 60cm
**Flowers:** single, early season
**Scent:** light
**Staking:** no

*Paeonia* 'Montezuma'

## 'MONTEZUMA'

Opening into a brilliant-scarlet goblet, as the flower matures the petals, which remain scooped along the edges, evolve into a deep cup. In the centre a mass of unruly, yellow stamens form a big flat mound. Despite its single flowers, the thick stems are so long and lax they tend to fall over. The mid-green leaves are very like those of *Paeonia officinalis* 'Rubra Plena'.

**Breeder:** Saunders, 1943
**Height:** 100cm
**Flowers:** single, early season
**Scent:** light
**Staking:** yes

*Paeonia* 'Moonrise'

## 'MOONRISE'

Big, round, green buds open into beautiful, pale-lemon flowers with two rows of petals that form a lightly ruffled, wide dish around a golden dome of stamens and large, white-tipped, soft-green carpels. The strong, light green stems carry three or four side buds and semi-glossy, light green leaves. It grows really well for me in soil that can be wet during the winter.

**Breeder:** Saunders, 1949
**Height:** 90cm
**Flowers:** single, early season
**Scent:** none
**Staking:** no

## 'NOSEGAY'

One of the most perfect early flowering varieties, the softly coloured blooms are washed with soft-pink as they open. As the petals widen into a broad saucer, the pink tints fade, leaving the flower softest apricot. The slim, gold stamens with red-based, white filaments form a circle around the woolly coated, soft-green carpels that are tipped with red. The deeply divided, mid-green leaves make a beautiful loose clump.

**Breeder:** Saunders, 1950
**Height:** 70cm
**Flowers:** single, very early season
**Scent:** none
**Staking:** no

*Paeonia* 'Nosegay'

Hybrid peonies | 133

*Paeonia* 'Picotee' blooms in early May along with *Chaerophyllum hirsutum* 'Roseum' (Hairy chervil) and *Aquilegia vulgaris* 'Alba'

### 'OLD FAITHFUL'

Glorious, rich dark raspberry-red – a colour that is evenly spread across the velvety, evenly sized petals. These unfurl to reveal a few gold stamens that disappear as an inner cluster of petals enlarges with age to create a double bloom. Matt, mid-green leaves are borne on strong stems that have no side buds and hold the flower reasonably upright. May need staking in windy, wet conditions.

**Breeder:** Glasscock/Falk, 1964
**Height:** 90cm
**Flowers:** double, midseason
**Scent:** none
**Staking:** sometimes

*Paeonia* 'Paula Fay'

### 'PICOTEE'

(opposite) At first the petals of the goblet-shaped, white flowers are touched with lilac-pink along the edges. As the bloom widens into a deep cup, the pink tones disappear. An upright ring of fine yellow stamens with magenta filaments encases the wavy-tipped, green carpels. Each fleeting bloom is borne neatly, just above a tidy clump of very large, fresh-green leaves. In my garden, this is the best of the very early blooming peonies.

**Breeder:** Saunders, 1949
**Height:** 70cm
**Flowers:** single, very early season
**Scent:** none
**Staking:** no

### 'PAULA FAY'

Five ruffled layers of waxy, vivid-pink petals form a deep cup. In the middle a dense little boss of gold stamens allows the soft pink-tipped, soft-green carpels to poke through. I have grown this plant for so long I can recognise it simply from the shiny, light green leaves. The flowers are at their best in warm springs because the large buds, which are borne on stiff stems, can take forever to open. Named after the breeder's sister-in-law.

**Breeder:** Fay, 1968
**Height:** 90cm
**Flowers:** semi-double, early season
**Scent:** none
**Staking:** no

*Paeonia* 'Old Faithful'

*Paeonia* 'Pink Pom Pom'

### 'PINK HAWAIIAN CORAL'

The short, rich salmon-pink petals, which are notched along the top, open into a shallow bowl. As the bloom opens further, the petals uncurl and fade in colour to create a frilly, soft-pink dome. The few golden stamens twist around pale pink-tipped, green carpels and gradually turn into a flat ring. Strong stems, which carry a few side buds, bear long, semi-double, mid-green leaves. Good for cutting.

**Breeder:** Klehm, 1981
**Height:** 90cm
**Flowers:** semi-double, early season
**Scent:** light
**Staking:** no

*Paeonia* 'Pink Hawaiian Coral'

### 'PINK POM POM'

Bright rose-pink and short, the petals are deeply serrated – like sharks' teeth – along the tops. These open into a tight ball, but as the large, lightly ruffled guard petals curl back, the inner petals form a perfect swirling dome. A yellow glow emanates from deep down within the petals. The strong stems produce a few side buds that may open together plus dark green leaves. Not the most robust plant, this has a lovely fruity fragrance.

**Breeder:** Reath, 1991
**Height:** 90cm
**Flowers:** double, midseason
**Scent:** light
**Staking:** no

### 'PRAIRIE MOON'

Small, slightly furry buds unfurl into pale-lemon cups. As they open further into a wide saucer the petals pale to softest cream and become almost translucent. The flowers are filled with light yellow stamens and have large, white-tipped, green carpels. No side buds are produced on the stiff stems that carry slightly shiny, mid-green leaves. I find this difficult to grow in our heavy, rather wet soil and it would fare better in a dryish soil.

**Breeder:** Fay, 1959
**Height:** 60cm
**Flowers:** single, very early season
**Scent:** none
**Staking:** no

*Paeonia* 'Prairie Moon'

### 'RASPBERRY CHARM'

Resembling a big, vivid-pink waterlily, the flower is composed of deeply notched petals. These open to reveal a broad ring of dark yellow stamens and bright pink-tipped, soft-green carpels. The colour of the bloom does not fade until the petals drop. Strong, straight stems with semi-shiny, mid-green leaves each carry a single bloom. Recommended for cutting.

**Breeder:** Wissing/Klehm, 1985
**Height:** 80cm
**Flowers:** semi-double, midseason
**Scent:** none
**Staking:** sometimes

*Paeonia* 'Red Grace'

### 'RED CHARM'

(opposite) If you want a rich-red peony, this is the one to choose. Long, notched petals, sometimes with silver tips, are arranged into V-shaped layers that form a tightly packed ball. Around the base sits a circle of large guard petals. Strong flower stems, which carry mid-green leaves but no buds, support the large double blooms well, staying upright except in the windiest of weather. AGM

**Breeder:** Glasscock, 1944
**Height:** 90cm
**Flowers:** double, early season
**Scent:** none
**Staking:** no

*Paeonia* 'Raspberry Charm'

### 'RED GRACE'

Long, shiny, deep scarlet petals are so tightly packed they create a ball. At first the guard petals are obvious, but as the inner petals grow and enlarge, all the petals grow to a similar size. The stems are stiff and do tend to relax sideways but don't entirely collapse. They carry mid-green leaves and a few side buds are present.

**Breeder:** Glasscock/Klehm, 1980
**Height:** 80cm
**Flowers:** double, midseason
**Scent:** none
**Staking:** yes

*Paeonia* 'Red Red Rose'

### 'RED RED ROSE'

The bright-red flowers have two rows of very large, wavy petals that are slightly notched along the tops. These open into a goblet, but as the flower ages it forms a wide, ruffled bloom. The gold stamens, which are borne on red filaments, make a big, loose mound around pink-tipped, soft-green carpels. Thick stems with glossy, fresh-green leaves carry the flowers but they are too long to stay reliably upright.

**Breeder:** Saunders, 1942
**Height:** 100cm
**Flowers:** semi-double, midseason
**Scent:** none
**Staking:** yes

*Paeonia* 'Red Charm'

*Paeonia* 'Requiem'

### 'REQUIEM'

Opening into a very pale pink, faintly apple-scented bloom, the waxy petals turn almost white with age. Long, slender staminodes, which are red at the bottom and curl at the top, create a central dome that is punctured by the bright-pink tips of the soft-green carpels. Strong flower stems carry one or two side buds and dark green leaves. If any unforeseen very late-spring frosts happen to catch the blooms, some of the staminodes will inevitably become blackened.

**Breeder:** Saunders, 1941
**Height:** 85cm
**Flowers:** single, early to midseason
**Scent:** light
**Staking:** no

*Paeonia* 'Rosedale'

### 'ROSEDALE'

Held in loose layers, the petals of this deep cerise-red flower curve inwards to form a rose-shaped bloom. Neither form nor colour changes as the flower ages and the petals remain largely cupped around a broad ring of rich-yellow stamens and red-tipped, soft-green carpels. A dwarf plant, the upright stems bear dark green leaves but no side stems.

**Breeder:** Auten, 1936
**Height:** 55cm
**Flowers:** semi-double, early season
**Scent:** light
**Staking:** no

*Paeonia* 'Rose Garland'

### 'ROSE GARLAND'

A single layer of spoon-shaped, bright-pink petals opens into a shallow goblet around a large, tight ring of golden stamens and reddish pink-tipped, soft-green carpels. As the petals become bigger with age, the flower evolves into an unruly, loose cup and the petals develop lightly serrated edges. The upright stems carry soft-green leaves but no side buds.

**Breeder:** Saunders, 1943
**Height:** 75cm
**Flowers:** single, midseason
**Scent:** none
**Staking:** no

### 'ROSELETTE'

In a good spring, this is a truly delightful plant. Smooth, apple-blossom pink petals unfurl into a cup around the rich-yellow stamens and furry, soft-green carpels with small red tips. With age, the bloom opens into a large saucer and the petal colour fades quickly, and sometimes unevenly, to pale-pink. The strong red stems, which carry glossy, slim, mid-green leaves, are bare of side buds.

**Breeder:** Saunders, 1950
**Height:** 85cm
**Flowers:** single, very early season
**Scent:** light
**Staking:** no

*Paeonia* 'Roselette'

*Paeonia* 'Salmon Beauty'

### 'SALMON BEAUTY'

Seen at their best, the deep shrimp-pink flowers are perfectly formed, if sparsely produced. As they open fully, the tightly packed layers of curved petals form a low dome and a ring of large guard petals sits around the base of the flower. In time, the petal colour fades unevenly to leave paler edges. The long, unbranched flower stems, which have mid-green leaves, are unable to stay upright owing to the weight of the blooms.

**Breeder:** Glasscock/Auten, 1939
**Height:** 75cm
**Flowers:** double, early season
**Scent:** none
**Staking:** yes

*Paeonia* 'Salmon Dream'

### 'SALMON DREAM'

Four rows of round, ruffled, thick, soft salmon-pink petals open into a cup. In time, the bloom widens into a rather flat frilly flower with a ring of slim, gold stamens and pale pink-tipped, soft-green carpels. The strong, unbranched stems produce handsome broad, glossy, bright-green leaves. An illustrious parentage of *Paeonia* 'Paula Fay' and *P.* 'Moonrise' has produced this good, early blooming and upright offspring.

**Breeder:** Reath, 1979
**Height:** 85cm
**Flowers:** semi-double, midseason
**Scent:** medium
**Staking:** no

*Paeonia* 'Scarlet O'Hara'

### 'SCARLET O'HARA'

Enticing big, round flower buds unfold into deep scarlet-red goblets with two rows of large petals. In the middle, the neat, thick ring of gold stamens edges the pink-tipped, light green carpels. In time, the petals grow bigger and soften in tone to a pinkish red. Strong flower stems carry a few side buds and mid-green leaves whose jagged edges make this plant easy to identify. AGM

**Breeder:** Falk/Glasscock, 1956
**Height:** 90cm
**Flowers:** single, early season
**Scent:** light
**Staking:** sometimes

### 'SHOW GIRL'

Large, slightly ruffled, mid-pink guard petals with lightly scalloped tops form a deep bowl around the wide centre of rich butter-yellow staminodes. These pale with age and as the guard petals fall flat, the centre develops into a large, pale-cream dome. If it wasn't for the thick, mid-green leaves this plant could easily be mistaken for a lactiflora, which explains the absence of a category alongside its entry in the American Peony register.

**Breeder:** Hollingsworth, 1984
**Height:** 90cm
**Flowers:** Japanese, midseason
**Scent:** none
**Staking:** no

*Paeonia* 'Show Girl'

### 'SOFT SALMON SAUCER'

The soft-pink blooms are at their loveliest when they first open into a small goblet. At the base of each inward-curved petal is a flush of deep pink. Soft-yellow stamens create a thick fluffy ring around the lipstick pink-tipped, soft-green carpels. With age, the thick petals unfold into a flat saucer and the tops fade nearly to white, leaving the bottom half of each petal pink. Borne on stiff stems, the leaves are bright-green.

**Breeder:** Cousins/Klehm, 1981
**Height:** 80cm
**Flowers:** single, early season
**Scent:** light
**Staking:** no

*Paeonia* 'Soft Salmon Saucer'

### 'SUGAR N' SPICE'

Eight extremely large, bright rich-pink petals, which are very lightly ruffled, unfold from big buds into a saucer. They are set round an immense, low dome of disorderly gold stamens that hide the carpels. As the flower matures, the petals become untidy. Red-tinged flower stems, although strong, never grow straight and carry big shiny, light green leaves but no side buds. With us, this peony starts into growth before almost any other.

**Breeder:** Rogers, 1988
**Height:** 85cm
**Flowers:** single, very early season
**Scent:** none
**Staking:** yes

*Paeonia* 'Sugar n' Spice'

### 'STARLIGHT'

On opening into a cupped soft-yellow flower, the crinkled petals are lightly flushed with pink. As they unfold further, they form a big, flat, palest cream saucer. The tight ball of golden stamens, which surround woolly, white-tipped, small green carpels, thins out with age and then turn wispy. Broad, semi-glossy, mid-green leaves are carried on thick stems with one or two side buds. A peony with the same parentage as *P.* 'Claire de Lune'.

**Breeder:** Saunders, 1949
**Height:** 80cm
**Flowers:** single, very early season
**Scent:** light
**Staking:** no

*Paeonia* 'Starlight'

### 'SUMMER GLOW'

When first open, the many-layered petals create a big, soft-apricot ball, which is quite extraordinary and very beautiful. In time, the petals fade to pale-lemon with hints of peach radiating from deep inside the flower. A deep central dip develops but no stamens or carpels are visible. Not a particularly free-flowering plant, the thick stems carrying one or two side buds and large, glossy, bright-green leaves.

**Breeder:** Hollingsworth, 1992
**Height:** 85cm
**Flowers:** double, mid to late season
**Scent:** light
**Staking:** no

*Paeonia* 'Summer Glow'

*Paeonia* 'Sunny Girl'

## 'SUNNY GIRL'

Apricot tones glow from deep inside the large petals creating a soft ochre-yellow flower. Two layers of guard petals open flat, forming a plate around a low, broad dome of loose, ruffled petals. A few upright, curling stamens and red-tipped carpels are just visible. Surrounding the flowers are large, thinly textured, light green leaves and a few side buds. This is a most impressive flower even if the long, strong stems are so lax they fall over.

**Breeder:** Laning, 1985
**Height:** 75cm
**Flowers:** double, early season
**Scent:** none
**Staking:** yes

*Paeonia* 'Tango'

## 'TANGO'

This eye-catching flower has very big, gently wavy, scarlet petals that open into a wide cup when mature. They create a ruff around a low centre of yellow stamens with scarlet filaments, which in turn relax into a circle around shiny, soft-green carpels. The thick flower stems, which are too long to stay upright, bear semi-glossy, mid-green leaves.

**Breeder:** Auten, 1956
**Height:** 100cm
**Flowers:** single, early season
**Scent:** none
**Staking:** yes

*Paeonia* 'Walter Mains'

## 'WALTER MAINS'

A lovely flower with burgundy-red guard petals that are wavy, round and possess a satin sheen. In the centre the crimson stamens, which are edged with yellow, open into a low boss. As they age, the crimson colouration retreats and the stamens turn almost entirely gold. Slender, stiff, red stems carry glossy, mid-green leaves but no side buds.

**Breeder:** Mains, 1957
**Height:** 85cm
**Flowers:** Japanese, early season
**Scent:** none
**Staking:** no

## 'WHITE INNOCENCE'

This surprising bloom is also unique. The stamens have been replaced by a small, tight dome of curling, pale-cream pistils (I usually refer to these as carpel tips). Inside the dome are two furry, green carpels. Fluttering around the edge is a row of large, pure white guard petals. Although beautiful, this peony produces only a few flowers on very long stems that carry a few long side stems and mid-green leaves.

**Breeder:** Saunders, 1947
**Height:** 120cm
**Flowers:** single, very early season
**Scent:** none
**Staking:** yes

*Paeonia* 'White Innocence'

Hybrid peonies | 141

# INTERSECTIONAL PEONIES

Stunning is the word that best describes the very large flowers of this wonderful group of peonies. The blooms are usually semi-double or single and although double forms are slowly becoming available, some are still incredibly expensive. The earliest intersectional in my garden blooms in mid-May; the majority are in flower towards the end of May into early June, creating a rainbow of colour that can last until the end of the month. Opening one at a time, the blooms crown a clump of woody stems that carry leathery, much-divided leaves.

Intersectionals result from crossing two distinctly different peonies – a woody tree peony with a herbaceous type. Their offspring are F1 hybrids and to date none has produced fertile seed. To develop a new hybrid, breeders have to start from scratch with parent plants, which explains why there are currently relatively few varieties and why they are similar in appearance.

## Itoh Hybrids

Intersectionals are also known as Itoh hybrids to acknowledge the Japanese breeder who first raised these plants. Dr. Toichi Itoh began breeding peonies as a hobby in Japan during the 1940s. Realising there was a distinct lack of herbaceous peonies in yellow – a colour found only in tree-peony flowers – he decided to cross Paeonia 'Alice Harding', a tree peony known in Japan as 'Kinko', with P. 'Kakaden', a white lactiflora peony. It is said that he attempted this cross over 2,000 times before raising just six seedlings. Finally, in 1964 the seedlings bloomed and included plants with double yellow flowers. Sadly, Dr. Itoh died in 1956 so didn't witness his great achievement.

Thankfully, the seedlings were not lost. Retired American accountant Louis Smirnow, now a nurseryman and peony collector, acquired the surviving plants from Itoh's widow. In 1974 Smirnow registered four of them under the names 'Yellow Crown' (a plant still readily available) 'Yellow Dream', 'Yellow Emperor', and 'Yellow Heaven'. This momentous move encouraged peony breeders and hybridisers around the world to create more intersectional peonies.

## The Next Generation

A decade after Itoh's peonies were registered, Don Hollingsworth and Roger Anderson introduced their own intersectional varieties. They were not the first American hybridisers to attempt to cross tree peonies with herbaceous types. In the 1960s Roy Pehrson managed to raise a few intersectional seedlings but the flowers were incomplete on opening and the leaves spotty – two traits seen as genetic defects. In 1976 Roger Anderson started his own breeding programme, although it took him a number of years to find the right combination of parents that would produce viable seeds.

## Intersectional Parents

Anderson stuck with the same two reliable parent plants to create his first intersectionals. Woody Paeonia 'Golden Era', a yellow lutea hybrid introduced by David Reath, proved excellent in combination with herbaceous pink, single-flowered Paeonia 'Martha Washington', a lactiflora peony little known in the UK.

When I visited Don Hollingsworth in Kansas some years ago, he explained how one of his introductions came about. Rushing out to visit friends, Don was determined not to waste the pollen from lutea hybrid Paeonia 'Alice Harding'. Flower in hand, he searched around for another bloom to transfer the pollen onto and came across Paeonia 'Martha Washington' in full flower at the front of his house. One of the seedlings of this fortunate cross was Paeonia 'Garden Treasure', introduced in 1984 and winner of the American Peony Society gold medal. Ten years later a similar plant raised by Roger Anderson, Paeonia 'Bartzella', also won gold.

## Micropropagation

Having raised new intersectionals, the next step was to propagate them in sufficient numbers to sell. Conventional methods are slow, particularly as the crowns of intersectionals are incredibly woody and therefore difficult to divide.

In the early years of this century, Canadian company Plantek began propagating intersectionals using the laboratory-based method of micropropagation. A technique used to multiply plants rapidly, it has not been as successful with older peony cultivars. To start the process, clean, disease-free material must be collected from stem and leaf cells but in older plants this tends to be 'dirty', leading to contamination and failure. Progress has been made with some peonies and as newcomers, intersectionals are the perfect subjects.

While it can take many decades for a peony, once registered, to become widely available, micropropagation has speeded up the process. Many intersectional varieties are now so freely available that plants once costing over US$200 now sell for the same price as a tried-and-tested herbaceous peony bred 50 years ago.

*Paeonia* 'Morning Lilac' is often produced by micropropagation. In the initial years the petals can be smooth, in later years they open crumpled with ragged edges

Peach *Paeonia* 'Singing in the Rain' (front) and dark pink *P.* 'Yankee Doodle Dandy' in a long border with lactiflora *P.* 'Golden Frolic' and *Stipa gigantea* (rear)

## THE INTERSECTIONAL PLANT

Intersectional peonies are as easy to grow as any other peony, and in some ways they are more satisfactory. With one or two exceptions, all the intersectional peonies I have planted don't grow too tall, reaching no more than 75cm in height. While reminiscent of tree peonies in habit, they are herbaceous, leafy plants with foliage that dies back over winter. Intersectionals have two distinct shapes: upright and wide, or forming a broad dome. The blooms are large and spaced at even intervals across the plant.

**The flowers** of intersectional peonies can be yellow, pink or red. The colours can also change over the life of the bloom. Flashes and smears of other tones often add further decoration to the petals, while flares of a richer colour stain the base of each. Almost all the varieties currently available produce semi-double or single flowers with one or two layers of wavy or ruffled petals. Owing to their impressive size, the leaves on some varieties can obstruct the unfurling petals so the flower is unable to achieve a symmetrical shape.

In the centre sits a group of large, eye-catching carpels, adding further drama to the flower. The number of carpels can differ from year to year and some are thickly coated with hairs, while the tips provide further colour. As the petals unfurl, the sheath that covers the young carpels splits to leave a low rim between the carpels and the stamens, which carry very little or no pollen. The absence of guard petals allows for a graduation in petal size as the bloom matures.

The blooms of *Paeonia* 'Cora Louise' are spaced neatly around the plant

*Paeonia* 'Julia Rose' blooms freely here in June, despite being grown on the north side of a hawthorn hedge

Initially, the soft-green carpels of *Paeonia* 'First Arrival' are covered by a red sheath

In a different year, the same *Paeonia* 'First Arrival' plant can produce more carpels

*Paeonia* 'Garden Treasure' with a large centre of hairy, pink-tipped carpels

Intersectionals produce many buds over a number of weeks

New shoots on intersectionals will appear on unpruned stems and from the soil

In October the foliage of *Paeonia* 'Unique' displays autumn tints

**The leaves and stems** share similarities with herbaceous and tree peonies but also have unique features. In spring, small, pink eyes can be seen round the base of the plant, poking out of the soil. These are produced from a thick crown that also carries the roots. When the stems first grow they are soft; in time they turn sufficiently stiff and woody that no staking is required. The leaves emerge on the new stems and from any old woody stems that have not been pruned out and are still alive. Leaving old stems to grow, however, will result in an unevenly shaped plant: the old growth will be taller and rise up above the new, shorter stems and leaves.

In size and shape the leaves are similar to those of tree peonies, but are carried on a much shorter plant. Consequently, the canopy they form will reach the ground and completely cover the soil beneath the plant. The leaves, which are truly handsome, are so thick and leathery they don't suffer from diseases associated with other herbaceous peonies. In autumn, they are often attractively tinted with red and as the days get shorter, they will simply and cleanly drop from the stems, leaving a pile at the base of the plant.

As the stems reach their ultimate seasonal height, flower buds form at the top and on the lower side branches. Two or three side buds are carried on each stem. These open gradually, often one at a time over a period of three or four weeks, giving intersectionals a longer flowering period compared to other herbaceous peonies.

### A–Z of Intersectional: Terms (pp.147–153)

**CARPELS** on most peonies contain an ovary that develops into a seed when pollinated. Intersectional peonies are generally sterile, so no seeds are likely to be produced. The tip (the stigma) is often a different colour to the carpel.

**AGM** The Award of Garden Merit given to the most garden-worthy peonies. Updated in 2021 after five-year trials at RHS Wisley.

**BREEDER NAME & DATE,** where known and date of registration.

**FLOWERS** i) the flower form (see p.9)
ii) the period when the peonies are in bloom on our nursery:
**Early** mid- to late May
**Midseason** early to mid-June
**Late** mid-June

At the base of the woody growth, the pink eyes will grow into new stems in spring

*Paeonia* 'Bartzella' is capable of producing one or two flowers in autumn

*Paeonia* 'Bartzella' in winter, before its spring prune

*Paeonia* 'Bartzella'

### 'BARTZELLA'

Soft-yellow flowers open into a shallow dish with narrow, soft-red flares staining the base of each ruffled petal. Yellow stamens assemble themselves into a straggly ring around white-tipped, soft-green carpels. A short plant that carries its lemon-scented blooms just above a round dome of semi-glossy, mid-green leaves stained here and there with red. In autumn, my plant has one or two new shoots that often produce flowers. AGM

**Breeder:** Anderson, 1986
**Height:** 75cm
**Flowers:** semi-double, midseason
**Scent:** medium

### 'CALLIE'S MEMORY'

The wash of raspberry-red over the pale-yellow petals is so pronounced it turns the bloom soft-apricot. As the red tint fades, the edges remain lightly stained but hefty smudges are left at the base of the petals. These form a broad ring around the slim stamens and soft yellow-tipped, green carpels. When fully open, almost the entire bloom has turned soft-yellow. The flowers are carried on a level with the broad mound of mid-green leaves that are soft-green beneath and slightly glossy above.

**Breeder:** Anderson, 1999
**Height:** 80cm
**Flowers:** semi-double, midseason
**Scent:** light

*Paeonia* 'Callie's Memory'

### 'CORA LOUISE'

On opening, the ruffled petals are very light pink – a diluted shade of the strong magenta that flares upwards from the base. As it evolves into a shaggy bloom, the pink tones disappear, leaving the flower bright white. A sparse gathering of loose yellow stamens sits around yellow-tipped, soft-green carpels. Each flower is evenly spaced around the upright clump of wide, mid-green leaves that are pale-green underneath. AGM

**Breeder:** Anderson, 1986
**Height:** 75cm
**Flowers:** semi-double, midseason
**Scent:** none
**Staking:** no

*Paeonia* 'Cora Louise'

### 'DARK EYES'

Small but handsome, the flower has ten wavy, thick, dark burgundy-red petals. These unfurl to create, an irregularly shaped bloom. At the centre, the soft-yellow stamens, which are carried on red filaments, are scattered around pale-green carpels with long, pale-pink tips. The blooms open at the same level as the dark green leaves.

**Breeder:** Laning, 1996
**Height:** 60cm
**Flowers:** single, early to midseason
**Scent:** none

### 'FIRST ARRIVAL'

True to its name, this is the earliest intersectional to bloom in our garden. Initially this lovely large flower is a rich lavender-pink, then the petals fade to pure pink. Within, a ring of golden stamens is outlined by a wide circle of magenta. Decorative white carpels with big, white-lined, pink tips, are divided into many sections. Long, branched stems bear matt, soft-green foliage. Not excessively leafy, the plant grows into a round bush and is perfect for borders. AGM

**Breeder:** Anderson, 1986
**Height:** 75cm
**Flowers:** semi-double, early season
**Scent:** light

*Paeonia* 'First Arrival'

*Paeonia* 'Dark Eyes'

*Paeonia* 'Garden Treasure'

### 'GARDEN TREASURE'

Lemon-scented and lemon-yellow, the bloom opens from a beautifully shaped bud into a big rosette. The ruffled petals decrease in size around the woolly, pink-tipped, dark green carpels which are highlighted by short red flares. Hugging the carpels are the remnants of the soft-yellow sheath and a single ring of yellow stamens. Growing into a wide dome of mid-green leaves, this resembles *Paeonia* 'Bartzella' (p.147) but was introduced two years earlier.

**Breeder:** Hollingsworth, 1984
**Height:** 70cm
**Flowers:** semi-double, midseason
**Scent:** medium

### 'HILLARY'

From a distance, the loose-petalled flowers look lake-red, a shade favoured by watercolour painters. Up close, the petals are actually soft-yellow but heavily stained and speckled with red. As they open into a shaggy flat bloom, small red flashes appear around the pale-yellow stamens and the cluster of cream-tipped, soft-green carpels. In time, the red wash diminishes and the strongly scented flower fades to very pale pink. The blooms nestle among mid-green leaves and the plant forms a spreading bush.

**Breeder:** Anderson, 1999
**Height:** 75cm
**Flowers:** semi-double, midseason
**Scent:** heavy

### 'JOANNA MARLENE'

This chameleon-like flower opens a similar colour to *Paeonia* 'Julia Rose'. Loose layers of petals that are scooped, like the bowl of a spoon, are paler along the edges and backs. As the bloom ages, the pink tints disappear on the inner petals, leaving a wash of pink on the outer layer. Pointed red flares form a star around a wide, wispy ring of stamens and cream-tipped, soft-green carpels. The blooms open just proud of the slender, mid-green foliage.

**Breeder:** Anderson, 1999
**Height:** 75cm
**Flowers:** semi-double, midseason
**Scent:** none

*Paeonia* 'Hillary'

*Paeonia* 'Joanna Marlene'

### 'JULIA ROSE'

On opening, the long petals display rich tones of dark red-apricot that dissolves over time to soft-lemon, leaving a wash of apricot and red staining the edges. The petals curl slightly inwards and form two rows, creating a wide bowl around very fine stamens and cream-tipped, soft-green carpels. The blooms, which have a spicy scent, are borne on long stems with mid-green leaves that create a free-flowering, wide but dense mound.

**Breeder:** Anderson, 1991
**Height:** 75cm
**Flowers:** semi-double, early season
**Scent:** light

*Paeonia* 'Julia Rose'

#### 'LEMON DREAM'

The lightly ruffled, lemon petals are lacking the characteristic splashes of colour apparent on other intersectional blooms. Just an occasional streak or a few very short strokes of magenta can be detected under the small circle of golden stamens. Semi-double in shape, the blooms are not dissimilar to those of one of its parents, white lactiflora 'Minnie Shaylor'. Not a particularly free-flowering plant, the blooms are carried just above a round mound of glossy, dark green leaves.

**Breeder:** Anderson, 1999
**Height:** 75cm
**Flowers:** semi-double, midseason
**Scent:** none

*Paeonia* 'Lemon Dream'

#### 'LOVE AFFAIR'

Pure white flowers on intersectionals are, as yet, rare and such plants are not very robust. With their cupped white petals, these blooms resemble those of lactiflora peonies in shape. The stamens are produced sparsely and the soft-green carpels have large, salmon-pink tips. Matt, mid-green leaves, which are not abundant, create a short, round clump. A mutation of a primrose-yellow flowered plant called *Paeonia* 'Prairie Sunshine', also introduced by Don Hollingsworth.

**Breeder:** Hollingsworth, 2005
**Height:** 60cm
**Flowers:** semi-double, late season
**Scent:** light

#### 'LOLLIPOP'

Something of a curiosity, this peony produces flowers that are totally inconsistent in terms of petal colour and markings. Lines and splashes of magenta thickly overlay the soft-yellow petals, sometimes appearing in distinct vertical 'candy' stripes up the petals. At other times, this strong tone is so diffused, the bloom turns almost apricot in colour. The flowers open level with the semi-glossy, mid-green leaves.

**Breeder:** Anderson, 1999
**Height:** 70cm
**Flowers:** semi-double, midseason
**Scent:** none

*Paeonia* 'Love Affair'

*Paeonia* 'Lollipop'

#### 'MAGICAL MYSTERY TOUR'

When in full bloom this peony is simply glorious. A low, broad dome of slightly glossy, fresh-green leaves is studded with reasonably large, peach-coloured blooms, which when they first open are rose-pink. Over time, some of the gently ruffled petals fade to pale-yellow. Behind the sparse ring of gold stamens, the dark red stains form a lovely star shape, and in the middle is a cluster of cream-tipped, soft-green stamens.

**Breeder:** Smith, 2002
**Height:** 75cm
**Flowers:** semi-double, midseason
**Scent:** light

*Paeonia* 'Magical Mystery Tour'

### 'MORNING LILAC'

In its first flowering season, the vivid purple-red blooms have smooth, even-coloured petals. In subsequent years, fine white lines run down the ragged-topped petals giving them a streaked appearance. Soft-yellow stamens encircle soft pink-tipped, pale-green carpels and you can just see the remains of the bright-pink sheath curling around the base of the carpels. A dark purple star is also visible. Long stems carry the blooms above the mid-green foliage.

**Breeder:** Anderson, 1999
**Height:** 70cm
**Flowers:** semi-double, early season
**Scent:** none

*Paeonia* 'Morning Lilac'

### 'NEW MILLENNIUM'

This lovely plant has lots of bright coral-pink flowers, a colour that is rather fruity. Three rows of gently ruffled petals open flat around a centre of small, gold stamens that splay out around small, soft-green carpels with cream-tips. As the bloom ages, the base of the coral-pink petals fades, turning them soft-yellow. Borne on long stems, the blooms are carried above an upright clump of mid-green leaves that have a dull sheen. AGM

**Breeder:** Anderson, 2012
**Height:** 70cm
**Flowers:** semi-double, midseason
**Scent:** none

*Paeonia* 'Norwegian Blush'

### 'NORWEGIAN BLUSH'

Not particularly free-flowering, this peony produces pure pink blooms consisting of eight to ten large petals with lightly frayed edges. Fine, soft-yellow stamens skirt the soft-yellow-tipped, pale-green carpels that are topped with small, pale-pink tips. The foliage is, unusually, a matt dark green in colour and the leaves are fairly large.

**Breeder:** Anderson, 1999
**Height:** 75cm
**Flowers:** single, midseason
**Scent:** none

*Paeonia* 'New Millennium'

### 'PASTEL SPLENDOR'

On first opening, the petals are bright pink and this colour is spread thickly around the edges. As the bloom evolves it turns mainly apricot, although very fine lines of pink remain along the petal edges. Dramatic, broad burgundy-red flares appear at the base of the petals, set round a thick dome of curling stamens. Hidden beneath them are white-tipped, pale-green carpels. In hot summers, the blooms may fade to white. Mid-green foliage grows into a broad mound.

**Breeder:** Anderson/Seidl, 1996
**Height:** 75cm
**Flowers:** single, midseason
**Scent:** none

*Paeonia* 'Pastel Splendor'

*Paeonia* 'Scarlet Heaven'

### 'SCARLET HEAVEN'

A single row of scarlet petals, slightly pointed at the top, is cupped around a slender ring of soft-yellow stamens with red filaments. Right in the middle sit large, soft cerise-pink, pale-green carpels. Slender stems carry semi-glossy, mid-green leaves and the plant forms a neat dome. Similar in colour to *Paeonia* 'Unique', but blooms later and is much shorter in stature.

**Breeder:** Anderson, 1999
**Height:** 60cm
**Flowers:** single, late midseason
**Scent:** light

*Paeonia* 'Sequestered Sunshine'

### 'SEQUESTERED SUNSHINE'

Almost all the same tone of soft-lemon, the petals are very lightly touched at the base with soft-red. Not particularly free-flowering, this plant carries each perfectly shaped, large, fluffy bloom neatly above the rich-green leaves. One of its parents is the lovely semi-double, white lactiflora *Paeonia* 'Miss America'.

**Breeder:** Anderson, 1999
**Height:** 75cm
**Flowers:** semi-double, midseason
**Scent:** none

*Paeonia* 'Singing In The Rain'

### 'SINGING IN THE RAIN'

Opening cupped and rosy-pink, the blooms are evenly spaced over a wide but low mound of glossy, rich-green leaves. As the two rows of petals unfurl, only the edges of the long, heart-shaped petals stay peach; the rest of the flower quickly turns lemon. A thick ring of gold stamens encases white-tipped, soft-green carpels.

**Breeder:** Smith, 2002
**Height:** 70cm
**Flowers:** semi-double, midseason
**Scent:** light

### 'SONOMA SUN'

One of a series of intersectional peonies with 'Sonoma' as the first name, this California-raised plant carries its single flowers well above the leaves. On opening, the two rows of round petals, which have small nicks along the top, are ever so lightly tinted with pink and appear rich-apricot. This tone disappears as the petals uncurl into a rich-yellow flower with small, round, red flares encasing a ring of sparse yellow stamens.

**Breeder:** Tolomeo, 1996
**Height:** 75cm
**Flowers:** single, midseason
**Scent:** none

*Paeonia* 'Sonoma Sun'

*Paeonia* 'Unique'

### 'UNIQUE'

The cup-shaped, scarlet bloom looks beautiful against the contrasting dark green foliage carried on long, red-tinged stems. Two layers of wavy, heart-shaped petals that are lightly pleated on the surface open to reveal long, yellow stamens. These are carried on red filaments and surround red-tipped, green carpels. Similar in appearance to *Paeonia* 'Scarlet Heaven' but much taller in my garden. AGM

**Breeder:** Anderson, 1999
**Height:** 90cm
**Flowers:** single, midseason
**Scent:** none

### 'WATERMELON WINE'

Vivid-pink blooms unfurl into a deep chalice, borne level with matt, mid-green leaves that spread into a low dome. On close inspection, you can see faint white lines running down the petals. At the base of each, a dark pink flare radiates upwards from golden stamens. The sage-green carpels have large, twisting rich-pink tips. AGM

**Breeder:** Anderson, 1999
**Height:** 70cm
**Flowers:** single, midseason
**Scent:** light

*Paeonia* 'Watermelon Wine'

### 'WHITE EMPEROR'

One of the few white intersectional peonies, this is a mutation of the original plant raised by Toichi Itoh, *Paeonia* 'Yellow Emperor'. Not a free-flowering plant, it carries small, pure white blooms just above a low dome of mid-green leaves. The petals are almost translucent and form a cup around a wide ring of soft-yellow stamens. These seem to whirl around laurel-green carpels with hairy, salmon-pink tips lined with deep pink.

**Breeder:** Seidl, 1989
**Height:** 60cm
**Flowers:** semi-double, late season
**Scent:** none

*Paeonia* 'White Emperor'

### 'YANKEE DOODLE DANDY'

A profusely flowering plant, it produces deep rose-pink blooms over a long period above a broad mound of mid-green leaves that have a matt surface. On opening, the single row of petals, which have dark red patches at the base, are perfectly shaped. As they age, the petals loosen, exhibit thin red veins and become unruly. Creating a dramatic contrast against the petals, tall yellow stamens almost hide the red-tipped, furry, mid-green carpels.

**Breeder:** Smith, 2002
**Height:** 75cm
**Flowers:** semi-double, midseason
**Scent:** medium

### 'YELLOW CROWN'

One of the original plants raised in Japan by Toichi Itoh then imported by Louis Smirnow and registered in the US. Unlike the dozens of intersectionals that have followed, this is more like a short tree peony. Large, lemon-scented, shallowly domed, pure yellow flowers are so double in form that the small red stains at the base of the curling petals are virtually hidden. The mid-green leaves are similar to those of a tree peony and produced on stems that are not strong enough to hold the flower upright.

**Breeder:** Itoh/Smirnow, 1974
**Height:** 50cm
**Flowers:** double, midseason
**Scent:** light

*Paeonia* 'Yellow Crown'

*Paeonia* 'Yankee Doodle Dandy'

# TREE PEONIES

For almost two centuries, these beautiful plants have been known as tree peonies – a term that is technically incorrect. Despite producing woody, perennial stems, they are actually shrubs not trees. Some peony enthusiasts would even prefer to call them woody peonies. In China, where they grow in the wild and have been revered since ancient times, they are known as Moutan or Mudan. In Japan, where many of our garden tree peonies originate, their name is Butan. For the sake of tradition, I shall continue to refer to them as tree peonies.

## China

Tree peonies have been in cultivation for considerably longer in China than herbaceous types, with a history that stretches back over two thousand years. Grown principally for medicinal use, the most beautiful cultivars were greatly admired and highly sought after by the rich who saw them as a symbol of wealth, power and class. Over the centuries they have been celebrated in poems and songs, embroidered on robes and depicted in exquisite paintings. Colourful myths and legends also grew up around tree peonies, especially in regions where they are grown commercially. On a trip to Heze in 1996, I was told the story of the heartbroken 'Peony Fairy' and how a peony grew where her tears fell. Another legend is associated with Luoyang, home of the famous peony festival. During the time of the Tang dynasty, Empress Wu Zetian was said to be so furious that the peonies failed to bloom in the city of Chang'an (now X'ian) one snowy spring day, she had all four thousand plants removed from the imperial gardens and replanted in Louyang. The following year, the peonies flowered in abundance and the Empress moved her court there.

## Chinese Tree Peonies in Europe

When trade with China began to open up, the Dutch East India Company managed to import tree peonies into Europe, with the first shipments arriving sometime around 1656. There are also records of tree peonies being grown in Britain around that time, and accounts of their beauty encouraged further attempts to import more plants from China. Joseph Banks arranged for a specimen, probably the first, to be brought to the Royal Botanic Gardens, Kew, in 1789. Unfortunately, the plant died, but records describe another tree peony growing in the gardens in the same period. It apparently survived for 53 years before being dug up to make way for a new building.

In the early 19th century, the Horticultural Society of London (later the RHS) engaged John Reeves, a tea inspector for the East India Company in Canton (now Guangzhou), to record Chinese flowering plants never seen in the west. Of more than 130 paintings he commissioned from local artists, 13 were tree peonies, most in colours never seen before including apricots and yellows as well as double forms with fringed petal edges. They had been brought south from colder areas of China – a common practice according to an account printed in *The Gardeners' Chronicle* of 1847. Each January, quantities of dormant tree peony plants were sent from northern China to the cities of Canton and Macao to decorate houses for Chinese New Year. In the warmer south, they failed to flower in the second season and were discarded. Foreign merchants managed to exported some plants to Europe, but they rarely survived the journey.

## Japan

Although not native to Japan, tree peonies have been cultivated there for over a thousand years, and probably grown from seed for medicinal purposes. Evidence exists that they were grown in temple gardens long before the 15th century but it was not until Chinese plants arrived that they were cultivated as ornamentals. Very soon they became 'must-have' plants and peonies were painted on temple doors and in Osaka castle. However, the appeal of the traditional Chinese forms with big double flowers that hung downwards began to fade and the Japanese set about breeding plants with single or semi-double flowers. They also preferred colours that lacked the 'undesirable' flares on the petals. By the end of the 17th century, more than 300 cultivars were recorded, with flowers in many colours and forms. Following the end of military government in Japan in 1868, these stunning plants began to be exported to Europe and in the later years of Victoria's reign, tree peonies would go on to become more popular in British gardens than the traditional herbaceous types.

Statue of the Peony Fairy in the gardens in Heze, China, 1996

Paintings of tree peonies have adorned walls in China for centuries

Tree peony growing in a Chinese garden, photographed c.1939

Japanese *Paeonia* 'Shimane Chojuraku' (front) with lutea hybrid *Paeonia* 'Gauguin' (behind) growing in the garden at White Hopton Farm

### Tree Peonies in Europe

Among the few accounts of the availability of tree peonies in the early 19th century, one, dated 1827, mentions their inclusion in wholesale flower markets in Paris along with roses and gardenias. They were certainly grown in the gardens of some British estates, according to an article published in the same year by James Nash, flower-gardener to Lady Farnborough in Kent. It explains how to graft tree peonies using brass wire to bind the scions and then suggests leaving them in a cold frame for a year before planting out.

In her book *The Ladies' Companion to the Flower Garden*, first published in 1841, Mrs. Loudon notes that Robert Fortune, having obtained plants through Canton 12 years earlier, had introduced some 'splendid kinds' of Mouton (tree peonies) from China that included shades from salmon to purple. Thirty years later, in *The Amateur's Flower Garden* (1871) (James) Shirley Hibberd advised his readers that tree peonies specifically required "the assistance of distant shelter, and a deep, rather dry, but exceedingly rich soil, and to be liberally aided with water all the summer".

In 1884, French missionary Père Jean Marie Delavay discovered *Paeonia delavayi* and *P. lutea* in China and sent plants to Paris. Hybridisation of these plants proved straightforward and it revolutionised the development of tree peonies, resulting in hardy, easy-to-grow garden varieties. Victor Lemoine (see p.32) introduced the first lutea hybrid *Paeonia* 'L'Espérance' in 1909, two years after Louis Henry's rich-yellow, heavy-bloomed *P.* 'Souvenir de Maxime Cornu'.

### New Tree Peony Discoveries

While tree peonies had been grown in Europe for several decades, it wasn't until 1914 that one was seen growing wild by a European. On an expedition to the uplands of the Chinese-Tibet border, Reginald Farrer sat down to survey the surrounding hillside and saw a plant with beautiful large white blooms. Farrer was convinced this was a tree peony but it was not identified until Joseph Rock came across a similar plant in about 1925, photographed it and collected the seeds. This is now known as *Paeonia rockii*.

Other explorers of the time went to incredible lengths to collect plants. Frank Ludlow and George Sherriff first met in the British Consulate in Kashgar, the most westerly Chinese city in the foothills of the central Asian mountain ranges. During the long, cold winter evenings, talk turned to travel and they discovered a mutual passion for Tibet. Through the Consul General, they obtained permission to visit Tibet in 1933 – the first of many trips. Travelling on foot and by donkey the pair, along with a team of helpers, explored the foothills and passes of Tibet and Bhutan discovering its rich flora and bird life. By 1949 they had visited the area seven times and collected over 24,000 plants, including *Paeonia lutea* var. *ludlowii*, known today as simply *P. ludlowii*.

Apart from a small number introduced by French breeders, very few new tree peonies were registered until the mid-20th century. Kelway's of Langport listed tree peonies with English names in their catalogue, but, lacking breeding notes, it was assumed these were imported Japanese varieties that had been renamed.

### American Breeders

While raising hybrid peonies in the US, Professor A. P. Saunders saw the need to create tree peonies with flowers that instead of drooping downwards, were more visible. He crossed *Paeonia lutea* (now *P. delavayi* f. *lutea*) and *P. delavayi* with Japanese tree peonies introducing the first of many lutea hybrids, *Paeonia* 'Argosy', in 1928. Over 70 more were registered between 1940 and 1952.

It was to be another 30 years and the combined energy of two creative amateurs before new cultivars were registered in any volume. Encouraged by his friend A. P. Saunders, artist and horse-breeder William Gratwick began collecting all Saunders' tree peonies and imported more plants from Japan. Gratwick introduced a dozen of his own tree peonies, but his friendship with artist Nassos Daphnis resulted in many more wonderful plants.

Born in Greece, Daphnis moved with his family to New York in 1930. He was 26 and working in his uncle's flower shop when he began teaching himself to paint. Captivated by the tree peonies he saw in Gratwick's Linwood Gardens, New York State, Daphnis started painting them and by 1945, encouraged by Gratwick, he was hybridising tree peonies himself. It was assumed that Saunders' tree peonies, which produced no seed, were sterile – an assumption that proved false. Selecting a few of them, plus *Paeonia lutea* and Japanese tree peonies, Daphnis made over 500 crosses and introduced 48 new plants, the last in 1996. Also famous as an artist, his abstract paintings hang in US museums and galleries.

Peony enthusiast, horse-breeder and artist William (Bill) Gratwick in the 1980s

Nassos Daphnis among the tree peonies at Linwood Gardens in 1994

*Paeonia* 'Artemis' was introduced by Daphnis and named after his daughter

## THE TREE PEONY PLANT

All tree peonies produce woody stems and enormous blooms. For the purposes of this book the individual species are described first, then hybrids, which are organised into three separate groups. A description of the group is given at the start of each section.

**Names** of tree peonies often start with *Paeonia × suffruticosa* followed by the cultivar name. No such peony ever existed, and it is simply a convenient way of categorising those cultivars whose heritage is unknown. It is often applied to Chinese and Japanese tree peonies.

**The plant** itself can grow very big so these peonies, especially the species types, are suitable only for the largest gardens. Tree peonies from China, if you can find them, may be shorter and densely covered with leaves. The flowers are usually semi-double or double. Japanese tree peonies are the most suitable for smaller gardens because they are generally upright, not spreading. These have been used to raise lutea hybrids, which are wider at the top than at the base.

**The flowers** of all tree peonies are usually unscented and carried on new growth that appears at the top of the previous year's woody stems. *Paeonia delavayi* and its hybrids produce several buds on each stem, while Chinese and Japanese tree peonies have only one, very large bud per stem. If this single flower bud emerges too early in spring it can be damaged by late frost, so always grow Japanese tree peonies in a spot where frost will not linger for long. Lutea hybrids have two or three buds per flower stems, which results in smaller blooms.

**The stems and leaves** of shrubby tree peonies are markedly different to those of herbaceous peonies. The stems are woody, but not very wide and create a framework for the leaves and flowers. *Paeonia rockii* and its hybrids have the prettiest leaves, which are small and nicely coloured. Those of Chinese tree peonies may be thick and quite coarse, while Japanese tree peony leaves can be particularly beautiful. Like all peony foliage, tree peony leaves are mid-green, but some are attractively stained with purple in spring. Lutea hybrids and Japanese tree peonies don't always form a thick canopy of foliage, and the leaves tend to be carried towards the top, allowing other plants to be grown under and around the base of the peony.

In the centre a white, or red, sheath covers the green carpels of tree peonies

New shoots containing the flower buds emerge from the top of old woody stems

Japanese tree peony buds are very handsome, but there is just one per stem

Chinese tree peonies produce abundant foliage and often have double flowers

Japanese peonies such as *Paeonia* 'Hana Kisoi' often have a very upright habit

Lutea hybrids such as *Paeonia* 'Black Pirate' make excellent garden shrubs

## DELAVAYI

In recent decades, Chinese botanists have made a distinction between *Paeonia delavayi* with red flowers and yellow-flowered *P. lutea*. They consider the latter a form (*forma*) of *P. delavayi*. Botanists living outside China don't always agree with this change.

Both plants are large, easy to grow and vigorous but there are clear differences between the two species. Their natural habitat is forest clearings at high altitudes that cover a great swathe of eastern China ranging from Yunnan in the south to Tibet in the north. Named after their discoverer, Père Delavay (see p.156), they cross and set seed readily and the resulting plants can produce a wonderful array of beautifully coloured blooms.

***Paeonia delavayi*** produces small flowers with short petals in dark tones of red. These open in a single layer around a wide circle of stamens that can be orange, red or rich-yellow with wide, green bracts. The flower stems dip forward and carry further buds. A tall plant with woody, spreading stems, it has deeply divided, mid-green leaves carried towards the top.

***Paeonia delavayi* f. *lutea*** has yellow, upward-facing flowers with big petals that open into a goblet then into a cup. Behind the petals sit distinctive narrow, light green bracts. Far more upright than *P. delavayi,* it bears big, mid-green leaves.

(for both plants)
**Height:** 180cm
**Flowers:** May to early June
**Scent:** sometimes

*Paeonia delavayi*

A yellow variant of *Paeonia delavayi*

An unusual apricot-flowered *Paeonia delavayi* with sweetly scented blooms growing in my garden

*Paeonia delavayi* f. *lutea*

*Paeonia delavayi* in winter

## LUDLOWII

A robust shrub bearing yellow flowers and light green leaves with a tall spreading habit – a feature that distinguishes it from *P. delavayi* f. *lutea*. It was collected from the wild by Ludlow and Sherriff (see p.156) on one of their many plant exploration trips. Thought to be a Tibetan form of *Paeonia lutea*, this peony was originally named *P. lutea* var. *ludlowii* but is now considered to be an entirely separate species. This hybridises readily with *P. delavayi* and freely sets seed.

**Height:** 180cm
**Flowers:** May to early June
**Scent:** sometimes

*Paeonia ludlowii*

*Paeonia 'Feng Dan Bai'*

## OSTII

Not considered a separate species until 1992, this tree peony was named after Gian Lupo Osti, Italian peony enthusiast and botanist. Native to central and north-central Chinese provinces and long valued for the medicinal properties of its roots, *P. ostii* is now rare in the wild owing to over collection. Plants sold under this name are likely to be a similar but more robust hybrid known as *Paeonia* 'Feng dan bai', also cultivated for its roots. Like *P. ostii* this has one large, lightly scented, white bloom per stem and dark green leaves. The blooms are often stained with pale-pink.

**Height:** 120cm
**Flowers:** single, early season
**Scent:** sometimes

*Paeonia 'Feng Dan Bai' is probably a hybrid of Paeonia ostii*

## ROCKII

Introduced by American botanist and explorer Joseph Rock who found a plant growing in a monastery garden in Gansu, China. Seeds were sent to the UK, US and Sweden, where they germinated to produce plants that bloomed in 1938. A tall shrub with finely shaped, mid-green leaves that are particularly beautiful. The very large white flowers have the most perfect centre of gold stamens backed by big, darkest maroon 'thumb prints'. *P. rockii* crosses readily with *P.* × *suffruticosa* cultivars, resulting in many fine hybrids.

**Height:** 180cm
**Flowers:** May to early June
**Scent:** none

*Paeonia rockii*

## CHINESE TREE PEONIES

Of the many hundreds of different cultivars grown, very few have been sold outside China. In past catalogues, I listed a number of varieties but many of these failed to thrive, probably because our temperate climate is too warm and wet for plants raised and grown on a continent where winters are very cold and summers hot. The flowers range from single to double and the leaves can vary from thick and round, to long and slender. The most outstanding plants among those I have grown are described on this page.

**Bloom time: Early season** late May; **Midseason** week 1, June; **Late season** week 2, June

### 'FEI YAN HONG ZHUANG'

Similar to a rose in shape, the flower has mid-pink petals that curl inwards in a whorl around the dome of small, gold stamens. A spreading plant carrying slender stems with mid-green leaves, it was raised in Heze province in 1964.

**Height:** 90cm
**Flowers:** semi-double, midseason
**Type:** Chinese hybrid
**English translation:** 'Flying Swallow Lady in Red'

*Paeonia* 'Fei Yan Hong Zhuang'

### 'QING LONG WO MO CHI'

Beautiful flowers of reddish-purple (described by Chinese growers as black) have round petals and an immense centre of yellow stamens. This classic variety is said to be double, but the plant I grew never gained further petals and remained resolutely single. Refined soft-green leaves grow into a mound.

**Height:** 90cm
**Flowers:** single to semi-double, midseason
**Type:** Chinese hybrid
**English translation:** 'Green Dragon Lying on a Chinese Ink Stone', 'Green Dragon in a Dark Pool'

*Paeonia* 'Qing Long Wo Mo Chi'

### 'ROU FU RONG'

An easy variety even in our garden, this is classed by Chinese breeders as 'chrysanthemum shaped'. Short, soft-pink petals are arranged in tightly packed layers. At first ruffled, the petals become smoother as they unfurl around a ring of yellow stamens and a cluster of many, soft-green carpels that are tipped pink. The fragrant blooms are carried above a short shrub densely covered with long, deeply cut mid-green leaves.

**Height:** 60cm
**Flowers:** semi-double to double, midseason
**Type:** Chinese hybrid
**English translation:** 'Pink Water Lily'

### 'YIN FEN JIN LIN'

According to Chinese tradition, the fully double flowers of this old variety are the most desirable shape. The soft-pink blooms, which are lightly scented, contain such an abundance of short, intertwined petals the stems cannot hold the flowers upright. Look deep into the bloom and you'll notice dark purple markings at the base of the petals. A dwarf, rather spreading plant with nicely shaped, mid-green leaves.

**Height:** 60cm
**Flowers:** double, midseason
**Type:** Chinese hybrid
**English translation:** 'Silver Pink and Golden Fish'

*Paeonia* 'Yin Fen Jin Lin'

*Paeonia* 'Rou Fu Rong'

## JAPANESE TREE PEONIES

All these plants are bred in Japan and their blooms face upwards. Flower stems produce just one bud and the leaves are particularly lovely. The shrub is usually very upright, although some stems may drift down to soil level and increase the spread. Most Japanese tree peonies sold by garden centres are categorised only by colour. To buy a named plant, seek out a peony specialist who will usually have imported them, often via the Netherlands, from Japan. Even then there is no guarantee they will will be true to name.

**Bloom time: Early season** mid-May; **Midseason** late May

## 'HAKUOJISI'

At first the pure white flowers of this robust variety open into a cup. As the flower ages, the petals, which are lightly pleated and ruffled along the tops, loosen into a fine, rose-shaped bloom. A sparse ring of slender, light yellow stamens sits in the centre, and the occasional petaloid might appear among them. Mid-green leaves cover a spreading shrub.

**Breeder:** unknown, pre-1910
**Height:** 90cm
**Flowers:** semi-double, midseason
**Type:** Japanese hybrid
**English translation:** 'King of White Lion', 'White-tailed Lion'

*Paeonia* 'Hakuojisi'

## 'HANA DAIJIN'

A stunning plant that grows into a wide, low shrub with large, purplish-red blooms opening evenly just above the leaves. The round petals are gently crimped along the edges and decrease in size towards the gold stamens. Initially the petals curl into a shallow goblet before unfurling into a loose, ruffled flower. Reasonably erect in habit, although certain longer stems may spread sideways.

**Breeder:** unknown, pre-1910
**Height:** 90cm
**Flowers:** semi-double, midseason
**Type:** Japanese hybrid
**English translation:** 'Messenger of Fowers', 'Magnificent Flower'

*Paeonia* 'Hana Daijin'

## 'HANA KISOI'

A neatly shaped, upright plant, this is a very beautiful peony with mid-pink flowers, sometimes double in form, carried on sturdy stems. The petals are lightly ruffled along the edges and their surface texture is similar to crêpe paper. The petals can fade around the margins with age, while in the centre, the gold stamens form a thick mound.

**Breeder:** unknown, pre-1910
**Height:** 90cm
**Flowers:** semi-double, early season
**Type:** Japanese hybrid
**English translation**: 'Floral Rivalry'

## 'HOKI'

Each bright-crimson petal of this medium-sized bloom weaves itself around the next petal to create a thick, fluffy ruff. In the centre, a circle of small gold stamens just about hides the round, red carpels. As the bloom ages, the petal edges fade slightly to pale-red. The shrub, which is vigorous, has a very erect habit.

**Breeder:** unknown
**Height:** 80cm
**Flowers:** semi-double, early season
**Type:** Japanese hybrid
**English translation:** 'Charming Age'

*Paeonia* 'Hoki'

*Paeonia* 'Hana Kisoi'

*Paeonia* 'Kamata-fuji'

### 'KAMATA-FUJI'

On opening, the extremely ruffled, short, soft-pink petals are so numerous the bloom resembles a flat powder puff. As the bloom ages, the tight dome of stamens becomes visible and the petals fade heavily to soft-pink around the edges. The large blooms are carried at the same level as the foliage on a short spreading shrub.

**Breeder:** unknown, pre-1937
**Height:** 75cm
**Flowers:** double, midseason
**Type:** Japanese hybrid
**English translation:** 'Kamata's Wisteria', 'Wisteria of Kamata'

### 'KAOW'

Variously listed over the years as 'Kao', 'Kaoh' and 'Kaou', this vigorous plant produces a big fluffy, scarlet flower that, as the shrub matures, will become even bigger and often double. The petals, which are serrated at the tops and lightly ruffled, open into a loose dome around a thick mound of yellow stamens. The blooms are evenly distributed just above a tidy mound of mid-green foliage.

**Breeder:** Watanabe, 1931
**Height:** 90cm
**Flowers:** semi-double, midseason
**Type:** Japanese hybrid
**English translation:** 'King of Flowers', 'King of Blossoms'

*Paeonia* 'Kaow'

### 'NANIWA-NISHIKI'

Brilliant reddish-pink blooms with two or three rows of incurved petals open into a deep goblet then, as the petals loosen and curl back, a ring of yellow stamens is revealed. The petal edges may gain the occasional very fine white line. The colour of the flowers, which are borne on a strongly upright plant, can be quite startling if the surrounding planting is not carefully considered.

**Breeder:** Unknown
**Height:** 90cm
**Flowers:** semi-double, midseason
**Type:** Japanese hybrid
**English translation:** 'Naniwa Brocade'

*Paeonia* 'Renkaku'

### 'RENKAKU'

The petals of the beautiful, pure white flower are tightly ruffled and, as they age, become almost translucent. Fully unfurled, they form a flat, frilly bloom with a ring of yellow stamens that sits in wonderful contrast to the purity of the petals. The carpels are also white. This free-flowering plant carries the blooms on an arching shrub with dark green foliage.

**Breeder:** unknown, pre-1898
**Height:** 90cm
**Flowers:** semi-double, early season
**Type:** Japanese hybrid
**English translation:** 'Flight of Cranes'

*Paeonia* 'Naniwa-nishiki'

## 'SHICHIFUKUJIN'

A very large flower with silky, soft-pink petals that open into a big, loose bowl around a thick, neatly formed ring of yellow stamens. The bloom increases in size with age, while the edges of the petals fade to silver. Handsome when in flower, this creates a wide shrub with long stems that may hang down to the ground.

**Breeder:** unknown, pre-1927
**Height:** 90cm
**Flowers:** semi-double, midseason
**Type:** Japanese hybrid
**English translation:** 'Seven Gods of Fortune', 'Seven Gods Bring Good Luck'

*Paeonia* 'Shichifukujin'

## 'SHIMA DAIJIN'

Very ruffled and reddish-purple in colour, the blooms are lovely yet not particularly large. They open into a goblet with each round petal curling inwards to frame large, soft-yellow stamens that almost hide the purple-red carpels. A vigorous plant with long, spreading stems.

**Breeder:** Ikeuchi, 1952
**Height:** 120cm
**Flowers:** semi-double to double, midseason
**Type:** Japanese hybrid
**English translation:** 'Minister of the Islands'

*Paeonia* 'Shimane Chojuraku'

## 'SHIMANE CHOJURAKU'

One of the most magnificent Japanese tree peonies I have grown. Smooth, rich-lilac petals initially unfold into a deep cup, then form a perfectly shaped bloom with near-black flares outlining the ring of gold stamens. Not a large plant but nicely shaped and upright. The stems stretch out slightly, making the plant wider and quite open towards the top.

**Breeder:** unknown
**Height:** 90cm
**Flowers:** semi-double, midseason
**Type:** Japanese hybrid
**English translation:** 'Long life', 'Old Age of Shimane'

*Paeonia* 'Shima Daijin'

## 'SHIMA NISHIKI'

A mutation of the scarlet-red flowered tree peony *Paeonia* 'Taiyo' ('The Sun'). The slightly curved petals display irregular white stripes but these are variable. Not every flower has them and some plants have none at all. In the middle, in stark contrast, is a boss of golden stamens. A semi-erect shrub with extraordinary flowers, this might be difficult to combine with other plants but will certainly add early glamour to the border.

**Breeder:** unknown
**Height:** 90cm
**Flowers:** semi-double, early to midseason
**Type:** Japanese hybrid
**English translation:** 'Island Brocade'

*Paeonia* 'Shima Nishiki'

### 'TAISHO NO HOKORI'

Easy to grow and robust, this peony produces large flowers with silky, purple-red petals that unfurl into a big, loose bloom. Sometimes, small white markings are visible on the smooth petal edges. Gold stamens and carpels covered with a similiar-coloured sheath grace the centre. This produces a nicely domed shrub.

**Breeder:** unknown, pre-1931
**Height:** 90cm
**Flowers:** semi-double, midseason
**Type:** Japanese hybrid
**English translation:** 'Pride of the Taishow Dynasty'

Paeonia 'Taisho No Hokori'

### 'TAMASUDARE'

The petals of this big, frilly bloom are long, slender and pristine white. On opening, they create a goblet. As the flower matures, the petals turn nearly translucent and relax to show the centre of short, gold stamens that cover white carpels. A strong growing, upright plant.

**Breeder:** unknown, pre-1940
**Height:** 120cm
**Flowers:** semi-double, midseason
**Type:** Japanese hybrid
**English translation:** 'Jewelled Screen', 'Tracery of White Jade', 'Beautiful Bamboo Curtain'

### 'YACHIYO-TSUBAKI'

Opening coral-pink, the short but slender petals are curled at the edges and lightly serrated along the top. As the flower matures, the tips of the petals pale in colour. In spring the young leaves are bronze, not the characteristic green of other tree peonies, and cover an upright, domed shrub.

**Breeder:** unknown, pre-1931
**Height:** 90cm
**Flowers:** semi-double, midseason
**Type:** Japanese hybrid
**English translation:** 'Eternal Camellias'

Paeonia 'Tamasudare'

### 'YAE ZAKURA'

Soft-pink petals arranged in neat layers uncurl from a deep cup into a wide bloom that fades to very pale pink along the lightly ruffled, notched edges. In the centre, the ring of gold stamens surrounds red carpels. The large blooms are produced on an upright shrub.

**Breeder:** unknown, pre-1940
**Height:** 90cm
**Flowers:** semi-double, midseason
**Type:** Japanese hybrid
**English translation:** 'Host of the Cherry Blossom'

Paeonia 'Yae Zakura'

Paeonia 'Yachiyo-tsubaki'

## FRENCH & AMERICAN INTRODUCTIONS

The earliest of the featured cultivars were raised in France by Lemoine but the majority are American and the result of crosses made between *Paeonia delavayi*, *P. × suffruticosa* hybrids and *P. rockii*.

**Lutea hybrids** have *Paeonia delavayi* parents. Most are yellow or red, but pink-flowered plants are available. These shrubs are not large and can be upright or spreading in habit.

**Rockii hybrids** are raised from *Paeonia rockii* and have particularly fine foliage – deeply segmented with slender leaflets. The large blooms are white or purple.

All bloom in June. **Early season** week 1; **Midseason** week 2; **Late season** week 3

## 'AGE OF GOLD'

The nicely shaped, semi-double, soft-lemon blooms are filled with wavy petals that curl around each other to form a densely ruffled flower. The long, gold stamens and small, dark red flares are just visible. Although the blooms hang slightly forward, they are produced in profusion above a neatly domed shrub.

**Breeder:** Saunders, 1948
**Height:** 90cm
**Flowers:** semi-double, midseason
**Type:** lutea hybrid

*Paeonia* 'Age of Gold'

## 'ALICE HARDING'

This dwarf, spreading plant has large, flat-topped lemon flowers that droop gently forward. Among the abundant short petals, the golden stamens and red flares can just be seen. To experience the heavy lemon scent, however, you must get down on your knees to flower level. For reasons not recorded, the breeder gave the same name to both this plant and a herbaceous peony he also raised. Known as 'Kinko' in Japan, it is one of the parents of many intersectional peonies.

**Breeder:** Lemoine, 1935
**Height:** 60cm
**Flowers:** double, midseason
**Type:** lutea hybrid

*Paeonia* 'Alice Harding'

## 'ANGELET'

On opening, the three rows of round, scallop-edged petals are heavily washed along the margins with soft pink-red, but as the bloom ages, they turn entirely yellow. Dark red streaks are visible underneath a thick ring of gold stamens, creating a dramatic centre. The scented blooms face outwards on the nicely shaped bush and one or two extra side buds are produced on the flower stems.

**Breeder:** Saunders, 1950
**Height:** 90cm
**Flowers:** single, midseason
**Type:** lutea hybrid

*Paeonia* 'Argosy'

## 'ARGOSY'

Two rows of sulphur-yellow petals frame a dense ring of golden stamens, which are highlighted by a distinctive star of deep red. This was the first lutea hybrid to be introduced by Saunders, whose attempts to raise tree peonies with flowers that did not hang down paved the way for many other wonderful hybrids.

**Breeder:** Saunders, 1928
**Height:** 120cm
**Flowers:** single, midseason
**Type:** lutea hybrid

*Paeonia* 'Angelet'

### 'BLACK PIRATE'

Free-flowering and easy to grow, this forms a reasonably wide but upright shrub that is covered with slender leaves. The handsome, very dark red blooms with silky, ruffled petals tip gently forwards, but not so far that the thick cone of yellow stamens is hidden. *Paeonia* 'Black Panther' is very similar in colour but its flowers, having more petals, tend to droop further forwards and hide the stamens.

**Breeder:** Saunders, 1935
**Height:** 90cm
**Flowers:** semi-double, midseason
**Type:** lutea hybrid

*Paeonia* 'Black Pirate'

### 'BOREAS'

Evenly spaced around the plant, the deep raspberry-red, fragrant flowers tumble across a sloping mound of mid-green foliage. Named after the Greek god of the north wind, the large, wavy, almost square-topped petals seem to whirl around the centre. This is sparsely filled with yellow stamens carried on red filaments and white-tipped, green carpels. Right at the base of the petals, darkest red flares are apparent.

**Breeder:** Daphnis, 1977
**Height:** 120cm
**Flowers:** semi-double, midseason
**Type:** lutea hybrid

### 'CHINESE DRAGON'

Although this is one of the easiest lutea hybrids to grow, its scented, purple-magenta flowers with shiny petals hang down and obscure the centre. The bloom needs to be lifted up to see maroon flares, yellow stamens and magenta-tipped, soft-green carpels. A robust shrub that, although spreading, is taller than it is wide and covered with particularly lovely finely divided leaves.

**Breeder:** Saunders, 1948
**Height:** 120cm
**Flowers:** semi-double, midseason
**Type:** lutea hybrid

*Paeonia* 'Chinese Dragon'

*Paeonia* 'Boreas'

### 'EZRA POUND'

The stunningly beautiful pure white flower has crimped petals and dramatic black-magenta basal flares. When young, the blooms are stained with magenta, but this quickly disappears. Slender yellow stamens form an elegant circle around white-tipped, soft-green carpels. The leaves are typical of *Paeonia rockii* and entirely clothe the upright plant. Grow in a place where late spring frost won't linger and damage the single buds as the flower stems produce no side buds.

**Breeder:** Gratwick, 1985
**Height:** 150cm
**Flowers:** single, early season
**Type:** rockii hybrid

*Paeonia* 'Ezra Pound'

### 'GAUGUIN'

An upright, round shrub that is covered with scented, strawberry-red, cup-shaped flowers. The colour is spread over the face of wavy yellow petals, but the reverse remains largely yellow – a tone that is apparent as the blooms tip forward. Blackish-maroon flares radiate out from golden stamens carried on darkest red filaments that are a similar colour to the flares. Sage-green carpels have tomato-red tips.

**Breeder:** Daphnis, pre-1980
**Height:** 120cm
**Flowers:** single, midseason
**Type:** lutea hybrid

*Paeonia* 'Gauguin'

### 'GOLD SOVEREIGN'

When fully open, the rims of the lightly ruffled, lemon petals curl slightly outwards. They create a deep bowl around long, shaggy, yellow stamens and white-tipped, soft-green carpels. Not the most free-flowering lutea hybrid but the blooms are lovely and carried on a wide, leafy shrub.

**Breeder:** Saunders, 1949
**Height:** 100cm
**Flowers:** semi-double, midseason
**Type:** lutea hybrid

### 'GOLDEN BOWL'

Sitting right in the centre of the lightly ruffled, lemon petals, a five-pointed red star outlines a neat boss of golden stamens. The bowl-shaped blooms are borne on quite long, but stiff flower stems. These hold the flowers at an angle to the slender, divided leaves that grace this spreading shrub.

**Breeder:** Saunders, 1948
**Height:** 120cm
**Flowers:** single, midseason
**Type:** lutea hybrid

*Paeonia* 'Gold Sovereign'

### 'HESPERUS'

Large, glamorous, rose-pink blooms face outwards from this upright, rather leggy shrub. Two rows of petals are unevenly washed with deeper tones around the petal edges and in the centre is a ring of bright yellow stamens borne on red filaments. These surround the pink-tipped, green carpels and the remnants of a red sheath. Some growers have recorded a second flush of flowers but so far my plant has not obliged.

**Breeder:** Saunders, 1948
**Height:** 60cm
**Flowers:** single, midseason
**Type:** lutea hybrid

*Paeonia* 'Hesperus'

*Paeonia* 'Golden Bowl'

Tree peonies | 167

### 'HIGH NOON'

Butter-yellow petals form neat, lemon-scented blooms that adorn a wide, round shrub. The cupped flowers, which have four or five rows of round petals, raise their heads just high enough to display the boss of straggly, gold stamens. Also visible are little smudges of red that paint each petal's base. The same plant is sold by British nurseries under the name of *Paeonia* 'Hai Huang'.

**Breeder:** Saunders, 1952
**Height:** 120cm
**Flowers:** semi-double, midseason
**Type:** lutea hybrid

*Paeonia* 'High Noon'

### 'MARCHIONESS'

(opposite) A very beautiful and perfectly shaped flower that, with age, changes from soft peach-pink to apricot-yellow. When fully open some of the gently ruffled petals are suffused with rose-pink. A dramatic centre of loose yellow stamens is edged by almost black blotches. The whole plant is made more spectacular by the mid-green leaves that are heavily burnished with bronze.

**Breeder:** Saunders, 1942
**Height:** 120cm
**Flowers:** semi-double, midseason
**Type:** lutea hybrid

### 'L'ESPÉRANCE'

A lovely old variety has two layers of round, gently wavy, pale-primrose petals that are blotched with dark red at the base. These surround a mound of very long, yellow stamens, which are carried on red filaments. Each large bloom is tucked between the leaves of a neatly domed shrub. Raised in France, this was the first lutea hybrid to be recorded. It is sold in Japan under the name *Paeonia* 'Kintei'.

**Breeder:** Lemoine, 1909
**Height:** 120cm
**Flowers:** single, midseason
**Type:** lutea hybrid

*Paeonia* 'Murad of Hershey Bar'

### 'MURAD OF HERSHEY BAR'

The petals of the large, rose-purple flowers are nicked along the edges. Unfurling into a wide flower, they reveal a dense circle of gold stamens that are surrounded by spear-like, deep purple stripes. Both the foliage and habit are characteristic of a Japanese tree peony and although registered as a suffruticosa hybrid, no details about its named parents are known. It is therefore unclear what this lovely peony's heritage is.

**Breeder:** Gratwick, 1986
**Height:** 150cm
**Flowers:** single, early season
**Type:** suffruticosa hybrid

*Paeonia* 'Renown'

*Paeonia* 'L'Espérance'

### 'RENOWN'

In comparison with other lutea hybrids this is a short plant, but the flowers are very large with big heart-shaped petals. The outward-facing blooms open into a loose frill around long, gold stamens and white-tipped, soft-green carpels. They are carried just above stems with light green leaves that form a sparsely leaved shrub.

**Breeder:** Saunders, 1949
**Height:** 75cm
**Flowers:** single, late season
**Type:** lutea hybrid

*Paeonia* 'Marchioness'

### 'SOUVENIR DE MAXIME CORNU'

As the stems of this upright shrub are too slender to hold up the enormous, fragrant, pink-tinged, rich-yellow blooms the flowers dangle between the leaves. Named after an eminent French botanist who publicly remarked that lutea hybrids would never amount to anything. Originally *Paeonia* 'Souvenir du Professeur Maxime Cornu', it is sold in Japan as *P.* 'Kinkaku'. A similar plant, *P.* 'Chromatella', ('Kinshi' in Japan) bears flowers so heavily tinged with red they appear orange.

**Breeder:** Henry, 1907
**Height:** 90cm
**Flowers:** double, midseason
**Type:** lutea hybrid

*Paeonia* 'Souvenir de Maxime Cornu'

### 'THUNDERBOLT'

The glossy, slightly crumpled petals are deepest red, a tone that is almost brown. Unfurling into two ruffled rows, they frame a tight circle of gold stamens with red filaments and cerise-tipped, soft-green carpels. Opening to face outwards, the blooms are carried on short flower stems just proud of the heavily red-tinted leaves that cover this wide shrub. A lovely plant with one drawback: the fragrance is distinctive and unpleasant.

**Breeder:** Saunders, 1948
**Height:** 110cm
**Flowers:** single, early season
**Type:** lutea hybrid

### 'VESUVIAN'

An abundance of silky, rumpled, burgundy-red petals opens into a ruffled, shallow dome. Through the centre of the lightly fragrant double bloom poke a few yellow stamens. The flowers nod gently among the ample, finely divided foliage that covers a short, round bush. On some tree peonies very large drooping blooms can be a disadvantage but these are quite small and their nodding habit does not detract from the plant's beauty.

**Breeder:** Saunders, 1948
**Height:** 65cm
**Flowers:** double, midseason
**Type:** lutea hybrid

*Paeonia* 'Thunderbolt'

### 'WAUCEDAH PRINCESS'

Soft tones of lilac-pink are flushed across the large, crinkled petals, although the colour pales around the edges. As the flower opens into a classic rose shape, a ring of long, loose gold stamens outlined by black-maroon flashes of different sizes is visible. In later years, more petals are produced and create a domed bloom that resembles a powder puff. The flowers are carried at an angle to the handsome, light green foliage of this neat, round shrub.

**Breeder:** Reath, 1988
**Height:** 90cm
**Flowers:** double, midseason
**Type:** rockii hybrid

*Paeonia* 'Waucedah Princess'

*Paeonia* 'Vesuvian'

# THANKS

I would like to thank Anna Kruger for her unfailing enthusiasm when editing my adventures into writing gardening books, Jo Weeks for proof-reading, and Marie Lorimer for indexing. Thanks must also go to the nursery team for working tirelessly during many long-months of the Covid-19 crisis. Thanks to Greg Milner Photography for letting me use the photograph from my daughter's wedding and special thanks to Allison Walter for the generous hours she has spent reading the book. But most of all I would like to say lots of thanks to Ric, my husband, without whom I could never have written this book.

# BIBLIOGRAPHY

American Peony Society Bulletin (1983 - 2020)
American Peony Society *The American Hybrid Peony* (1990)
*Beeton's Shilling Gardening* (1910)
David C. Michener & Carol A. Adelman *Peony* (2017)
David Thomson *Handy Book of the Flower Garden* (1865)
F. C. Stern *A Study of the Genus Paeonia* (1946)
Gian Lupo Osti *The Book of the Tree Peonies* (1999)
Graham Stuart Thomas *Third Edition Perennial Garden Plants* (1990)
James Kelway *Garden Peonies* (1954)
Jo Bennison *Grafting tree peonies: The Plantsman March 2010*
John C. Wister, Editor *The Peonies* (1962)
Martin Page *The Gardener's Guide to Growing Peonies* (1997)
Martin Page *The Gardener's Peony: Herbaceous and Tree Peonies* (2005)
Michael Haworth-Booth *The Moutan or Tree Peony* (1963)
Mrs. Edward Harding *The Book of the Peony* (1917)
Phillip Miller *The Gardeners Dictionary* (1733)
Roger Phillips & Martyn Rix *Perennials Volume 1 Early Perennials* (1991)
Roy Genders *The Peony* (1961)
*The Garden An Illustrated Weekly Journal* (1886), (1887), (1893)
William Robinson *The English Flower Garden* (1903)
www.americanpeonysociety.org
www.biodiversitylibrary.org
www.paeon.de

# ABOUT THE AUTHOR

Claire Austin grew perennials for 20 years while working at her father's company, David Austin Roses. In 2001 she and her husband, Ric Kenwood, established Claire Austin Hardy Plants. Their nursery is situated in Mid-Wales on the border with Shropshire. They grow more than 1500 varieties of perennials, including extensive collections of peonies and bearded irises. A recipient of numerous medals and trophies, Claire is a trained illustrator and a skilful photographer.

Photograph © Clive Nichols

# INDEX

**GENERAL INDEX**

Page numbers in *italic* refer to illustrations

*Achillea* (Yarrow) 20, 29
  'Moonshine' *20*
*Aconitum* (Monkshood) 20
Adelman Peonies Gardens 38, *38*
*Alchemilla mollis* (Lady's mantle) 19, *20*, 29
American peony breeders 34, 35, 38, 113, 143, 156, 165–70
American Peony Society 6, 35, 36, 43, 45
Anderson, George 35
Anderson, Roger 43, 143
*Anemanthele lessoniana* 26
anemone-flowered peonies 9
  *see also* Japanese peonies
anthers 8
antiquity, peonies in 30
ants 15, *15*
*Aquilegia vulgaris* (Granny's bonnet) 19, *23*, *27*, 29, *29*
  'Alba' *20*, *134*
  'Ruby Port' *18*, *19*, 25
  'William Guiness' *28*, *104*
*Aruncus* 20
*Aster 24*, 25
  'Glow in the Dark' *25*
*Astrantia* (Masterwort) 19, *24*, 29
  *A. major 25*
  'Roma' *20*, *27*
Austin, David 36
Australian peony breeders 39
Auten, Edward 34, 113
Award of Garden Merit (AGM) 40

Bakers of Codsall 34–5
balling 15, *15*
Banks, Joseph 155
bare-rooted plants 8, 12, *12*, 43
Barr, Peter 33
bee-friendly plants 28
*Bergenia* (Elephant ears) 29
best companion plants 29
best peonies
  for colour 23
  for cutting 11
  by flowering season 16
  for scent 11
  for self-support 9

  for windy sites 26
Blooms of Bressingham 36
Boekel, Ron 39, *39*
*The Book of the Peony* (Alice Harding) 34, *34*, 36
borders, peonies in the 16–26
  colour 22–3
  companion plants 19, 20, 25, 26, 29
  flowering season 16
  intersectionals 25
  planting distances 16
  shade tolerance 28
  spring 17
  summer 19–20
  tree peonies 26
  windy sites 26
breeding peonies
  Australia 39
  Britain 33, 34–5
  France 32, 34, 156, 165, 168
  Japan 143
  USA 34, 35, 38, 113, 143, 156, 165–70
British peony breeders 33, 34–5
*Brunnera* (Siberian bugloss) 19
buds 10, 115, 157
  balling 15, *15*
  side buds 8, 11, 15, 47, 145
buying peonies 12

*Calamintha* (Calamint) 25
Calot, Jacques 32
camellias 28
*Campanula* (Bellflower) 20, 29
  *C. persicifolia* 'Blue Bloomers' *29*
carpels 8, 10, 114, 144, 145
*Centaurea* (Perennial cornflower) *17*, 19, 25, 29
*Centranthus ruber* (Valerian) 20, 29
*Chaerophyllum hirsutum* 'Roseum' (Hairy chervil) 19, *19*, *134*
Charles Klehm & Son 36
Chelsea Flower Show 40, *40*
China
  lactiflora peonies 45
  peony festivals 39, *39*
  tree peonies 7, 36, 39, 155, 157, 160
Coit, John 35
colour 22–3
  hybrid peonies 7, 22, 23, 114

  intersectional peonies 7, 22, 23, 144
  lactiflora peonies 7, 22, 23, 46
  tree peonies 23
commercial growers
  Austin family business 36–9, 40, 41, 43
  lifting and dividing peonies 41, *41*
  photographic records 37
  plant descriptions 37
  selling peonies 43
  stock numbers 43, *43*
  weed control 41
companion plants 19, 20, 25, 26, 29
Conrad Loddiges & Son 33
container planting 28
container-grown peonies 12, *12*, 43, *43*
coral flowers 22, 23
*Corydalis flexuosa* 28
  'China Blue' *104*
cottage peonies *see P. officinalis*
cross-fertilisation 105
Crousse, Félix 32
culinary spice 30
Culpeper, Nicholas 30
cultivation *see* growing peonies; propagation
cut flowers 11, 43, 45

Daphnis, Nassos 156, *156*
David Austin Hardy Plants 37
David Austin Roses 36, *37*, 38, 41
Delavay, Père Jean Marie 156, 158
Dessert, Auguste 32, 34
*Dianthus* (Hardy pink) 20, 29, *29*
  *D. carthusianorum 21*
*Digitalis* (Foxglove) 29
  *D. grandiflora* 20
  *D. purpurea* 19
Dimmock, Charlie *40*
diseases 13, 15
division 13, 41
Doriat & Son 34
double flowers 9, 10
Dutch East India Company 155

*Epimedium* (Bishop's mitre) 29
  *E. pubigerum* 17, *17*
*Euphorbia* (Spurge) 29
  *E. dulcis* 'Chameleon' *27*

  *E. palustris 18*
  *E. polychroma 19*
eyes 8, *8*, 12, 13, 145, *145*

failure to flower 15
Falk, Elizabeth 113
Farrer, Reginald 156
Fenwick-Owen, G. 110
fertilising 13
festivals, peony 39, *39*, 155
flower shows 40, *40*
flowering season 16
  hybrid peonies 7, 20, 113, 115
  intersectional peonies 7, 143
  lactiflora peonies 20
  species peonies 105
  tree peonies 7, 20
flowers
  colour *see* colour
  failure to flower 15
  flower parts 8
  hybrid peonies 113, 114
  intersectional peonies 143, 144
  lactiflora peonies 46
  shapes 9
  species peonies 105, 113
  tree peonies 157
foliage 10
  autumn tints 10
  hybrid peonies 7, 10, 19, 115
  intersectional peonies 144, 145
  lactiflora peonies 10, 47
  mounds 10, 16
  rogue leaves 15
  species peonies 10, 105
  tree peonies 10, 157
Fortune, Robert 156
French National Horticultural Society 32
French peony breeders 32, 34, 156, 165, 168
frost 15
fungal diseases 13, 15

Galen 30
*Galium odoratum* (Sweet woodruff) 26
*Geranium* 19, 20, *22*, *24*, 25, 29, *29*, *51*
  'Brookside' *22*, 29
  *G. clarkei* 'Kashmir Blue' 20
  *G. maculatum* 'Vicky Lynn' 19, *131*

*G. psilostemon* 20
*G. renardii* 25
*G. sanguineum* 20
Gerard, John 30
*Geum* (Avens) *22*, 25, 29, 105
  'Mai Tai' *26*
  'Prinses Juliana' *19*, *22*, *27*, *131*
  'Totally Tangerine' *20*
Gilbert H. Wild & Son 38, *38*
*Gillenia trifoliata* (Bowman's root) 19, *19*, 29, *29*
Glasscock, Lyman 34, 113
grafted peonies 12, *12*, 14, *14*
Gratwick, William 156, *156*
growing peonies 12–15
  fertilising 13

  grafting tree peonies 12, *12*, 14, *14*
  growing from seed 14
  hardiness 12
  moving peonies 13
  planting 12
  pruning 13, *13*
  soil 12
  sun and shade 12
  supports 13, 45
  tidying 13
  troubleshooting 15
  *see also* propagation
guard petals 8, 47, 144
Guérin, Modeste 32

Hamilton, Geoff 40
*Handy Book of the Flower-Garden* (David Thomson) 33
hardiness 12
  hybrid peonies 114
  lactiflora peonies 46
Harding, Alice 32, 34, 36
Hardy Plant Society 40
Henry, Louis 156
herbaceous peonies 6, 7, 8
  leaf die-back 7, 10, *13*
  planting 12
  planting distance 16
  tidying 13
  *see also* hybrid peonies; intersectional peonies; lactiflora peonies
herbals 30
*Heuchera* 22
  *H. sanguinea* 20
Hibberd, Shirley 156
Higo peonies 45
history of peony cultivation 30–5
Hollingsworth, Don 38, *38*, 43, 143

hybrid peonies 7, 9, 10, 34, 43, 112–41
  breeding 113
  buds 10, 115
  colour range 7, 22, 23, 114
  cultivars 116–41
  flowering season 7, 20, 113, 115
  flowers 113, 114
  foliage 7, 10, 19, 115
  hardiness 114
  lactiflora heritage 113
  natural hybridisation 6
  scent 11
  stems 9, 115

identification 8, 46
imperial peonies 9
  *see also* Japanese peonies
intersectional peonies 7, 8, 9, 10, 142–53
  border plants 25
  breeding 143
  buds 10
  colour range 7, 22, 23, 144
  cultivars 147–53
  F1 hybrid offspring 143
  flowering season 7, 143
  flowers 143, 144
  foliage 144, 145
  height and shape 144
  micropropagation 143
  planting 12
  planting distance 16
  scent 11
  seeds and pods 10
  shade tolerance 28
  side buds 145
  stems 9, 145
  tidying 13
*Iris* *17*, 19, 25, 29, *94*
  'Fond Kiss' *29*
  *I. sibirica* 29
Itoh, Toichi 34, 36, 143
Itoh hybrids *see* intersectional peonies

Japanese peonies 9, 23, 26
  colour 23
  lactiflora peonies 45, 46
  tree peonies 7, 26, 36, 155, 157, 161–4
Japanese peony breeders 143
John Waterer, Sons & Crisp Ltd. 36

Kelway, James 33, 36
Kelway & Sons 33, 34, 35, 36, 156

Klehm, Carl 38, 113
Klehm, Roy 38, 43, 92
Klehm Peony Nurseries 38, *38*, 57, 64, 123
Klinkhamer, Luc 96
*Kniphofia* 25, *25*
Krekler, Alice 79
Krekler, William 38, 100

L. Van Leeuwen 34
lactiflora peonies 7, 10, 31, 45–103
  buds 10
  colour range 7, 22, 23, 46
  cultivars 48–103
  flowering season 20
  flowers 46
  foliage 10, 47
  hardiness 46
  name changes 45
  roots 46
  scent 11
  seeds 105
  shade tolerance 28
  side buds 47
  stems 9, 47
Landis, Henry 71
leaf blotch 15, *15*
leaves *see* foliage
Lemoine, Émile 32, 34
Lemoine, Victor 32, *32*, 113, 156
Lemon, Nicholas 32
Loudon, Mrs. 156
Ludlow, Frank 156, 159
Luoyang Peony Festival 39, *39*
*Lupinus* (Lupin) 20, 29
*Lychnis* (Dusty miller) 20, 29
Lynch, Richard 35

Male and Female Peony 30, *30*, 31
manure 13
Marx, Walter 38
Méchin, Etienne 32
medicinal uses 30, 31
micropropagation 143
Middle Ages 30
Miellez, Auguste 32
Miller, Philip 30, 31
Mlokosiewicz, G. 106
moving peonies 13

Nash, James 156
*Nepeta* (Catmint) 19, 29, *51*
  'Six Hills Giant' *29*
Olson, Christian 49
Osti, Gian Lupo 159
*Paeonia*
  *P. albiflora see P. lactiflora*

*P. algeriensis* 6
*P. anomala* 6
*P. arietina* 6
*P. bakeri* 35
*P. broteri* 6, 31
*P. brownii* 6
*P. californica* 6
*P. cambessedesii* 6
*P. cathayana* 6
*P. chinensis* 45
*P. clusii* 6
  subsp. *clusii* 6
  subsp. *rhodia* 6
*P. coriacea* 6
*P. corsica* 6
*P. daurica* 6, 105, 106
  subsp. *coriifolia* 6
  subsp. *daurica* 6
  subsp. *macrophylla* 6
  subsp. *mlokosewitschii* 6
  subsp. *tomentosa* 6
  subsp. *velebitensis* 6
  subsp. *wittmanniana* 6
*P. decomposita* 6
*P. delavayi* 6, 12, *14*, 26, *26*, *27*, 156, 157, 158, *158*, 159
  f. *lutea* 156, 158, *158*
*P. emodi* 6, 28, 106, *106*, 125
*P. x festiva* 108
*P. intermedia* 6
*P. jishanensis* 6
*P. kesrouanensis* 6
*P. lactiflora* 6, 7, 9, 31, *31*, 33, 34, 113, 114, 126
  'Adolphe Rousseau' 7
  *see also* lactiflora peonies
*P. ludlowii* 6, 26, 156, 159, *159*
*P. lutea see P. delavayi* f. *lutea*
*P. macrophylla* 114, 126
*P. mairei* 6
*P. mascula* 6, 30, *30*, 31, 33
*P. mlokosewitschii* 105, *105*, 106, *106*, 113, 114, 126
*P. mollis* 106, *106*
*P. obovata* 6, *6*, 107, *107*
  subsp. *willmottiae* 6
*P. officinalis* 6, 13, 30, *30*, 31, *31*, 33, 108, 113, 114, 126
  subsp. 'Anemoniflora Rosea' 107, *107*
  subsp. *banatica* 105, 107, *107*, 119
  subsp. *humilis* 105, 107
  hybrids 108
  'Lize Van Veen' 108, *108*
  'Rosea Plena' 105, 108, *108*
  'Rubra Plena' 30, *30*, 31, 105, 108, *108*
  subsp. *villosa* 6, 105, 107, *107*

*P. ostii* 6, 159
*P. parnassica* 6
*P. peregrina* 6, 33, 120, 125
  'Otto Froebel' *33*, 109, *109*
*P. qiui* 6
*P. rockii* 6, *28*, 156, 157, 159, *159*
*P. rotundiloba* 6
*P. sinensis* 45
*P.* x *smouthii* 109, *109*
*P. steveniana* 6, *6*
*P.* x *suffruticosa* 157
*P. tenuifolia* 6, 109, *109*, 133
  'Plena' 109, *109*
  'Rosea' 109, *109*
*P. veitchii* 6, 28, *105*, 125
  var. *woodwardii* 28, *28*, *104*, 105, 110, *110*
*P. wittmanniana* 105, 110, *110*
  subsp. 'Rosea' 12, 16, *16*, 28, *28*, 110, *110*, *111*
  see also species peonies
*Paeonia* genus 6
  buds 10
  Delavayanae subsection 6
  flower parts 8
  flower shapes 9
  foliage 10
  global distribution 6
  history of peony cultivation 30–5
  Moutan group 6
  Onaepia group 6
  Paeon group 6
  scent 11
  seeds and pods 10
  stems 9, 10
  taxonomy 6, 35, 105
  Vaginatae subsection 6
  in the wild 6, 30
*Papaver orientalis* (Oriental poppy) 19
Parkinson, John 30
Pehrson, Roy 143
'Peony Fairy' 155, *155*
Peony Society 40
peony wilt 15
*Perennial Garden Plants* (Graham Thomas) 37
*Persicaria affinis* (Bistort) 25, 29
petaloids 8, 47
pink flowers 22, 23
plant collectors 6, 31, 43, 156
Plantek 143
planting 12

moving peonies 13
  planting distance 16
  too deeply 15

Pliny 30
*Polemonium* (Jacob's ladder) 29
  'Lambrook Mauve' 19
*Potentilla rupestris* (Cinquefoil) 19, *23*, 29
*Primula* 25
propagation
  commercial growers 41
  division 13, 41
  grafting 12, *12*, 14, *14*
  micropropagation 143
  seed, growing from 14
pruning 13, *13*
*Pulmonaria* (Lungwort) 26, 29, 105
Pyke, Doreen 36

Reath, David 36, 143
red flowers 22, 23
Reeves, John 155
Rock, Joseph 156, 159
Rogers, Al and Dot 36, 38, 71
root rot 12, 15
roots 8, 12, *12*, 13, 14, 15, 16
  lactiflora peonies 46
  species peonies 105
*Rosa* 23, 36
  'Boscobel' *23*
  'James Galway' *26*
Royal Horticultural Society 32, 34, 40

Salter, John 33
*Salvia* (Hardy sage) 20, 25, 29
  *S. nemerosa* 'Amethyst' *22*
*Sambucus nigra* f. *porphyrophylla* 'Eva' *24*, *70*
Sang, Tao 6
*Sanguisorba* 25
  *S. menziesii* 20
Sass, Henry 69
Saunders, A.P. 34, *34*, 39, 80, 106, 113, 114, 124, 156
scent 11
Scotts of Merriot 36
*Sedum* 25
seeds 10
  collecting 14
  germination 14
  growing from seed 14
  lactiflora peonies 105
  seed pods 10, *145*
  species peonies 105, *105*
self-supporting peonies 9, 10
semi-double flowers 9

shade 12, 15, 28
Sherriff, George 156, 159
side buds 8, 11, 15

intersectional peonies 145
lactiflora peonies 47
single flowers 9
*Sisyrinchium striatum* 20, *21*, 29, *29*
small gardens, peonies in 28
Smirnow, Louis 36, 39, 143
Snelling, Lilian 35
soil requirements 12
species peonies 104–11
  flowering season 105
  flowers 105, 113
  foliage 10, 105
  garden-worthy 105–11
  name changes 105
  roots 105
  seeds 105, *105*
  subspecies (subsp.) 105
  variety (var.) 105
spring-flowering peonies 17
*Stachys* (Lamb's ears) 29, *29*
  *S. byzantina* 19, *20*, *21*, *22*, *23*, *84*, *121*
staking 13, 45
stamens 8, 114
staminodes 8, 47
stems 9, 10
  hybrid peonies 9, 115
  intersectional peonies 145
  lactiflora peonies 46
  tree peonies 9, 157
Stern, Sir Frederick 6, 35, *35*, 105
stigma (pistil) 8
*Stipa gigantea* *24*, *142*
*A Study Of The Genus Paeonia* (F.C. Stern) 6, 35
summer-flowering peonies 19–20
supports 13, 45
Sweerts, Emanuel 31

temperatures 46, 113, 114
Thomas, Graham 37
Thomson, David 33
tree peonies 6, 7, 9, 10, 154–70
  border plants 26
  buds 10, 157, *157*
  Chinese 7, 36, 39, 155, 157, 160
  colour range 23
  flowering season 7, 20
  flowers 157
  foliage 10, 157
  French and American introductions 165–70
  grafting 14, *14*
  introduction to Europe 155, 156

Japanese 7, 26, 36, 155, 157, 161–4
legends 155
lutea hybrids 7, 156, 157, 165
names 157
planting 12
planting distance 16
*rockii* hybrids 157, 159, 165
rogue leaves 15
seeds and pods 10
shade tolerance 28
statement plants 16
stems 9, 157
tidying 13
see also intersectional peonies
Turner, William 30

Veitch Medal 32
*Veronica* (Speedwell) 25, 29, *29*
  'Ellen Mae' *23*, 25
*The Visions of Piers Plowman* (William Langland) 30

Ware, Thomas S. 33
waterlogging 15
White, Earle B. 113
white flowers 22, 23
White Hopton Farm *17*, *27*, *29*, *41*, *43*
Wild, Gilbert 36
windy sites 26
Wissing, Samuel 113
Wister, John C. 34
Woodward, Robert 110
woody peonies *see* tree peonies
Wu Zetian, Empress 155

yellow flowers 22, 23

## PEONY CULTIVARS

Page numbers in *italic* refer to illustrations

'Adolphe Rousseau' 7, 9, 26, 48, *48*
'Age of Gold' 165, *165*
'Albert Crousse' 48, *48*
'Alexander Fleming' 9, 11, 16, 48, *48*
'Alice Harding' 11, 48, *48*, 143, 165, *165*
'Ama-no-Sode' 49, *49*
'Amabilis' 49, *49*
'Amalia Olsen' 11, 49, *49*
'America' 22, 116, *116*
'Angel Cheeks' 23, 49, *49*
'Angelet' 16, 165, *165*
'Angelo Cobb Freeborn' 116, *116*
'Ann Cousins' 11, 50, *50*
'Argentine' 50, *50*
'Argosy' 156, 165, *165*
'Artemis' *156*
'Athena' 116, *116*
'Auguste Dessert' 20, 22, 29, 42, 50, *50*, *51*
'Auten's 1816' 116, *116*
'Avant Garde' *33*, 16, 117, *117*

'Balliol' see 'Lord Kitchener'
'Barbara' 9, 11, 23, *44*, 50, *50*
'Baroness Schroeder' 52, *52*
'Barrington Belle' *47*, 52, *52*
'Bartzella' 11, 16, 23, 145, *146*, 147
'Belle Center' 117, *117*
'Bess Bockstoce' 117, *117*
'Best Man' 11, 52, *52*
'Better Times' *47*, 52, *52*
'Black Monarch' *37*, 117, *117*
'Black Panther' 166
'Black Pirate' *157*, 166, *166*
'Blaze' 118, *118*
'Blush Queen' 53, *53*
'Border Gem' 53, *53*
'Boreas' 166, *166*
'Bouquet Perfect' 9, 11, *11*, 16, 26, 53, *53*
'Bowl of Beauty' 8, 16, 23, *46*, 53, *53*
'Bowl of Cream' 11, 54, *54*
'Break o' Day' 54, *54*
'Bridal Icing' 9, 11, 22, 23, 54, *54*, *55*
'Bright Knight' 118, *118*
'Buckeye Belle' 9, 23, 118, *118*
'Bunker Hill' 9, 54, *54*
'Burma Midnight' 118, *118*

'Burma Ruby' 116, 119, *119*
'Butch' 56, *56*
'Butter Bowl' 56, *56*

'Callie's Memory' 147, *147*
'Carol' 119, *119*
'Catharina Fontijn' *10*, 56, *56*
'Chalice' 119, *119*
'Chameleon' 119, *119*
'Charles Burgess' 57, *57*
'Charles White' see 'Charlie's White'
'Charlie's White' 56, *56*
'Charm' 57, *57*
'Cheddar Charm' 57, *57*
'Cheddar Cheese' 57, *57*
'Cheddar Gold' 58, *58*
'Cherry Hill' 58, *58*
'Cherry Ruffles' 120, *120*
'Chiffon Clouds' 58, *58*
'Chinese Dragon' 166, *166*
'Chocclate Soldier' 120, *120*
'Chromatella' 170
'Christmas Velvet' 120, *120*
'Chromatella' 170
'Cincinnati' 58, *58*
'Clair de Lune' 11, 16, 17, *17*, 113, *113*, 120, *121*
'Claire Dubois' 59, *59*
'Claudia' 120, *120*
'Color Magnet' 122, *122*
'Command Performance' 122, *122*
'Cora Louise' *25*, 144, 147, *147*
'Cora Stubbs' *8*, 29, 59, *59*
'Coral Charm' 11, *13*, 23, 29, *40*, 122, *122*
'Coral Fay' 122, *122*
'Coral 'n Gold' 123, *123*
'Coral Sunset' 11, 123, *123*
'Cornelia Shaylor' 59, *59*
'Couronne d'Or' 60, *60*
'Cream Puff' 60, *60*
'Crusader' 123, *123*
'Cuckoo's Nest' 59, *59*
'Cutie' 26, 123, *123*
'Cytherea' 11, 16, 23, 124, *124*, 130

'Dancing Butterflies' see 'Little Medicine Man'
'Dandy Dan' 124, *124*
'Dark Eyes' 147, *147*
'Dawn Pink' 60, *60*
'Dayton' 60, *60*
'Defender' 124, *124*
'Dinner Plate' 11, 16, 61, *61*
'Do Tell' 61, *61*
'Don Richardson' 61, *61*

'Doreen' 16, 61, *61*
'Doris Cooper' 63, *63*
'Dr. Alexander Fleming' see 'Alexander Fleming'
'Duchesse de Nemours' 11, *32*, 62, 63
'Early Glow' *114*, 124, *124*
'Early Windflower' 16, 17, *17*, 106, *115*, 125, *125*
'Edulis Superba' 11, 32, *32*, 45, 63, *63*
'Eliza Lundy' 7, 9, 16, 23, 26, *112*, 125, *125*
'Elizabeth Foster' 125, *125*
'Ellen Cowley' 125, *125*
'Elsa Sass' 16, *20*, 23, *46*, 63, *63*
'Emma Klehm' 9, 16, 26, 63, *63*
'Etched Salmon' 126, *126*
'Eventide' 126, *126*
'Ezra Pound' 166, *166*

'Fairbanks' 64, *64*
'Fairy Princess' 126, *126*
'Fairy's Petticoat' 64, *64*
'Fei Yan Hong Zhuang' 160, *160*
'Félix Crousse' 16, *32*, 64, *64*
'Fen Yu Nu' see 'Little Medicine Man'
'Feng Dan Bai' 159
'Festiva Maxima' 11, *32*, 64, *64*
'Fiona' 65, *65*
'Firelight' 126, *126*
'First Arrival' 16, *16*, 23, 25, 29, 144, 147, *147*
'Flame' *8*, 127, *127*
'Florence Nicholls' 11, 65, *65*

'Garden Lace' 127, *127*
'Garden Peace' *115*, 127, *127*
'Garden Treasure' 11, 143, *144*, 148, *148*
'Gardenia' 65, *65*
'Gauguin' 26, *154*, 167, *167*
'Gay Ladye' 33
'Gay Paree' 11, 23, 66, *66*
'Gayborder June' 65, *65*
'Germaine Bigot' 11, 66, *66*
'Gilbert Barthelot' 11, 66, *66*
'Glory Hallelujah' 11, 16, 26, 67, *67*
'Glowing Candles' 67, *67*
'Gold Sovereign' 167, *167*
'Golden Bowl' 167, *167*
'Golden Era' 143
'Golden Frolic' *10*, 11, 24, 66, *66*, *142*
'Goldilocks' 23, 127, *127*
'Guidon' 67, *67*

'Hai Huang' see 'High Noon'
'Hakuojisi' 161, *161*
'Hana Daijin' 161, *161*
'Hana Kisoi' *157*, 161, *161*
'Helen Hayes' 23, 26, 67, *67*
'Henry Bockstoce' 128, *128*
'Henry Sass' 68, *68*
'Hermione' 68, *68*
'Hesperus' 7, 167, *167*
'High Noon' 168, *168*
'Hillary' 7, 11, 148, *148*
'Hit Parade' 68, *68*
'Hoki' 161, *161*
'Honey Gold' 16, 23, *47*, 68, *68*
'Honor' 16, *19*, 23, 128, *128*
'Horizon' 128, *128*
'Hot Chocolate' 69, *69*

'Illini Belle' 128, *128*
'Illini Warrior' 129, *129*
'Inspecteur Lavergne' *8*, 9, 23, 64, 69, *69*
'Instituteur Doriat' 69, *69*

'James Pillow' 69, *69*
'Jan Van Leeuwen' 16, 23, 70, *71*
'Jean Ericksen' 71, *71*
'Joanna Marlene' 148, *148*
'John Harvard' 129, *129*
'Joker' 9, 26, 71, *71*
'Joyce Ellen' 129, *129*
'Julia Rose' *144*, 148, *148*
'June Rose' 71, *71*

'Kakaderi' 143
'Kamata-fuji' 162, *162*
'Kansas' *19*, 72, *72*
'Kaow' 162, *162*
'Karen Gray' 72, *72*
'Karl Rosenfield' 9, 72, *72*
'Kelway's Glorious' 72, *72*
'Kinkaku' see 'Souvenir de Maxime Cornu'
'Kinko' see 'Alice Harding'
'Kintei' see 'L'Espérance'
'Krekler's Red' 46
'Krinkled White' 11, 16, 23, 73, *73*
'LaDonna' 130, *130*
'Lady Alexandra Duff' 11, 73, *73*
'Lady Liberty' 45
'Lady Orchid' 16, 23, 73, *73*
'Lancaster Imp' 26, 73, *73*
'Largo' 74, *74*
'Late Windflower' 16, 106, 129, *129*
'Laura Dessert' 74, *74*
'Lavender Whisper' 130, *130*
'Le Cygne' 74, *74*, 96

'Lemon Chiffon' *8*, 16, *17*, *22*, 23, 130, *131*
'Lemon Dream' 149, *149*
'Leslie Peck' 74, *74*
'L'Espérance' 34, 156, 168, *168*
'Lian Tia' *45*
'Liebchen' 75, *75*
'Lilac Time' 75, *75*
'Lillian Wild' 75, *75*
'Little Joe' 75, *75*
'Little Medicine Man' *45*, 76, *76*
'Lois Kelsey' 76, *76*
'Lollipop' 149, *149*
'Lord Kitchener' 76, *76*
'Lotus Queen' 76, *76*
'Louis Barthelot' 77, *77*
'Love Affair' 149, *149*
'Lovebirds' 17, *17*, 130, *130*
'Lovely Rose' *115*, 130, *130*
'Lowell Thomas' 77, *77*

'Machanic Grand' *see* 'Mackinac Grand'
'Mackinac Grand' 132, *132*
'Madame Calot' *9*, *44*, 77, *77*
'Madame Ducel' *32*, 77, *77*
'Madame Edouard Doriat' 78, *78*
'Madame Emile Debatène' *16*, 78, *78*
'Magenta Moon' 78, *78*
'Magical Mystery Tour' *22*, 149, *149*
'Mai Fleuri' 132, *132*
'Many Happy Returns' 132, *132*
'Marchioness' 168, *169*
'Margaret Clark' 79, *79*
'Margaret Truman' *26*, 78, *78*
'Marie Lemoine' *9*, 11, 16, 79, *79*
'Marietta Sisson' 11, 79, *79*
'Martha Reed' *26*, 79, *79*
'Martha Washington' 143
'Matilda Lewis' 80, *80*
'May Lilac' 132, *132*
'Merry Mayshine' 133, *133*
'Midnight Sun' 16, 80, *80*, *81*
'Minnie Shaylor' 80, *80*, 123, 149
'Mischief' 80, *80*
'Miss America' 82, *82*, 151
'Miss Eckhart' 82, *82*
'Mister Ed' *37*, 82, *82*
'Monsieur Jules Elie' 11, 52, 82, *82*, 113
'Montezuma' *114*, 133, *133*
'Moon of Nippon' *8*, 83, *83*
'Moon River' 83, *83*
'Moonrise' 16, *18*, 23, *29*, 133, *133*, 139

'Morning Lilac' *25*, *143*, 150, *150*
'Mother's Choice' 83, *83*
'Mr. G.F. Hemerik' 11, 83, *83*
'Mrs. Edward Harding' 85, *85*
'Mrs. F.D.R' *see* 'Mrs. Franklin D. Roosevelt'
'Mrs. Franklin D. Roosevelt' 85, *85*
'Murad of Hershey Bar' 168, *168*
'My Pal Rudy' 85, *85*
'Myrtle Gentry' *9*, 11, 16, *20*, 23, *26*, *29*, *84*, 85

'Nancy Nicholls' 16, 85, *85*
'Nancy Nora' *9*, 11, *26*, *46*, 86, *86*
'Naniwa-nishiki' 162, *162*
'Nellie Saylor' 86, *86*
'Neon' 86, *86*
'New Millennium' 150, *150*
'Nice Gal' 11, 23, 86, *86*
'Nick Shaylor' 11, 87, *87*
'Nippon Beauty' *47*, 87, *87*
'Nippon Gold' 87, *87*, 130
'Norma Volz' 87, *87*
'Norwegian Blush' 150, *150*
'Nosegay' *114*, 133, *133*
'Nymphe' 16, 88, *88*

'Old Faithful' 135, *135*

'Pastel Splendour' 150, *150*
'Paul M. Wild' 16, *22*, 23, *29*, 88, *88*
'Paula Fay' 23, *23*, *115*, 135, *135*, 139
'Petite Elegance' *26*, 88, *88*
'Petite Porcelain' *23*, 88, *88*
'Philippe Rivoire' 89, *89*
'Philomèle' 89, *89*
'Picotee' *9*, *10*, 16, *19*, *26*, *134*, 135
'Pillow Cases' 89, *89*
'Pillow Talk' 11, 16, 23, 89, *89*
'Pink Dawn' *see* 'Pink Princess'
'Pink Delight' 90, *90*
'Pink Giant' 90, *90*
'Pink Hawaiian Coral' *114*, 135, *135*
'Pink Lemonade' 90, *90*
'Pink Parfait' 11, 16, 90, *90*
'Pink Pom Pom' 135, *135*
'Pink Princess' 91, *91*
'Prairie Moon' 136, *136*
'Prairie Sunshine' 149
'President Lincoln' 91, *91*
'President Wilson' 11, 91, *91*

'Qing Long Wo Mo Chi' 160, *160*
'Queen of Sheba' 23, 91, *91*

'Raspberry Charm' 136, *136*
'Raspberry Sundae' *46*, 92, *92*
'Red Charm' *9*, *9*, 11, 16, 23, *115*, 136, *137*
'Red Emperor' 92, *92*
'Red Grace' 136, *136*
'Red Red Rose' 136, *136*
'Red Satin' 92, *92*
'Reine Hortense' 93, *93*
'Renato' 93, *93*
'Renkaku' 162, *162*
'Renown' 168, *168*
'Requiem' 138, *138*
'Roland' 92, *92*
'Rose Garland' 138, *138*
'Rose Heart' *see* 'Bess Bockstoce'
'Rosedale' 138, *138*
'Roselette' 16, 138, *138*
'Rou Fu Rong' 160, *160*
'Ruth Cobb' 93, *93*

'Salmon Beauty' 139, *139*
'Salmon Dream' 139, *139*
'Santa Fe' 93, *93*
'Sarah Bernhardt' 11, 95, *95*
'Scarlet Heaven' 151, *151*
'Scarlet O'Hara' 11, 14, 23, *115*, 139, *139*
'Sea Shell' 16, 95, *95*
'Sequestered Sunshine' 151, *151*
'Serene Pastel' *26*, 95, *95*
'Shichifukujin' 163, *163*
'Shima Daijin' 163, *163*
'Shima Nishiki' 163, *163*
'Shimane Chojuraku' *7*, *26*, 154, 163, *163*
'Shirley Temple' 11, 12, *20*, *46*, *47*, *94*, 95
'Show Girl' 139, *139*
'Singing in the Rain' *142*, 151, *151*
'Snowflake' 33
'Soft Salmon Saucer' 140, *140*
'Solange' 11, 95, *95*
'Sonoma Sun' 151, *151*
'Sorbet' 96, *96*
'Souvenir de Maxime Cornu' 156, 170, *170*
'Stardust' 96, *96*
'Starlight' 140, *140*
'Sugar n' Spice' 140, *140*
'Summer Glow' 140, *140*
'Sunny Girl' *114*, 141, *141*
'Surugu' 11, *21*, *26*, *26*, *29*, 96, *96*
'Sweet 16' 97, *97*
'Sweet Marjorie' *45*

'Sword Dance' 97, *97*

'Taisho No Hokori' 164, *164*
'Taiyo' 163
'Tamasudare' 164, *164*
'Tamate-boku' 97, *97*
'Tango' 141, *141*
'The Fawn' *9*, 23, 97, *97*
'The Mackinac Grand' *see* 'Mackinac Grand'
'The Mighty Mo' 98, *98*
'Thunderbolt' 170, *170*
'Tom Eckhardt' *9*, 23, 98, *98*, *99*
'Top Brass' *45*, 98, *98*
'Topeka Garnet' 98, *98*
'Toro-no-maki' 100, *100*
'Touch of Class' 100, *100*
'Tria' *7*

'Unique' *145*, *152*, 153
'Ursa Minor' 100, *100*

'Vesuvian' 170, *170*
'Victorian Blush' *26*, 100, *100*
'Vivid Rose' 11, 101, *101*
'Vogue' 11, 101, *101*

'Walter Mains' 23, 141, *141*
'Watermelon Wine' 153, *153*
'Waucedah Princess' 170, *170*
'Westerner' *19*, 101, *101*
'White Cap' 101, *101*
'White Emperor' 153, *153*
'White Grace' 103, *103*
'White Innocence' 34, 141, *141*
'White Ivory' 103, *103*
'White Wings' *102*, 103
'Whitleyii Major' 36
'Wiesbaden' 103, *103*

'Yachiyo-tsubaki' 164, *164*
'Yae Zakura' 164, *164*
'Yankee Doodle Dandy' *142*, 153, *153*
'Yellow Crown' 143, 153, *153*
'Yellow Dream' 143
'Yellow Emperor' 143
'Yellow Heaven' 143
'Yin Fen Jin Lin' 160, *160*

'Zuzu' 103, *103*